PHILOSOPHY FOR CHILDREN

Theories and praxis in teacher education

Edited by Babs Anderson

Routledge
Taylor & Francis Group

LONDON AND NEW YORK

First published 2017
by Routledge
2 Park Square, Milton Park, Abingdon, Oxon OX14 4RN

and by Routledge
711 Third Avenue, New York, NY 10017

Routledge is an imprint of the Taylor & Francis Group, an informa business

British Library Cataloguing in Publication Data
A catalogue record for this book is available from the British Library

Library of Congress Cataloging in Publication Data
Names: Anderson, Babs, editor.
Title: Philosophy for children: theories and Praxis in teacher education / edited by Babs Anderson.
Description: Abingdon, Oxon ; New York, NY : Routledge is an imprint of the Taylor & Francis Group, an Informa Business, [2017]
Identifiers: LCCN 2016007717| ISBN 9781138191747 (hardback) | ISBN 9781138191754 (pbk.) | ISBN 9781315640310 (ebook)
Subjects: LCSH: Reasoning–Study and teaching–Great Britain. | Persuasion (Rhetoric)–Study and teaching–Great Britain. | Educational psychology–Great Britain. | Teachers–Training of–Great Britain.
Classification: LCC LB1590.3 .P5563 2017 | DDC 370.15/2–dc23
LC record available at https://lccn.loc.gov/2016007717

ISBN: 978-1-138-19174-7 (hbk)
ISBN: 978-1-138-19175-4 (pbk)
ISBN: 978-1-315-64031-0 (ebk)

Typeset in Bembo
by Cenveo Publisher Services

Philosophy for Children

Philosophy for Children (P4C) is a movement that teaches reasoning and argumentative skills to children of all ages. This book looks at the progress that P4C has made in the UK in addressing issues of literacy, critical thinking, PSHE, education for sustainable development and wider issues such as bullying.

Chapters identify the different theories and practices that have emerged and discuss the necessity for the reflective approach that P4C brings to education. The book highlights how this movement can fit into the early years, primary and secondary curricula and the challenges and rewards that come with it. Chapters include:

- evolution of Philosophy for Children in the UK
- pedagogical judgement
- negotiating meaning in classrooms: P4C as an exemplar of dialogic pedagogy
- impact of P4C on teacher educators
- being and becoming a philosophical teacher.

This will be an invaluable guide for all those interested in P4C and undertaking Early Childhood Studies, Education Studies and Initial Teacher Training courses.

Babs Anderson is a lecturer in Early Childhood at Liverpool Hope University, UK and teaches on a number of Early Childhood undergraduate and postgraduate courses.

CONTENTS

CONTRIBUTORS

Babs Anderson is a lecturer at Liverpool Hope University in the Early Childhood department. She has a long-standing interest in young children's thinking skills, undertaking training with SAPERE in P4C over 15 years ago. She is currently researching how communities of enquiry can be used to enable students to develop as autonomous learners in higher education. She is book review editor for *Child Care in Practice* journal.

Clive Belgeonne is an education advisor at the Development Education Centre, South Yorkshire (DECSY), and one of the national leaders of the Global Learning Programme (England). He is also Course Leader for PGCE Citizenship at Sheffield Hallam University. Clive is a SAPERE approved trainer in Philosophy for Children and a qualified 'Global Trainer' who has facilitated training with a wide range of educators in the UK and Europe. A former secondary school teacher and currently a primary school governor, he has taught in the UK, Latin America and West Africa.

Fufy Demissie has worked in ITE at Sheffield Hallam University for the past 12 years, originally training as an early years teacher. She teaches on the Professional Learning, Early Years Pedagogy and Educational Enquiry modules at undergraduate and master's level. She is a passionate advocate of P4C and has introduced P4C to all early years and primary students in the second year of ITE, education studies students and early years teachers. Fufy has also recently become an accredited Level 1 trainer. Her research interests are on developing student teachers' capacity for reflection through enabling pedagogies such as P4C and the impact of P4C on young children's thinking.

Lynda Dunlop is a lecturer in Science Education at the University of York where she teaches on undergraduate and postgraduate education programmes, including the BA Education and Secondary Science PGCE. Lynda has introduced a module on Philosophy for Children for final-year undergraduate students. Prior to joining York, Lynda was a teacher of science and theory of knowledge, working in schools in the UK and Mexico. She has recently completed a PhD in Science Education that focused on communities of enquiry and the discussion of social and ethical issues in science with young people aged 11–14.

Darren Garside philosophised with children from 2000 to 2008, and then he started philosophising with undergraduates at Bath Spa University where he currently uses P4C to introduce philosophy of education to students on the BA Education Studies degree. His research interests include post-Deweyan and post-humanist pragmatism – specifically the work of Colin Koopman and the concept of transitionalist pragmatism. He is also interested in educational judgement, P4C/PwC as a pedagogy for twenty-first-century higher education, and the role of arts education in countering educational and social injustice. Currently he is exploring arts and indigenous education in British Columbia, Canada.

Joanna Haynes is Associate Professor at the University of Plymouth. Following undergraduate studies in philosophy, Joanna taught in primary schools in inner-city Glasgow and Bristol, before completing a Master's degree in Education at Bristol University. Her PhD (University of Exeter) is in philosophy with children. She is author of *Children as Philosophers* (Routledge), which has been translated into several languages. Joanna has been involved in writing, presenting, teaching and leading courses on Philosophical Enquiry and Philosophy with Children for over 20 years and is a member of the national and international Philosophy for Children networks, SAPERE and ICPIC. She belongs to the Philosophy of Education Society (PESGB). Her research interests are in philosophy with children, troublesome knowledge, and critical and transformative pedagogies.

Lizzy Lewis was initially a primary school teacher, school governor, then teacher trainer and is now a UK-based consultant and speaker, specialising in Philosophy for Children (P4C). Her current roles include P4C school training (as a registered SAPERE Trainer), Development Manager for SAPERE, Partner of A Level Philosophy and Secretary of ICPIC (International Council of Philosophical Inquiry with Children). Lizzy has published articles on P4C and co-edited *Philosophy for Children through the Secondary Curriculum* (Continuum). She is Director of Thinking Space, and on the advisory board of BRILA Youth Projects.

Sue Lyle has been an educator for over 40 years as a classroom teacher, advisory teacher for language and intercultural education, curriculum developer for both primary and secondary schools and for 20 years in higher education as a teacher educator. In this role she has trained primary and secondary school teachers and led CPD for practising teachers. Retired from full-time work at Swansea Metropolitan University, she established Dialogue-Exchange, a consultancy to promote dialogic education and the rights of the child. Sue is a senior trainer in P4C for SAPERE and an active researcher.

Julie McCann is a SAPERE trainer and Advanced Skills Teacher based in School Improvement Liverpool where she supports and trains colleagues in primary, secondary and special schools. Julie is passionate about developing P4C in a sustainable and meaningful way for each school community. She received *Citizenship Magazine*'s 'Outstanding Teacher Award' in recognition of her work around challenging prejudice, promoting emotional well-being, and engaging with the wider community. Julie is also a member of the PSHE Association Advisory Council.

Naomi McLeod teaches Early Childhood and leads the MA in International Approaches to Early Childhood Education at Liverpool John Moores University. Her doctorate focused on developing pedagogical participation for young children and continued professional development for teachers and early years professionals. She currently works with families and early years curators at Tate Liverpool nurturing a sense of self in young children through artwork as a provocation for philosophical enquiry. She is engaged in a collaborative comparative study involving four universities looking at the 'multiple identities of Early Childhood students for a quality workforce'.

Sarah Meir is Faculty Executive Officer for the Faculty of Education at Liverpool Hope University. Prior to this she spent over 20 years in marketing and research roles, latterly specialising in qualitative behavioural and social marketing research, including service evaluations, and undertaking work with a wide range of public sector stakeholders, particularly schools and PCTs, as well as emergency services and charities.

Georgia Prescott is Senior Lecturer in Primary Religious Education at the University of Cumbria. Prior to that, she was a primary teacher in schools in London and Cumbria. Her research interests and publications include a focus on Religious Education, Philosophy for Children (P4C), and Spiritual, Moral, Social and Cultural Development (SMSC). She has been involved in P4C for many years and works with children, student teachers and practising teachers developing and researching into P4C, particularly its use in RE. She is beginning work with SAPERE as a partner institution, training student teachers to Level 1 in P4C.

Grace Robinson is founder and Managing Director of Thinking Space CIC and a teaching fellow of Leeds University. She is a philosophy teacher, trainer and consultant. She founded Thinking Space in 2008 believing that philosophical dialogue and enquiry can help people think and communicate their thinking more clearly. Grace is an accredited SAPERE trainer and an associate of the Philosophy Foundation – both leading UK charities promoting philosophical enquiry with children and young people.

Karen Rogan has worked in secondary education in Merseyside for 32 years in a wide variety of teaching and managerial roles, including Head of Drama, Head of English, National Strategies English Consultant and Assistant Principal. Over the past three years she has worked in secondary ITE as PGCE English Course Leader and Head of Secondary PGCE at Liverpool Hope University. Her professional interests in teaching and learning encompass a wide range of pedagogical approaches to the teaching of English with a particular focus on how dialogic (and the role of oracy overall) works in the classroom to develop pupils' metacognition.

John Smith was a primary school teacher, developing a keen interest in children's language and reasoning. In 2000, as a senior lecturer at Manchester Metropolitan University, he discovered P4C and the enormous potential offered to children by this approach. He became a SAPERE P4C Trainer in 2009 and his book *Talk, Thinking and Philosophy in the Primary Curriculum* was published in 2010. John has led many courses for teachers, trainee teachers and others and has written a range of articles on P4C and dialogic teaching. He now works independently and his website can be found at www.talkandreason.com.

Kathy Stokell is a senior lecturer at Liverpool John Moores University in Initial Teacher Education and is Programme Leader for the Foundation Subjects in Education. Prior to this she worked as a primary school teacher for 18 years and was the SENCo and Professional Mentor for ITT students in school. While teaching she was seconded to Wirral Local Authority as their Recruitment and Well-being Coordinator where she worked for three years, looking at the health and well-being of all staff in primary schools.

Roger Sutcliffe read Philosophy at Oxford, graduating in 1975. After five years' teaching in a junior school, he took an Open University degree in Maths and joined the Maths Department at Christ's Hospital School, Horsham. In the early 1990s he left full-time teaching for private study, and trained in Philosophy for Children with Matthew Lipman, and in Creative Thinking with Edward de Bono. Roger was a founder member of SAPERE, and was Chair from 1996 until 2003, then elected President. In the same year he was elected President of ICPIC, the international equivalent of SAPERE, and served two terms.

Diane Swift has extensive experience in schools as a teacher, senior leader and a governor. She regularly contributes articles to a variety of professional journals and has authored a variety of materials both online and paper-based that support teachers to develop both their curriculum and pedagogic thinking. She has worked extensively with teacher colleagues on a variety of projects in relation to Philosophy for Children and Communities (P4C). Diane is currently Director of the Keele and North Staffordshire Primary SCITT (KNSPS). Within the KNSPS, P4C is promoted as a pedagogy for beginning teachers, encouraging conceptual and reflective thinking about practice.

FOREWORD

This book is a result of a symposium held at Liverpool Hope University in June 2014. This symposium arose from a collection of like-minded individuals in education, who had a lively interest in the approach of Philosophy for Children (P4C) in the UK. Other chapter contributors were contacted personally as they are active in this field and worked alongside SAPERE (The Society for the Advancement of Philosophical Enquiry and Reflection in Education).

In the chapters in the book, the abbreviation P4C is mostly commonly used; one uses an alternative, Philosophy with Children (PwC). This was left to the individual author's choice, as befitting the democratic nature of a community of enquiry approach. In Chapter 1, Roger Sutcliffe gives the rationale for these abbreviations.

As for my part, I am privileged to work with such talented and inspiring individuals. I hope that you gain a sense of their commitment to education in its fullest, richest sense throughout.

Babs Anderson
February 2016

PART 1

The context

1

THE EVOLUTION OF PHILOSOPHY FOR CHILDREN IN THE UK

Roger Sutcliffe

Pointers from the past

The Greek historian Thucydides (*c.* 460–400 BC) was an almost exact contemporary of Socrates (*c.* 470–399 BC) and would surely have been familiar with the famous philosopher's project of seeing to the 'welfare of souls'. Soul, of course, is an English word, and only a rough equivalent of the word Socrates would have used: *psyche.* The modern English use of *psyche,* moreover, is different again. What Socrates meant might be better rendered as something like moral sense or sensibility.

Thucydides' vision of the purpose of philosophy, indeed, was probably not far removed from that of his illustrious contemporary. He is reputed to have said that history was 'philosophy teaching by example', meaning, presumably, that our philosophies – our understanding and appreciation of the world, especially of other humans, and our engagement with it, and with them – benefit from reflection on real life, such as historical examples.

Socrates' own reliance on examples in the building of understanding is surely consistent with this vision, even if his metaphysical beliefs – in divine influence in human affairs and, perhaps, the permanence of meanings – might not have gone down so well with Thucydides. He has earned the sobriquet of a founder of scientific method by his strict adherence to robust evidence gathering and careful analysis of cause and effect, without recourse to the power of the gods.

But what do these examples have to do with the theme of this chapter, the evolution of P4C in the UK? Well, they are clearly not examples of P4C in the UK. It would also be rash to claim that either Socrates or Thucydides regarded children as their prime clients, where the Latin *cliens* means 'follower', though it could be equally rash to claim that they would have excluded them. Their concepts, however, help set a context for this introductory chapter.

The models of philosophical (often ethical) enquiries that Socrates bequeathed, courtesy of Plato, were certainly an inspiration for Matthew Lipman in his development of Philosophy for Children. We can see this both in Lipman's own declared purposes and in his emphasis on the importance of dialogue in pursuing them.

The approach that I have created in Philosophy for Children is not about prescribing any one philosophy to children, but about encouraging them to develop their own philosophy, their own way of thinking about the world. It is about giving the youngest of minds the opportunity to express ideas with confidence and in an environment where they feel safe to do so (Lipman, 2009, p.166). He reiterates his views that: 'The aim of a thinking skills program such as P4C is to help children become more thoughtful, more reflective, more considerate and more reasonable individuals' (Lipman, 1980, p.15).

It was surely significant, moreover, that Lipman agreed for this inspiration to be recognised in the title of the 1990 BBC documentary, *Socrates for Six Year Olds*. This broadcast was itself seminal in the history of P4C in the UK, since it led to the founding of the network that became SAPERE, the charitable Society for Advancing Philosophical Enquiry and Reflection in Education. More of that anon.

The significance of Thucydides to our argument is more oblique. For certain, he gives us an important reminder that philosophy in its Western birthplace was regarded as the moral foundation, if not the model formula, for good education and for the good life. This was a perspective maintained by most educated people in Europe into the Middle Ages, but has sadly been minimised by designers of 'educational' curricula since then – and especially since 'mass education' emerged in the nineteenth century, in the service of industrialised societies.

But I have a more particular and peculiar purpose in quoting Thucydides: namely, to draw attention to the fact that I shall be able to provide only a few examples – of practices and people – among many thousands who have played their part in the evolution of P4C in the UK. I hope the examples will be illuminating, of course, but, as *selected* examples, they cannot tell the whole story. If I fail to mention any individuals who might better have been mentioned, I apologise in advance. Let it be thought, simply, that my purpose is to 'teach P4C by examples', rather than to write a comprehensive history.

Crossroads in 1990

So, what was the philosophy behind *Socrates for Six Year Olds* and why was this television documentary a seminal event?

Most viewers have naturally assumed that, since Matthew Lipman was the chief spokesperson in the film, it primarily reflected his own project, which he had labelled 'Philosophy for Children' and which had already by 1990 become commonly abbreviated to P4C. And perhaps that is true. But it also reflected a practice and philosophy that was different from his, and deserves clear recognition, namely the COPI (Community of Philosophical Inquiry) approach developed by Dr Catherine McCall, who also appeared in the film. The model of practice with 6 year olds that it showed, indeed, was hers. Now is not the place to go into full details about the commonalities and differences between Lipman's P4C and McCall's COPI, but it should be certainly be registered that both saw the 'community of inquiry' as central to their practice.

One distinctive difference between the two approaches was that COPI placed more emphasis on developing the skills of the philosophical facilitator by learning about philosophical traditions and practising some models in particular (especially Hegelian dialectic). In contrast, Lipman relied more on teachers' immersion in the large body of stories for children and support materials that he and his associates at Montclair University had produced in the 1970s and 1980s.

This writer takes an even-handed view of these two emphases, which are mixed to varying degrees in different countries, and indeed continue to be represented in different ways and approaches within the UK itself. It is probably fair to say that the COPI approach has had more traction in Scotland, McCall's native country, where she returned after several years of working with Lipman in USA, while the more gradual (but less reliable) approach of encouraging teachers to get going and 'learn on the job' is more prevalent in other countries in the UK.

Notwithstanding, many of those who came to Philosophy for Children as a result of the BBC documentary and contributed to the development of SAPERE might still regard Lipman's materials as the Gold Standard, or at least the benchmark, of philosophical resources for children, and McCall's COPI as a benchmark for philosophical facilitation with children.

Mapping a route

Did SAPERE set off with the best of both worlds, then? Not exactly. There were good reasons for developing a new route map, and not least of these was that SAPERE was certainly not setting off in the 'best of all possible worlds'. 1990, when 200 viewers of the BBC documentary met for a first conference at the West London Institute, was a turbulent enough year in world politics – the Berlin Wall had been opened in the previous year – but, more to the point of this chapter, the educational world in the UK (or, to be more accurate, in England and Wales) was literally coming to terms with a new National Curriculum, whose first programmes of study came into effect in September 1989. This was a process that one high-profile chief education officer referred to as 'death by a thousand files', and the imposition of a state-determined curriculum was, at the time, much more controversial in principle than it is now.

In such circumstances, it would have been foolhardy to have staked the future of P4C in the country on the foundation of Lipman's (similarly voluminous) materials; and it would have been almost equally quixotic to have suggested that teachers, let alone schools, might invest money and time in extensive professional development. Yet this was clearly a moment to be seized, with over 2,000 people having contacted the BBC to ask what P4C, if any, was going on in the UK. Actually, there had been some pioneers who had introduced P4C into their practice before the documentary, and among them was Dr Will Robinson. He had even run a P4C course for teachers at Edge Hill College, and was an obvious person to serve as first chair of SAPERE.

But if Lipman's materials were only potential starting points, and full-blown training for teachers was a pipe dream, what sensible strategy could there be for giving P4C a chance in schools, let alone for its becoming established? Well, the strategy was still to offer training. One cannot start building a community of enquiry on the back of just reading a book – without any experience of it, still less any reflection on one's practice. But it would have to be very carefully designed training, and with some simple, inexpensive resources for teachers to use.

Happily, both of these things came to be. In the first place, a group of people with very varied expertise but common sense (I might say, *phronesis*) fairly quickly developed a three-stage training programme that has, in essence, stood the test of 25 years. Robert Fisher, a former primary head but by then a teacher educator at the West London Institute, soon to be part of Brunel University, was perhaps the most in tune with what would be suitable for teachers in these circumstances. But every voice was heard, and the outcome was a programme of training that provided exactly the right balance of theory and practice, of realism and idealism.

At roughly the same time, a key step was made by another member of the core group, Karin Murris, who had trialled the Lipman materials in some of her local schools with mixed results. As an experienced librarian, she recognised the potential of picture books for stimulating philosophical enquiry, especially with younger children, and her book, *Teaching Philosophy with Picture Books* (Murris, 1992), seized the imagination of every primary teacher introduced to it. This, together with the original publication *Stories for Thinking* (Fisher, 1996) and the subsequent Stories for Thinking series (1996–2000), also written by Fisher, provided models of the sort of resources that teachers could readily access and use effectively with their children.

True to say, P4C did not suddenly crop up all over the country. Several of the early courses did not recruit well; a few even ran at a loss financially. Schools were struggling to cope with 'curriculum overload' well into the 1990s (they still do) and many teachers still reacted with incredulity at the idea of 'adding' philosophy to the timetable. '*You can't be serious!*' must have been in the minds, if not specifically articulated, of many head teachers.

Every good project needs good people

So, more was needed than just an infrastructure of courses and resources. At least two other vital things had to be in place. One was a dedicated team that could hold the Society and central organisation together. The other was, in effect, an argument: a powerful rationale for doing philosophy with children.

At the start of this chapter I made clear that it would be only a partial account of the evolution of P4C in the UK, and I shall certainly not go into the intricacies of the development of SAPERE itself as an organisation. But it would be wrong not to mention Steve Williams and Sara Liptai, secretaries in its early days, and Will Ord and Alison Hall, later chairs. It is probably no exaggeration to say that without the efforts of any of these people, the Society – and almost certainly the P4C project – would have collapsed. And these people continue to influence its evolution in ways varying from strategic and intellectual guidance to project management and quality control. (Lizzy Lewis, the first appointed member of staff but still serving as development manager, has also been essential to the whole project's success.)

But back to the argument(s) …

A good rationale and evidence base

A preliminary argument needed to be met – one that Lipman himself spent years facing down in the USA – namely, that children (loosely defined, of course) were simply incapable of doing philosophy, and so it would be a complete waste of time to try and get them to do it. I will not now rehearse the reasons for and against this argument – partly because it has had less and less traction over time. But I do want to record that Joanna Haynes' book, *Children as Philosophers* (2001), was very instrumental in changing people's thinking for the better in this respect.

Children can and do wonder about the meaning of words (and the significance of 'things') just as adults do *qua* philosophers; moreover, they go on to figure out many meanings, causes, reasons, purposes and values for themselves, without over-reliance on ideas set in texts. In that sense, indeed, they are 'natural' philosophers.

What, though, were the positive arguments to promote P4C in schools? To be fair and accurate, some of them were, themselves, very instrumentalist – and SAPERE did not flinch from using them. So, if there was concern about children's confidence or competence in speaking, it was argued (with good reason) that P4C helped most children grow in either or both respects. If there was concern about children's literacy scores, it was argued (with evidence from Derby and Dyfed in the 1990s, supporting the welter of test scores from the USA in 1980s) that children's comprehension skills improved with P4C. And if there was concern about children's will or skill to think critically – or creatively – the 2003 'Clackmannanshire' project, run by Paul Cleghorn and validated by Professor Topping of University of Dundee, was often quoted to demonstrate the cognitive benefits of P4C.

There was, it must be admitted, a glossing over of the fact that not all of the research results involved Lipman's materials, and that different projects had facilitators who had experienced a diverse range of training. If anything, though, it could have been seen as both remarkable and the more significant that, despite such variety, 'results' seemed steadily positive. (And, of course, they continue to come. Very recent research projects in Texas and in England have added to the impressive collection.)

What can be said, with some security, is that a common strand to all of the projects has been the intended and actual practice of a community of enquiry approach, and this has increasingly been the banner under which P4C has been promoted, at least by SAPERE.

Extending the reach

What is more, even from the start it was recognised that this practice is as powerful for adults as it is for children and young people, and there was always an ambition to promote it in adult and informal contexts as well as in schools. Realistically, SAPERE's work on fulfilling this ambition could not begin in earnest until the idea of communities of philosophical enquiry in schools had taken root. But there were some early initiatives, which paved the way for further development.

One was a project in Barrow-in-Furness called 'Building Bridges', led by Barry Hymer, in collaboration with Paul Jenkins, of what was then called Age Concern. Senior citizens, having been introduced to philosophical enquiry in their own meetings, then built intergenerational communities of enquiry with pupils in local primary and secondary schools. It was a model that was also taken up in Northumberland, where Michelle Whitworth had a team of senior volunteers, who regularly visited schools for enquiry. Such projects are very dependent on lead individuals who, unfortunately, cannot commit their working lives to sustaining them, and both projects have ended now. One day, though, someone will not only see the societal value of such 'bridging' but also help provide the infrastructure for it to become part of the social landscape.

Another project with adults arose in the late 1990s out of the enthusiasm of Rob Lewis, who set up the first of what are now a number of 'pub clubs' in Liverpool, where adults meet for recreational philosophical enquiry. The 'Philosophy in Pubs' (PiPs) movement has spread to other cities, and remains one of a host of networks of adults that quite properly designate themselves as 'philosophical societies'.

There is a potential risk, however, in such organic developments: that different people come to such groups with different conceptions of 'philosophy', and different purposes, not to say agenda. This can be so, however cohesive and purposive the original group may have been. And, to some extent, this 'dilution' or 'diffusion' of purpose has afflicted PiPs. Nevertheless, the need remains for adults to deliberate, more or less formally, about important ideas (not merely political policies) that affect them, and SAPERE has always taken a 'let many flowers bloom' approach to adult philosophising.

It took a significant step to mark this in the early 2000s, when the SAPERE logo was changed to read 'Philosophy for Children, Colleges and Communities' – with self-directing adult communities specifically in mind (as well as reaching out to secondary schools and colleges, for whom the banner 'Philosophy for Children' never did hit the mark in the UK). It was a natural progression from this step for SAPERE to pilot courses in 'Community Philosophy', which it was able to do thanks to a grant from the Esmée Fairbairn Foundation. Steve Bramall, formerly of the Institute of Education, and Graeme Tiffany, a leading youth worker, led the project. To be fair, it has not resulted in a crop of adult communities of enquiry, but it was certainly an important 'proof of concept'. The change of logo was not merely a matter of signalling an extended aspiration; it was also a matter of bringing the concept of 'communities' more to the fore, as being what makes the P4C/SAPERE approach to philosophical enquiry distinctive.

The centrality of the community of inquiry

SAPERE recognises, of course, that philosophy can be 'done' in a variety of ways and with a variety of purposes, including formal teaching of the history of philosophical ideas, as well as the practice of facilitator-directed enquiry, in which a facilitator leads a student or class towards specific, predetermined ideas. (To some extent, it can be argued, Socrates himself followed this latter practice.)

But what Lipman made clear, when he changed the concept of the community of inquiry (originally used in the nineteenth century to refer to what we nowadays call 'the scientific community') into that of a 'community of philosophical inquiry', was that this was a radically different approach to 'philosophy'. The approach can – and arguably should – be supplemented by private study and reflection, but the community should 'follow the inquiry where it leads' (not where the facilitator says it should go), and indeed it should start from the shared interests of the group, rather than from a topic that is prescribed by a syllabus or by a (usually self-appointed) guardian of 'the' philosophic tradition.

SAPERE has remained true to this 'free spirit' of enquiry, even while recognising that sometimes children (and, for that matter, adults) might choose to enquire into a concept that may not have been held in much regard in 'the' Western tradition of philosophy, nor even by philosophers in other traditions. Often enough, though, the concepts chosen can turn out to be connected, in subtle or complex ways, with the 'big' ideas and questions of the 'great' philosophers.

Supporting and developing practice

SAPERE has also recognised from the start that the 'quality' of philosophical enquiry in communities does depend to a considerable extent on the skill with which the facilitator pushes for depth (e.g. by inviting conceptual distinctions) or for breadth (e.g. by inviting conceptual connections). Usually, the facilitator is a teacher, but SAPERE pioneered courses introducing secondary students to the art of philosophical facilitation, and is not averse to primary pupils 'giving it a go' under teacher guidance.

In general, though, it is a big enough challenge encouraging teachers to take their 'teaching hats' off and get into enquiry mode, and much of the thrust of SAPERE courses in the twenty-first century has been towards equipping them with the skill, as well as the will, to advance the children's philosophical thinking – that is, *questioning* and *testing* meanings, *expressing* and *clarifying* understandings, *evaluating* and *arguing* for points of view, etc. One example was the creation of an 'enrichment' course called 'Tools for Thinking Together' (partly inspired by *20 Thinking Tools*, the excellent resource written by Phil Cam (2006), an admired colleague and P4C leader in Australia, who has been over to the UK several times to offer his expertise).

Philosophical thinking in education

These 'tools' need not be regarded as unique to philosophical thinking, even if they might have been first used, or at least systematically practised, by philosophers. If anything, they are of even more use and value in twenty-first-century life with all of its complexities. This makes them particularly appealing to thoughtful teachers, who see it as a duty of schools to equip their pupils with generic 'skills for life' as well as qualifications for university or further education. These skills include the capacity to think *critically* and *creatively*. When one adds to these two capacities another two, one conceived by Lipman himself and the other particularly promoted by SAPERE – respectively, *caring* and *collaborative* thinking – the full complement of the 4Cs of P4C provides a well-balanced model for educators at all levels.

More precisely, the community dimension of the community of enquiry is conditioned by the aim of developing caring and collaborative thinking, while the enquiry dimension is conditioned by the aim of developing critical and creative thinking. Yet this is a holistic model, with the overall aim of keeping each dimension and each mode of thinking in harmony with the others. Therefore models of teaching and learning that overemphasise the critical at the expense of the caring (or vice-versa), or the creative at the expense of the collaborative (or vice-versa), do not follow the direction of evolution of P4C in the UK.

Proof against a narrow conception of knowledge

Moreover this model shows the distortion provided by a brief 'educational' movement in the early 2000s that can be characterised as 'the rise (and derisiveness) of anti-therapists', at least in so far as P4C might have been targeted. The basic argument of this movement was that 'therapeutic forms of teacher training' had infiltrated higher education, demonstrating an undervaluing of hard measurable outcomes, not least of knowledge. Notwithstanding the aim of therapy as one of healing and renewal, this view of education is reductionist in both the proper purposes and the refined processes of teaching and teacher education as socially just practices.

The reality is that teachers and educators in the twenty-first century know very well that knowledge is important, but also that it is the servant of *understanding*, which is the prerequisite for sound *judgement* and sane *action*. What is more, they appreciate that 'knowledge' is not merely about objective, physical matters of fact (knowing that) but is also about knowing how (skills, of various sorts) and, importantly, about knowing why (in a conative sense rather than a causal sense, that is knowing about will and *post hoc* justifications). In short, these embody human aims and principles.

Educating for knowledge in this broader sense asks a lot of modern teachers and they need all the encouragement they can get to practise the best means of doing so. Such means will include any that improve the learning environment for their pupils – that is, an environment where positive emotions towards fellow learners, and towards teachers themselves, predominate. Creating such an atmosphere may well involve 'healing' or 'curing' in their proper senses (Old English *haelan* = 'to make whole', Latin *curare* = 'to care for'). This is not to say that such 'therapy' is the ultimate purpose of education (though it could be thought of as a positive side-effect). The precise point is that it can play a healthy part in the processes that better conduce to those purposes of education in its broader sense.

Thinking carefully about caring thinking

A final note to 'lay the ghost' in this regard: it would be easy to seize upon the Lipman/P4C language of caring thinking and claim that it shows a forsaking of critical thinking in favour of something softer, with regard to expressing and sharing emotions rather than evaluating ideas and arguments. But this would be to show precisely the lack of both the caring and critical thinking that Lipman himself argued for.

In P4C terms, caring thinking is as much about taking care to understand people's ideas and experiences as it is to appreciate their values and the affective side of their thinking, including their feelings. In itself this is good thing, but also it is a necessary ingredient of (good) critical thinking. Failure to attend to such consideration(s) may lead to poor judgement, the end that critical thinking is aiming to avoid.

There is one more aspect of caring thinking that can, but should not, be overlooked, and that is the value it places upon clear and considerate expression of one's thinking (and feeling), namely the cognitive and affective aspects of ideas and beliefs. Again this is an important, if not essential, ingredient of criticality and good judgement. P4C is not, in short, against rigour in thinking and learning – quite the opposite.

Philosophy an end in itself

That might be a suitably 'big picture' statement with which to finish, but there are a few loose ends that need to be tied up before a rounded conclusion.

The first is to be clear that, for all the talk above about 'instrumentalism' and 'tools', SAPERE has never lost a sense that philosophical enquiry is quite simply worth doing for its own sake. It is an actual ingredient of, as well as an itinerary towards, a/the 'good life'. The fact that P4C continues to grow in reputation and scale of practice in the UK (though it still has a long way to go to be present in even half the schools in the country) is *prima facie* evidence that many teacher and pupils share this sense. The growth of P4C has been steady and organic, largely as a result of personal and professional recommendations, and not at all as a result of governmental backing.

Two further clarifications: PwC, and inquiry/enquiry

A couple of other points of clarity – less significant in themselves, but important for seeing how P4C has evolved in the UK, and also what 'developments' do not share the same genetic roots, so to speak. The first clarification is to note that what might appear to be major departures from Lipman's original vision (which he regarded, incidentally, as a reconstruction of both education and philosophy) are not essentially different.

One such departure was the creation of a new term and abbreviation, namely Philosophy with Children or PwC. This did, indeed, mark a proper distinction, being a term that Karin Murris preferred when she pioneered picture books and other 'stimuli' for philosophical enquiry, rather than Lipman's philosophical novels. But she has never undervalued the building of a community of enquiry as the essential process with which to undertake philosophical enquiry with children. Indeed, she has been among the most distinguished writers and thinkers in refreshing the concept of the community of enquiry, as well as taking forward the 'vision of the child' that Lipman had. Although he devised P4C for use within schools, he was not enamoured of conventional schooling in his day. He would have seen P4C, like philosophy itself, as a liberation for teachers and children alike from many of the constraints of the educational system.

Another simple (but again not hugely significant) distinction should be drawn, as between 'enquiry' and 'inquiry'. On the face of it, the general use of 'enquiry' in the UK (though we have noted Catherine McCall's preference of 'inquiry') might seem to suggest a distancing from the practice, as well as the original and general designation, of the 'community of inquiry' in the USA. There was never such distancing. SAPERE and its various supporters and partners have always had cordial and mutually respectful relations with the IAPC and its supporters. The reason for using 'enquiry' rather than 'inquiry' in the UK was as simple and pragmatic as that it better fits the acronym, SAPERE. It is not a 'principled' difference. (Nor, for that matter, was it argued to be a more 'correct' word for the process. Some have indeed argued this for the use of 'inquiry', but usage is not so clear cut, either as between American and English usage, or as between the meaning of 'making an enquiry' and 'having an inquiry'.)

On a more significant point of difference, there are those who have taken over the phrase '(doing) philosophy with children' as more or less a descriptive term for what they do. Consistent with its policy of letting 'flowers' bloom, SAPERE has not sought in any way to limit the use of the phrase. But, as hinted before and now made clear, where the process of 'doing philosophy' is not centrally that of the community of enquiry, SAPERE does not regard it as appropriate to refer to it as P4C. This does seem to be a suitable point at which to take stock and draw to a conclusion.

Taking stock – philosophy for/with children taken seriously

So, P4C has come a long way in the UK in the last 25 years. It has moved from meeting that 'You can't be serious!' sort of response to being taken very seriously as a pedagogy and philosophy. This has American 'pragmatic' roots certainly, but with a remarkably open blend of ancient and modern philosophical roots, reflecting Lipman's own broad philosophical education at the post-war American University in Shrivenham and in the Sorbonne.

The increasing attention being given by the SAPERE community to the scholarly heritage of P4C, especially in the education and development of its trainers, is one mark of the seriousness with which the Society itself treats the P (Philosophy) in P4C. Notable scholars in P4C and related fields have led the annual Advanced Seminar at Winchester University, which Pat Hannam initiated a few years ago. Indeed, one of the seminars was organised in collaboration with the Philosophy of Education Society Great Britain.

Another project, on a smaller scale, focused on the need for P4C to engage more with scholarship in regard to the contested concept of racism. Darren Chetty, who had a proper concern about the extent to which SAPERE and its trainers were ignoring important issues in this field, inspired this highly relevant and timely project.

There is, to be fair, much more that could be done to raise the standards and sights of SAPERE and P4C in the UK. However, I sometimes remind people of my reckoning from the start that 'P4C' in the UK would be a 50-year project. I had in mind that the UK, or at least England, where I received my own education, was a society that undervalued (indeed at times denigrated) philosophy as an academic discipline (not to mention as a discipline of life), and that it would take more than a single generation to restore its respect.

The project to be undertaken was that which Dewey had set in motion in 1917: 'Philosophy recovers itself when it ceases to be a device for dealing with the problems of philosophers and becomes a method, cultivated by philosophers, for dealing with the problems of men [sic].' It was a project that Lipman surely gave new impetus to even though the ground in the USA was no more fertile than in England. Nevertheless, as I hope this and succeeding chapters show, the first 25 years or so of P4C in the UK have seen encouraging changes and developments and there is good reason for optimism for the next 25 years.

SAPERE has seen educational fashions come and go, such as Circle Time and Learning to Learn, not to mention governmental initiatives such as Literacy Hour and SEAL. During this time it has established itself as a unique intervention that meets most of the goals of those initiatives, such as communicative, reading, metacognitive, social and emotional skills, in addition to generic thinking skills. It may also influence numeracy skills positively, as shown in the Education Endowment Foundation research project (Gorard *et al.*, 2015).

A pedagogy for the twenty-first century

Truly, it is a 'pedagogy for the twenty-first century', overlapping importantly with other pedagogies that will only grow in significance as humans (and especially their education systems) come to terms with the knowledge 'explosion' and cultural complexity. Enquiry-based Learning (better termed 'Enquiry-driven Learning') is one such pedagogy, as is Dialogic Teaching (also better termed 'Dialogical Learning'). Both of these, arguably, draw much of their strength from constructivist theory, such as the ideas of Vygotsky, which influenced Lipman himself.

That theory, however, and its associated pedagogies still tend to talk about 'knowledge constructs', whereas Lipman was more focused on 'concept construction' (or what he called 'concept-formation'). This, I suggest, is the better way of thinking. In education 'knowledge' is typically traded in and with words, and words are all more or less concepts. The educational challenge is not primarily that of accumulating knowledge of more and more facts, but that of making *sense* of the language in which those facts are presented. This language for many students becomes overwhelming in its denseness as well as its sheer volume.

What teachers, as well as students, need to concentrate on is not knowledge so much as understanding, especially of key concepts in each of the subjects. In that sense, we need not a core knowledge curriculum, nor even an enquiry-based curriculum, but quite simply a core concept curriculum. If the focus were indeed on understanding core concepts, students, led by good teachers, would inevitably pick up valuable knowledge, through asking good questions and applying good reasoning, precisely the skills that P4C prizes and practises above all others.

This, then, is the direction that P4C will be pushing in the coming years, making the link with curricula and good teaching clearer and more manageable. To this end, SAPERE has two recently developed projects.

Ways ahead

One of these projects is a more sustainable model (known as 'Going for Gold') of embedding P4C in whole schools over two to three years. After initial training, teachers are given support, mainly by distance but some in-class, in the practice of philosophical skills and, more generally, the cultivation of philosophical dispositions or 'habits of mind'.

The other is a partnership model whereby teacher educators in higher education are given 'fast-track' training so as to become 'partner educators', approved to introduce P4C to teacher trainees. With their background already in introducing students to good models of teaching and learning, offering approved training in P4C could be the icing on their (students') cake. No one would be expecting them all to become teachers of philosophy; the point would be to help them all teach more philosophically – whatever their subject and age speciality.

It would be especially pleasing if, by this and other means, P4C could become as widely respected in the institutions of teacher education as it is in UK schools themselves. Not only would that ensure even greater sustainability, it could also contribute to the restoration of philosophy at the heart of education, and to the recognition that education is a proper business, if not the heart, of philosophy.

References

Cam, P. (2006) *20 Thinking Tools*. Camberwell, VIC: ACER Press.

Dewey, J. (1917) The need for a recovery of philosophy. In J. Dewey (ed.) *Creative Intelligence: Essays in the pragmatic attitude* (pp. 3–69). New York: Holt.

Fisher, R. (1996) *Stories for Thinking*. Oxford: Nash Pollock.

Gorard, S., Siddiqui, N. and Huat See, B. (2015) Philosophy for Children Evaluation Report and Executive Summary. Education Endowment Foundation. Available at: https://educationendowment foundation.org.uk/uploads/pdf/Philosophy_for_Children.pdf (accessed 4 January 2016).

Haynes, J. (2001) *Children as Philosophers: Learning through enquiry and dialogue in the primary classroom*. Abingdon: Routledge.

Murris, K. (1992) *Teaching Philosophy with Picture Books*. London: Infonet.

Lipman, M. (1980) *Philosophy in the Classroom*, 2nd edn. Philadelphia: Temple Press.

Lipman, M. (2003) *Thinking in Education*, 2nd edn. Cambridge: Cambridge University Press.

Lipman, M. (2009) *A Life Teaching Thinking*. Montclair: Institute for the Advancement of Philosophy for Children.

Socrates for Six Year Olds (1990) BBC film.

2

EDUCATION AS A PHILOSOPHICAL ENDEAVOUR

Naomi McLeod

This chapter starts by considering different historical philosophical perspectives on the purpose and value of education. The legacy of Aristotle is used to explore how education is viewed and how this influences the purpose it serves. The distinction between education as a process and/or a product is examined as a starting point, particularly in relation to the relevance of developing thinking and questioning skills (Barnes, 1976). Here the need for practical wisdom to inform ethical judgements as a source of moral action is considered as an application of *phronesis* (Carr and Kemmis, 1986; Kemmis, 2010). This process of *phronesis praxis* begins with a question or situation, which then leads to thinking about a situation in the light of personal understandings of what is good or what makes for human flourishing (Kemmis, 2010). At the core of this open questioning process is the necessity for a critically reflective approach by the adult, teacher or facilitator. As such, Dewey's attitudes, competencies and lenses for critical reflection are offered as an alternative to a mechanistic product-driven view of teaching (Moss, 2008). In doing so, Schön's 'new epistemology' through 'convergence of meaning' for praxis is used so the teacher can adopt a creative and reflective way of facilitating an open process of 'deep-level', experiential child-led learning (Laevers, 2000; Claxton, 2003; Schön, 1987). This chapter concludes with consideration of how adults can nurture a critically reflective process so that education as a process of phronesis can be facilitated.

A historical overview of the purpose of education: the legacy of Aristotle, Dewey and Schön: knowledge as a process or product?

The distinction between the technical (productive/product related) and practical (process/ knowing why) is important as a starting point in determining the function of education. Here the legacy of Aristotle (384–322 BC) and his classification of knowledge is drawn on as a way of showing how knowledge was viewed and how this influenced the purpose it served (Barnes, 1976). If the purpose of knowledge was the pursuit of making action, its function was the attainment of knowledge to make or produce something. According to Aristotle, this kind of knowledge and enquiry is involved in productive disciplines. Aristotle associated this form of thinking and doing with the work of craftspeople or artisans. Making action is dependent upon the exercising of skill (what the Greeks called *techne*), which always results from the idea, image or pattern of what the artisan wants to make. In other words, a person has a guiding plan or idea. This way of thinking is dominated by the plan, and actions are directed towards the given end product (Grundy, 1987).

In contrast, the *practical* (process of knowing why), according to Aristotle (Barnes, 1976), deals with an awareness of ethical and political life: the intention being on developing practical wisdom and knowledge (Carr and Kemmis, 1986) involving the making of moral judgements and human interaction. Kemmis (2010) and Grundy (1987) consider this type of knowing as *phronesis praxis*, or the knowing why, the source of moral action. The process, beginning with a question or situation, invokes deliberation and reflection on what is good, either for the self or for human society (Kemmis, 2010). This process or *phronesis* results in a doing-action or *praxis*, and is therefore process centred. The 'idea' in the interaction is personal, subjective and never fully formed; rather it is constantly being formed and influenced by the situation in a very organic way (Grundy, 1987). This process is held together by a way of 'saying, doing and relating – so that each informs the other' (Kemmis, 2010, p. 419). This is influenced by the identity of an individual as a result of their experiences, beliefs, values and understandings of education as a whole (Reed and Canning, 2010).

Such an understanding of education in this sense involves personal and professional attributes that merge as one takes ownership of why different approaches are taken as part of teaching. During this process, the relationship between theory (the thinking process) and practice (the action as a result) fuse and the teacher develops a personal responsibility for the outcomes experienced by the learner. Rather than a mechanistic approach to teaching (Moss, 2008, p. xvi) as a 'technician' reliant on 'unreflective induction' (Claxton, 2003, p. 2), the teacher is viewed as an artist and reflective practice as an art form (Schön, 1987), a creative, open process in collaboration with others. In a similar way, van Manen (1995) questions the appropriateness of implicit theory in relation to practice and suggests that instead, actions should give purpose to the words used as part of a teaching context so that purpose is demonstrated through action. The importance of understanding and recognising different behaviours involving words and actions as part of communication is identified by Gilroy (1993). Within teacher–child interactions, Gilroy emphasises the value of making sense by questioning personal interpretations and giving reasons, so that interpretations by the teacher of the shared interaction are accurate.

Praxis: informed knowledge for a moral intent

This open form of reasoning known as praxis or an intentional and committed action with moral intent involves behaving 'for the good of humankind in acts consciously and *collectively* performed to contribute to the good' (Kemmis, 2010, p. 419). By reflecting on collective and individual action and its consequences, Kemmis argues that this is 'how we learn *wisdom* and how we develop what Aristotle called *phronesis*' (2010, p. 419). As such we are guided to behave wisely. For Aristotle, *phronesis praxis* was guided by a moral disposition to act truly and rightly: a concern to further human well-being and the good life. In relation to reflection, Aristotle prioritised the quality of the experience and the principles and values that influence the reflective experience (Zeichner, 1983; Barnes, 1976). For Russell and Munby (1992, p. 3), the knowledge development and the application are equally essential as the key to reflection for professionals as part of the process of 'systematic and deliberate thinking back over one's actions'.

Aristotle's philosophical thinking on the value of education influenced Dewey and likewise Schön's (1983, 1987) work on reflection, in particular the emphasis on practical application and the requisite attitudes necessary for a critically reflective approach. These were viewed as essential to being able to question the product-driven dominant discourse seen within the processes of education today.

The legacy of Dewey: using critical reflection for new ways of seeing

John Dewey's (1929) theory of knowing and (1933) concept of reflection, from philosophical thinking to practical application in education by professionals, is offered as a practical way for promoting thinking about knowledge and understanding about the purpose of education in practice. According to Dewey, reflective action is 'careful consideration of any belief or supposed form of knowledge in light of the grounds that support it and the further consequence to which it leads' (1933, p. 9). For Dewey, reflective thinking involved a state of doubt or uncertainty and the resulting act of searching and inquiry to make sense of a concern, a question or a problem (1933). In this context it is helpful to consider Loughran's (2006) definition of the word 'problem', which he acknowledges tends to have negative connotations and conjures up images of mistakes and errors of judgement. He therefore identifies a problem as 'a situation that attracts attention; something that is curious or puzzling; something that invites further consideration beyond that which might initially have been anticipated' (p. 45).

Dewey used reflection to explain the principles of human thinking and distinguished between non-critical and critical (or reflexive) thinking. For Dewey (1933), reflection supported the development of knowledge as a guide for behaving wisely, which could then be applied to practice in a meaningful and purposeful way. He saw reflective thinking as a way to discover specific connections between actions and consequences, enabling learning from experience, developing further knowledge and improving problem-solving skills. As such, his understanding of reflection started by seeing a situation as a cause for concern or a problem with a variety of open possibilities that are considered in light of previous experience or understanding. Here we see praxis as an intentional and committed action with moral intent behaving 'for the good of humankind in acts consciously and collectively performed to contribute to the good' (Kemmis, 2010, p. 419). At the heart of this process, Dewey's attitudes are a crucial element of critical reflection and for behaving wisely or developing wisdom today.

Dewey's attitudes

At the heart of Dewey's (1933) reflective process, he emphasised three essential attitudes: (1) open-minded, (2) responsible and (3) wholehearted. Open-mindedness is, as Dewey noted, 'active desire to listen to more sides than one, to give heed to facts from whatever source they come, to give full attention to alternative possibilities, to recognise the possibility of error even in the beliefs which are dearest to us' (1933, p. 30).

Hassan (2005) clarifies the complexity of this, mainly because of the lifetime biases and beliefs attached to our own perceptions. In addition, Scharmer (2009) refers to the 'blind spot', the part we do not see because of our inability to see 'the inner place (source) from which our attention and action originate' (p. 464).

Still today, Dewey's (1933) attitudes are used and viewed as essential by many current writers on critical reflection, such as Moon (2008), Pollard (2002) and Brookfield (1995), who refer to Dewey's work in creating the right attitude for critical reflection. As part of Western culture, Levinas (Critchley *et al.*, 1996) articulates the danger of not seeing and turning the new into the same (Rinaldi, 2006) rather than something fresh and different to be valued. Scharmer explains: 'When we listen, we usually hear very little other than what we have heard before … we selectively hear only what we recognise, interpret what we hear based on our past views and feelings and draw conclusions much like those we have drawn before' (2009, p. xiv).

Similarly, Hassan echoes the words of Scharmer: 'Failure to see is the biggest barrier towards tackling our challenges' (2005, p. 6). As part of an open attitude, Dewey (1933) considered the ability to see situations in new and different ways: being open to new ideas and thoughts, which may not have previously been considered. This means being prepared to hear views and ideas that may be contrary to our own and being able to admit that a prior belief may be incorrect particularly in relation to pedagogy (Rinaldi, 2006).

This requirement of openness as an attitude also resonates particularly closely with Brookfield's four lenses of critical reflection (1995) and Moon's (2008) emphasis on creating the right atmosphere for deep self-awareness, critical reflection and phronesis.

The second attitude necessary for critical reflection and valuing education as phronesis, according to Dewey (1933), is the responsibility to consider the ethical consequences of a planned or intended action. This closely resembles praxis as an intentional action with a moral intent and as such embodies a commitment to human well-being and the search for truth and respect for others (Bernstein, 1983).

The third of Dewey's (Boydston and Rorty, 2008) necessary attitudes is wholeheartedness, which he suggested required energy and enthusiasm: 'There is no greater enemy of effective thinking than divided interest … A genuine enthusiasm is an attitude that operates as an intellectual force. The person is absorbed, the subject carries on' (p. 136). Dimova and Loughran (2009) reinforce the essential need for an authentic and personal engagement with reflection, so that interest is maintained, ideas are sought and there is a desire for knowing. Here the right atmosphere or attitudes as an integral part of facilitating a critically reflective approach are evident (Moon, 2008). However, Levinas warns that as part of the process of the will to know, there is the danger that the new knowledge is taken and turned into the familiar knowledge (Peperzak *et al.*, 1996).

The principles of reflection and the willingness to query values, as advocated by Dewey, are acknowledged as critical by Moon (2008) today, but at the same time as complex and difficult (Scharmer, 2009; Hassan, 2005). Marcos, Miguel and Tillema (2009) emphasise how hard it is to commit to Dewey's attitudes, particularly in the outcome-driven context of cultural forces and structures. Wilkins (2015) also acknowledges how externally imposed political policies and audits can prevent students and practitioners from asking open questions about the purpose of education.

Dewey's competencies

In relation to Dewey, Pollard (2002) offers three types of competence necessary for education as phronesis. These are (1) empirical, (2) analytical and (3) evaluative. Empirical competence relates to being aware of two types of observations: objective – that is, what is seen – and subjective – what people feel or think. Being aware of these is important but difficult when enquiring into our own practice (Davies and Artaraz, 2009; Hassan, 2009). Analytical competence relates to deciding how to interpret observations as part of a framework (such as in relation to participation and critical reflection). Evaluative competence refers to being aware of one's own values in order to understand and appreciate the experience of others. As already discussed, this can be difficult given personal cultural experiences (Rinaldi, 2006) and influences on values (Clough and Nutbrown, 2007).

Dewey's lenses

Brookfield (1995) presents four distinct but interconnecting 'lenses' as necessary for teachers to achieve the level of insight, critical reflection and wisdom. The four lenses of reflection are (1) personal self-reflection, (2) reflection from the children's perspective, (3) the lens provided by colleagues as critical friends, and (4) viewing practice through the lens of literature. The most distinguishing feature of the first lens, indeed of the reflective process as a whole, is the essential requirement to seek out underpinning assumptions (Brookfield, 1995). Here the term 'hunting' is used to reinforce the need for self-appraisal: 'Assumptions are the taken for granted beliefs about the world and our place within it that seem so obvious to us as not to need stating explicitly' (Brookfield, 1995, p. 2). In effect we embody our own assumptions and it is these that give purpose to who we are and what we do. Failure to search for these underpinning influences creates the danger that the whole process of reflection will be stifled and not adopted as intended.

Indeed as Marcos *et al.* (2009) found in many instances, the 'how' to reflect received much less attention than the 'what', thus contributing to the fragmented reflective processes identified. Similarly, the study by Davies and Artaraz (2009) identifies the need to explore the foundations of practitioners' views, attitudes and practice in relation to knowledge. This ability to see afresh is a very complex and difficult thing to acquire because of lifetime biases and embedded beliefs (Hassan, 2009). It is only through a genuine openness and willingness to examine personal beliefs, values and experiences that a teacher is able to put themselves in the position of the 'other' (a child). By reflecting on collective and individual action and its consequences, *wisdom* is learned and *phronesis* is developed.

However, Ashworth (2004) stresses how a lack of attunement to the other person as part of dialogue can have a subverting effect on behaving for the good of humankind. During reflective conversations about practice, colleagues need to be very sensitive about aspects of each other's practice that were previously hidden.

Schön's praxis: a new epistemology through convergence of meaning

In comparison to Dewey, Schön's (1983) views on critical reflection were closely linked with the notion of self-reflection and an optimistic vision of the power of individuals to better understand their work and improve their practice. For Schön, reflection was a medium for the acquisition of professional knowledge – a means of understanding 'tacit knowledge' (1983, p. 54), or ordinary practical knowledge (knowing-in-action), which he claimed could be understood through two forms of reflection that were central to his thinking: reflection-*in*-action, and reflection-*on*-action.

Reflection-on-action is comparable to Dewey's concept of reflection as a purposeful and conscious act, a reconstruction of an experience by looking and thinking back over one's practice. Reflection-in-action was what Schön referred to as 'a new epistemology of practice', that would stand the question of professional knowledge on its head (1983, p. xi).

According to Schön, reflection-*in*-action is more about 'thinking on your feet, keeping your wits about you, and learning by doing suggest[ing] not only that we can think about doing but that we can think about doing something while doing it' (1983, p. 54). Reflection-in-action involves consideration of experiences, connecting with personal feelings, and attending to theories used as part of practice. In addition, reflection-in-action entails building new understandings to inform personal actions in the situation that unfolds so that:

> The practitioner allows himself to experience surprise, puzzlement, or confusion in a situation, which he finds uncertain or unique. He reflects on the phenomenon before him, and on the prior understandings, which have been implicit in his behaviour. He carries out an experiment, which serves to generate both a new understanding of the phenomenon and a change in the situation.
>
> *(Schön, 1983, p. 68)*

As such, reflection-in-action is about how practitioners create new knowledge as part of dealing with and appreciating problematic situations in action. Grimmett (1988, p. 13) notes that it is the emphasis on the 'crucible of action' that sets Schön's (1983) work apart. The process of reflection-in-action was an idealised one and rare according to Schön. In proposing his 'new epistemology' Schön claimed a 'convergence of meaning' (1987, p. 99). By convergence of meaning, Newman (1999) clarifies Schön's interpretation of openness and agreed meaning of what is understood as part of communication between the master and the student (or in the case of this study, the teacher and the child). This depends on and occurs as a result of a dialogue having three essential features: (1) communication has to take place in context; (2) there is an understanding of language consisting of interwoven words and actions; and (3) there is reciprocal reflection-in-action on tacit knowing-in-action (Schön, 1987).

Schön (1983) considered that when the practitioner experienced something unexpected or unfamiliar, through 'convergence of meaning', reflection-in-action led to a rethink in-action so that there was an 'on the spot experiment of trying out new actions to explore newly intended phenomena or occurrences' (p. 28). These new actions could then be affirmed so that changes could be made for the better: 'for the good of humankind' (Kemmis, 2010). Therefore convergence of meaning acts consciously and is collectively performed, developing *wisdom* – what Aristotle referred to as *phronesis*. In creating such a new epistemology through convergence of meaning, Gilroy (1993) is conscious of the challenges in recognising or interpreting what is known. For Gilroy, 'the "knowledge" or phronesis, produced by reflection can only be recognised by further reflection, which in turn requires reflection to recognise it as knowledge, and so on' (1993, p. 138).

In many respects, Schön draws on Aristotle's different forms of knowledge and the practitioner who aspires to be more than a 'worker-as-technician' (Moss, 2008, p. xiii): a process that draws on ancient wisdom and multiple forms of knowing offering authentic connection with the self and a shift in awareness.

A philosophical endeavour committed to phronesis as a way forward

In contrast to outcome-driven views or a deficit model of education (Dockett and Perry, 2007), an open form of praxis as an intentional and committed action with moral intent behaving for the good of humankind (Kemmis, 2010) involves approaches to learning that draw on deeper dispositions and competencies, such as self-confidence, curiosity, exploration, intuition, imagination, creativity and expression. Without these, children are hindered in developing wisdom. For a philosophical approach, committed to phronesis as a way forward, children need to be able to interpret for themselves, make connections and make sense of situations. At the heart of this process is a curiosity linked to an intense awareness of feelings and thoughts and a desire to explore (McLeod *et al.*, forthcoming; Laevers, 2000).

Conclusion

Clearly the process of becoming wise, facilitating a process of phronesis, involves a meta-cognitive course of action requiring awareness and self-examination of what is thought and done, which then results in a conscious change. This apparently smooth neat process would not seem to represent the outcome-driven, product-focused dominant discourse approach to knowledge evident today. The question of whether it is possible to influence teachers' views, assumptions and understandings regarding knowledge as phronesis is grounded in underlying values and attitudes to listening (McLeod *et al.*, forthcoming) and facilitating appropriate conditions for change (McCormack and Boomer, 2007).

References

Ashworth, P. (2004) Understanding the transformation of what is already known. *Teaching in Higher Education*, 9(2), 147–58.

Barnes, J. (1976) *Introduction to Aristotle: The Nicomachean Ethics*. Harmondsworth: Penguin.

Bernstein, R. J. (1983) *Beyond Objectivism and Relativism: Science, hermeneutics and praxis*. Oxford: Basil Blackwell.

Boydston, J. and Edelston Toulmin, S. (eds) (2008) *The Later Works of John Dewey, Vol. 4, 1925–1953: The quest for certainty* (Collected Works of John Dewey, 1882–1953). Carbondale, IL: South Illinois University Press.

Boydston, J. and Rorty, R. (eds) (2008) *The Later Works of John Dewey, Vol. 8, 1925–1953: Essays and how we think*, revised edition (Collected Works of John Dewey, 1882–1953). Carbondale, IL: South Illinois University Press.

Brookfield, S. D. (1995) *Becoming a Critically Reflective Teacher*. San Francisco: Jossey-Bass.

Carr, W. and Kemmis, S. (1986) *Becoming Critical: Education, knowledge and action research*. Lewes: Falmer Press.

Claxton, G. (2003) *The Intuitive Practitioner: On the value of not always knowing what one is doing*. Maidenhead: Open University Press.

Clough, P. and Nutbrown, C. (2007) *A Student's Guide to Methodology*. London: Sage.

Critchley, S., Peperzak, A. T. and Bernasconi, R. (eds) (1996) *Emmanuel Levinas: Basic philosophical writings*. Bloomington: Indiana University Press.

Davies, S. and Artaraz, K. (2009) Towards an understanding of factors influencing early years professionals' practice of consultation with young people. *Children and Society*, 23(1), 57–69.

Dewey, J. (1933) *How We Think: A restatement of the relation of reflective thinking to the educative process*. New York: Heath and Co.

Dimova, Y. and Loughran, J. (2009) Developing a big picture understanding of reflection in pedagogical practice. *Reflective Practice*, 10(2), 205–17.

Dockett, S. and Perry, B. (2007) Trusting children's accounts in research. *Early Childhood Research*, 5(1), 47–63.

Gilroy, P. (1993) Reflections on Schön: An epistemological critique and a practical alternative. In P. Gilroy and M. Smith (eds) *International Analyses of Teacher Education* (pp. 125–42). Abingdon: Carfax.

Grimmett, P. P. (1988) The nature of reflection and Schön's conception in perspective. In P. P. Grimmett and G. L. Erickson (eds) *Reflection in Teacher Education* (pp. 5–15). New York: Teacher College Press.

Grundy, S. (1987) *Curriculum: Product or praxis*. Oxford: Routledge Falmer.

Hassan, Z. (2005) *Connecting to Source*. Online at: www.world changing.com (accessed 24 July 2010).

Kemmis, S. (2010). What is to be done? The place of action research. *Educational Action Research*, 18(4), 417–27.

Laevers, F. (2000) Forward to Basics! Deep-level-learning and the experiential approach. *Early Years*, 20(2), 20–9.

Loughran, J. (2006) A response to 'Reflecting on the self'. *Reflective Practice*, 7(1), 43–53. DOI: 10.1080/14623940500489716.

Marcos, J. J. M., Miguel, E. S. and Tillema, H. (2009) Teacher reflections on action: What is said (in research) but what is done (in teaching). *Reflective Practice*, 10(2), 191–204.

McCormack, B. and Boomer, C. (2007) *Creating the Conditions for Growth. Report on the Belfast City Hospital and the Royal Hospitals Collaborative Practice Development Programme*. Belfast, NI: Belfast Health and Social Care Trust.

McLeod, N., Wright, D., McCall, K. and Fuji, M. (forthcoming) Patterns and rhythms: Facilitating young children's engagement at Tate Liverpool. *Journal of Early Childhood Research*.

Moon, J. (2008) *Critical Thinking: An exploration of theory and practice*. Oxford: Routledge.

Moss, P. (2008) Foreword. In A. Paige-Smith and A. Craft (eds) *Developing Reflective Practice in the Early Years* (pp. xii–xvi). Maidenhead: Open University Press.

Newman, S. (1999) Constructing and critiquing reflective practice. *Educational Action Research*, 7(1), 145–63.

Peperzak, A. T., Critchley, S. and Bernasconi, R. (1996) *Emmanuel Levinas: Basic philosophical writings: Studies in continental thought*. Bloomington: Indiana University Press.

Pollard. A. (2002) *Reflective Teaching*. London: Continuum.

Reed, M. and Canning, N. (2010) *Reflective Practice in the Early Years*. London: Sage.

Rinaldi, C. (2006) *In Dialogue with Reggio Emilia: Listening, researching and learning*. London: Routledge.

Russell, T. and Munby, H. (1992) *Teachers and Teaching: From classroom to reflection*. Brighton: Falmer Press.

Scharmer, C. O. (2009) *Theory U: Leading from the future as it emerges*. San Francisco: Berrett-Koehler.

Schön, D. A. (1983) *The Reflective Practitioner: How professionals think in action*. New York: Basic Books.

Schön, D. A. (1987) *Educating the Reflective Practitioner: Toward a new design for teaching*. San Francisco: Jossey-Bass.

van Manen, M. (1995) Epistemology of reflective practice. *Teachers and Teaching: Theory and Practice*, 1(1), 33–50.

Wilkins, C. (2015) Educational reform in England: Quality and equity in the performative school. *International Journal of Inclusive Education*, 19(11), 1–18.

Zeichner, K. M. (1983) Alternative paradigms of teacher education. *Journal of Teacher Education*, 34(3), 3–9.

PART 2

P4C as a pedagogical approach

3

THE CONSTRUCT OF THE CHILD

The 'C' in PwC

Sue Lyle

This chapter reports on some professional development instituted to promote teachers' critical reflection on discourses of childhood that influence their everyday practice in Philosophy with Children. These professional development sessions, in the form of workshops with teachers, grew out of research carried out for the Philosophy for Children in Schools Project. This is an ongoing research project, which explores the impact of Philosophy with Children on classroom practice in schools in South Wales (UK). The research has identified discourses of childhood as a key construct that impacts on teacher engagement with PwC. It raises the question of how we imagine, construct or understand the 'C' in PwC and what this might indicate about society's values and adult–child power relationships (John, 2003).

Theoretical standpoint

The primary starting point for this chapter is a consideration of how we understand the 'C' in PwC by asking, 'Who is the child before us?' This is important, for it is the construction of child that provides the lens through which we view the children in our schools. In addressing this question I begin by outlining the particular theoretical lenses that shape the thinking in this chapter. My analysis is informed by social constructionism: that is, the view that our beliefs about and attitudes towards children (and everything else) are socially constructed. Furthermore, drawing on post-structuralist ideas, I problematise the ways in which children are constructed in the here and now in order to better understand how current educational policy impacts on the organisation of schools, and the influence this has on those wishing to introduce philosophy with children in classrooms.

I take the view that the concept of child is a social, cultural and historical construction – that is to say, there is no universal child waiting to be discovered through scientific means. This view entails a critique of a scientific view of the child coming from biology and psychology that purports to tell us what a child is. I also embrace a narrative turn in research that claims our world is produced through stories and that the stories we tell ourselves about children create the social and cultural location in which children are raised. In fact, stories of children from diverse contexts can disrupt our taken-for-granted understandings drawn from scientific research and explicate the constructed nature of childhood. Today the concept of 'child' and 'childhood' is being challenged by the diverse experiences of the world's children. Our globalised world shows us there are many different ways of being a child in the twenty-first century (Kehily, 2015). The blight of AIDS means that children as young as 8 lead households all over Africa, calling into question our assumptions about the relationship between chronological age and maturity. The media presents daily stories of the hundreds of thousands of children living in refugee camps across the world, and the resilience of these children.

Such narratives challenge the implication that children are passive victims of events. Rather, they present them as active meaning-makers, capable of understanding their lives and able to make decisions (Alderson, 2000). If we listen to the voices of children – the child soldier (Beah, 2007), those displaced (Eggers, 2006), the 8-year-old adopted Chinese girl creating meaning out of growing up in America (Ying Ying Fry and Klatzkin, 2001) or the inspirational Malala (Yousafzai and Lamb, 2013), joint winner of the 2014 Nobel Peace Prize at the age of 17 who engaged in political action to assert her right to education – we see how children's life experiences and contexts impact on their agency, actions and understanding. Such stories challenge Western, scientific conceptions of childhood. However, it is not my intention to compare and contrast different childhoods, important as this is: my focus here is on children attending schools in advanced capitalist democracies (itself a metaphor that separates such societies from the rest of the world that are not considered advanced) in order to identify and disrupt the many different kinds of discourses about 'child' that are available to teachers.

Even within advanced capitalism, there are many different stories to account for childhood. A report from UNICEF (2007) ranks the UK and USA at the bottom of the table of child well-being, suggesting that the experiences of children who grow up in poverty constructs childhood in particular ways. Each story we tell about children contains assumptions that are informed by particular sets of values and ethical standpoints. It is important therefore that we identify these different narratives and their associated discourses in order to disrupt them, as they directly inform the gaze that teachers bring to their ideas of 'child'.

An important corollary to this is the impossibility of thinking about the 'C' in PwC without considering the teacher who introduces PwC into their classroom. The binary adult/child is a relationship infused with power (John, 2003). This entails a consideration of how power operates in school and classroom in order to understand how children are positioned *vis-à-vis* adults and the impact this has on how PwC is enacted in practice. The gaze through which a teacher views children influences the teacher's capacity for dialogue in classrooms and it is to a consideration of these different gazes that I now turn.

Discourses of the child

The construction of the child and the subsequent treatment of children needs problematising if we are to genuinely reconceptualise our classrooms as 'communities of enquiry' that value dialogic approaches to learning and teaching (Lyle, 2008). As a SAPERE trainer in PwC, I want to promote critical reflection by helping teachers to identify the different ways in which children and childhood are conceptualised today. Previous research suggests that the discourses of childhood held by teachers influences their attitudes towards children's capacity to engage with PwC and informs their approach to classroom practice (Lyle, 2013, 2014).

For the purposes of this research, teachers were asked to identify, in collaborative groups, which discourses of childhood they considered to be in circulation. They were asked to create a mind-map stimulated by the words 'child/childhood today'. On all of the many occasions I have introduced this exercise, a complexity in the range of narratives of childhood upon which teachers draw has been evident. These tend to be narratives that reflect a diverse range of attitudes and values. To help teachers reflect on their mind-maps I introduced narratives of childhood and asked them to consider if any or all of these narratives were represented in their mind-maps, and if they were what we might learn from them.

Historical accounts of childhood are deeply embedded in our culture, and as philosopher John Wall (2010, p. 35) says, 'Overturning historical biases about childhood ... will also require ethical self-critique'. It is therefore essential that the professional development process promotes critical reflection so that teachers can both identify and explore their assumptions about children and childhood in order to problematise current discourses of child that influence their practice. Teachers were asked to consider what functions the different discourses performed in shaping attitudes and values and what concrete actions they influenced. Later on teachers were asked to apply their thinking to a consideration of PwC in order to identify how the different narratives of childhood discussed might act as either a barrier or an affordance to PwC.

Historical models of childhood

Two key narratives of childhood that are often presented as obvious binary tensions are 'child as innocent'/'child as evil'. Many authors (see, for example, philosophers such as Wall, 2010; Stables, 2008; Kennedy, 2006) have discussed how the narratives of children as naturally pure and innocent and therefore in need of protection, or as naturally wicked and in need of redemption, have been 'woven into the western cultural fabrication of the child since at least medieval times' (Stainton-Rogers and Stainton-Rogers, 1992, p. 27). All agree that these models continue to shape our contemporary ideas and disagreements about children.

Following Wall (2010), I modified this binary and presented the idea of 'child as innocent and child as unruly'. Child as 'unruly' rather than 'evil' better reflects teacher narratives of the child and equates to the idea of children as 'naughty'. Teachers have no difficulty in identifying from their mind-maps ideas that equate to these narratives. The binary innocent/evil-unruly is recognised as complex as they are used to categorise children as either/or (implying an essentialist discourse) and see that such categories can be used to describe the same child at different times indicating diversity. Often these discourses are equated with social categories such as gender, ethnicity and social class, with the 'unruly' discourse often linked to boys (particularly black boys) and children from disadvantaged backgrounds.

The third narrative of childhood I presented to the teachers could be located in the ideas of the philosopher John Locke, who in the seventeenth century emphasised the child as *tabula rasa*, or blank slate. Teachers are able to identify the assumption that children 'don't know anything' in their mind-maps and can see this reflected in the strictures of a centrally imposed National Curriculum that dictates what and when (and increasingly how) children are to learn. This discourse sees the child as always in the process of becoming, an adult-in-the-making with educational needs the teacher must meet. Teachers take seriously their responsibility to ensure that children learn and a preoccupation with curriculum coverage is closely related to the *tabula rasa* discourse.

A fourth narrative is presented, which has proved to be the most dominant. Promulgated by the discipline of psychology, the concept of developmentalism is very prevalent in teachers' minds; it deserves further discussion, as it has great power to influence teacher behaviour.

Developmentalism

The Western scientific study of childhood has produced a developmental model of the child (Burman, 1994). Epistemologically scientific study assumes that there are truths about human beings that can be discovered through rigorous, systematic study. Psychology purports to know what children are, what constitutes childhood, and what ought to be done about children. This epistemological stance has led to what is widely known as DAP (developmentally appropriate practice) being advocated in the education of children. In this model children are viewed as incomplete human beings and require teaching that is matched to their current developmental levels.

The development model arises from the Enlightenment focus on human progress. Younger human beings are to be viewed as those who should be observed for information concerning the advanced adult mind. Children's minds are believed to prefigure, to foreshadow, the adult (usually male) mind because they represent a lower evolutionary state of 'man'. Children are seen as the evolutionary baseline for revealing human truths. Developmental psychology, premised on Enlightenment ideas, was created as the avenue for observation/surveillance, measurement/judgement that would reveal human progress (Burman, 1994).

Development as a metaphor positions adults as 'developed' and children as 'developing' and reflects dominant assumptions in the West that the telos of childhood is adulthood. Just as European intellect and culture has been promulgated as more advanced and superior to others so that the goal of development for all countries is seen as akin to the progress achieved in the West, the Western adult (in particular the white, male adult) is considered superior to children, and the goal of development (Cannella and Viruru, 2004). The model creates the child/adult binary, presenting children as separate from adults. The child is innocent, savage, ignorant and dependent; the adult is knowledgeable, civilised and independent. Following this, children are labelled as a group for which surveillance, limitation and regulation is necessary for their own good.

In our research the assumption that children should be taught in a developmentally appropriate way was widely held by teachers, limiting their expectations. Developmentalism is linked to the tenets of natural science, and the growth of the child is presented as influenced by heredity and environment, which has gained the status of a 'regime of truth' (MacNaughton, 2005). As a result we find that DAP is widely advocated in the education of children.

Walkerdine (1984), an early critic of developmental psychology, claims that it constructs childhood as a 'becoming' rather than a 'being'; children are seen as developing persons, not persons already. The main point of interest of adults in children is in considering how they will become adults. More recently, Murris (2013, p. 245) describes the developmental model of child as akin to putting 'metaphorical sticks' in teachers' ears in their educational encounters with children 'which prevent them from hearing the child's voice'.

A developmental approach has led to a focus on the individual child and their development, measured against other children so that a normative account of childhood emerges that has led to labelling children as, for example, 'gifted and talented', 'average', 'slow', 'educationally subnormal'. Developmentalism is also influenced by the high value placed on individualism in the West. Kennedy (2001) reminds us that words like individuation, autonomy, differentiation and self-actualisation are typically used to describe the radical individualism valued in adults raised in Western culture. Developmentalism 'adopts the Western prioritization of the individual self, and of individual autonomy and freedom' (Stainton-Rogers, 2015).

These models of children as 'innocent', 'unruly-evil', 'blank slate' or 'developing' are identifiable in the mind-maps produced by teachers. Such models serve to limit children's participation in PwC and are deficit models of the child. They have one thing in common: adults are the protectors of children – to actively seek to tame the unruly, to preserve their innocence, to provide them with knowledge, or ensure that the topics covered are developmentally appropriate. None of these models of childhood is supportive of PwC as a practice suitable for children of all ages. The implications of such views are wide-ranging, as Dahlberg and Moss (2005) point out; by protecting children from the world in which they exist (innocent) or providing a predetermined developmental curriculum (developing/becoming), adults deny children their right to seriously engage in the world. Furthermore, such views assume that children's ways of engaging with a curriculum are different from those of adults.

Through professional development we can disrupt these taken-for-granted ideas that are part of our history in order to reconstruct them. We need to address not just the stories told in the different discourses of innocent/unruly/*tabula rasa*/developing, but to unpick their ideological motivations and consider whose interests they promote, in order to examine their practical consequences. We must examine not only the stories each one tells of children, but what conducts they foster and what ideologies they warrant. One way we can start to reconstruct our understanding of childhood is to consider other more recent models that inform the process of deconstruction. To this end, a fourth model of childhood was presented to teachers to disrupt the deficit models described above.

A competency model of childhood

A competency model of childhood has its roots in anthropology and sociology and defines children as 'social actors who shape their identities, create and communicate valid views about the social world and have a right to participate in it' (MacNaughton *et al.*, 2007, p. 460). It is important for those practising PwC to recognise that other disciplines have much to offer our understanding of the 'C' in PwC. Within anthropology, for example, there has been a recent move to study children in their own right and not just in terms of what they will become (James, 2007). Anthropologist Bluebond-Langner's (1978) research with American children dying of leukaemia shows that they are aware that they are dying and take an active responsibility for the impact of their dying on others. Such research insists upon the social competence of children and can contribute to the task of dispelling the historic constructions of children as innocent, passive or 'adults-in-waiting'.

This model seeks to take into account a treatment of children as agents in their own right within the social context. It is not just a plea that they should be seen as persons, that their voice should be heard; it is also an assertion of their own self-constructive powers of personhood (that they are persons). Wall points out that to be human is to be an active constructor of meaning from birth:

> Even the youngest child under the most difficult of circumstances interprets their own worlds and relations, however much they are also constructed by them ... Each of us is and has been shaped by many layers of surrounding persons, communities and histories.
>
> *(2010, p. 5)*

To model the child as construc*ted* but not as construc*tive* diminishes the child. It permits us to see the young person as having their identity constructed by outside forces but not the young person constructing their identity out of what is culturally available (Stainton-Rogers and Stainton-Rogers, 1992).

To support understanding of a competency model, the following quotation is presented and teachers are asked to identify the assumptions made and to consider the implications for practice. This exercise helps teachers disrupt the adult/child binary and make the shift from seeing the child as a becoming to a being:

> I attribute to the child the same capacities, if not the same level or consistency of their realisation, for self-regulation and self-organisation that I find in or attribute to myself. I attribute to the child the same need I find in myself: for autonomous action, for personal choice, for privacy, for respect from others, for personal exploration, for moments or periods of psychological regression, for nurturance, for meaningful work, for a reasonable level of power in the personal politics of the 'microsphere' or near environment, for leisure, for equal treatment in situations of dispute, for, in every case of conflict or failure, the recognition of mediating circumstances of one kind or another.
>
> *(Kennedy, 2006, p. 159)*

As they discuss Kennedy's arguments for seeing adults and children as co-learners and co-enquirers, the child as a complete human being who may lack the experience of an adult but deserves the same respect, teachers consider the implications for practice. Commonly the concept of power is raised. Teachers, who are used to occupying a position of authority that has traditionally been exercised in an authoritarian manner, often find it difficult to imagine an alternative approach. Once teachers have had a chance to embrace Kennedy's ideas, I then introduce the work of philosopher Gareth Matthews (1980, 1992, 1996), whose writing on childhood includes the concept of 'rational authority' as a counter-discourse to authoritarian ways of thinking. This provides teachers with an alternative way of conceptualising classroom relationships.

Rational authority is based on respectful relationships between all adults and children in the classroom and school. It acknowledges a teacher's responsibility for the well-being of the children in their care, and expects them to sometimes make decisions on behalf of the child, but also expects such decisions to be justifiable. Actions taken must be based on sound logic, which the children can understand and will benefit from.

Building on this competency model, I ask teachers to reflect on the impact of a rights discourse on our conceptions of childhood.

A rights discourse

The relatively recent adoption of the United Nations Convention on the Rights of the Child (UNCRC, 1989) can build on the competency discourse of childhood outlined above. The view of the child as a rights-bearing citizen implies that there must be some limits on adult power over children. It is a recognition that adults don't always know best and may not always act with the best interests of the child at heart. James (2007) identified a key barrier to implementing children's rights as adult attitudes to them. There is considerable evidence that under the sway of DAP, teachers frequently assume that children cannot exercise their rights, as they are deemed developmentally inappropriate. This is not surprising; as Stainton-Rogers (2015, p. 105) points out, although the UNCRC is couched in terms of 'rights', in fact it is couched in terms of 'needs', which she argues arises from developmental psychology and serves to position the child in a paternalistic discourse that allows adults to abuse the power it gives them 'in the best interests of the child' (Article 3, UNCRC). Teachers use Article 3 to justify restricting children's participation. When they do this they restrict children's rights to be treated as humans, regardless of age, circumstances or context (John, 2003).

Similarly, the notion that childhood is an apprenticeship for adulthood with the assumption that there will be 'an arrival', 'an age of majority', when the rights and status of citizenship will be conferred, is commonly held (James *et al.*, 1998; Webb, 2014), and the adults in our research were no different. This was in spite of the fact that the research took place in Wales, where the UNCRC is a statutory obligation for all institutions; where the 'Children and Young Persons (Wales) Rights Measure' (Welsh Government, 2011) requires schools to put the UNCRC at the heart of its policies, practice and ethos. We found that the dominant discourse of child as 'citizen-in-waiting' supports attitudes that work against the rights of the child and, by implication, PwC.

Childhood in crisis

A view of childhood that was frequently represented on teachers' mind-maps can be linked to Palmer's (2006) idea of a 'toxic childhood'. Teachers frequently referred to children growing up in disrupted families; they were at risk from sexual predators and abusers. Children's health was seen as compromised by obesity or from pressure to be thin. Mental health was at risk from emotional abuse through cyber bullying or media access to pornography. Pressure on children to be consumers by owning the 'right' trainers or the latest electronic gadgets was commonly identified. The pressure on teachers to restrict children's lives through risk assessment reflects an emphasis on protection of children that is a contemporary version of child as innocent or unruly.

Implications for practice

The professional development process reported above continued by asking teachers to identify barriers to PwC that the dominant discourses of the child might imply. They were asked to consider how the presence of these discourses of childhood might impact on teachers' practice of PwC. Teachers suggested that those who see children as 'innocent' would be likely to withhold knowledge from them under the guise of protecting them. They would see their role as gatekeepers who should protect children from information inappropriate for them to deal with in an 'age appropriate' way. Such teachers would probably avoid 'controversial issues' such as racism, child abuse or religious differences and prevent them from being raised in PwC.

Teachers holding the view of child as 'evil-unruly' would prioritise a stance that focused on good behaviour and compliance. Unruly children need to learn 'how to behave' and be taught 'how to be good'. Such teachers would find it difficult not to intervene in enquiries – wanting to ensure the 'correct' response to an issue. Sometimes teachers would see 'unruly' children as potentially disruptive and subversive to the process of the enquiry in PwC, because they would, 'deliberately introduce issues that are inappropriate' (a comment made during training).

The views of children as 'innocent', 'unruly' or 'in crisis' support the notion of adults as gatekeepers of children. Teachers saw their role as 'protectors' and took this role very seriously. Further data collection from observations of PwC practice found that this had the effect of shielding children from full participation in enquiries, as teachers carefully chose topics they felt comfortable with or chose stimuli for enquiry that had clear moral messages. One teacher, who had been practising PwC for seven years, liked it because, 'I use it [PwC] to teach them what is the right thing to do'.

Teachers who took part in our research and those attending professional development all felt that the existence of a given curriculum that 'had to be covered' was a major barrier to PwC. It isn't a great leap to see that this approach to teaching reinforces a *tabula rasa* approach to children. Teachers frequently saw themselves as epistemologically dominant and often failed to acknowledge that children bring knowledge, understanding and experience to the curriculum. Teachers preoccupied with curriculum coverage and learning outcomes found the PwC practice (where children are required to identify questions for enquiry themselves and then follow where children lead) challenging to their ideas of teaching to a set curriculum. Curriculum requirements were frequently cited to justify limiting the practice of PwC.

Our research has given us an insight into what impact different discourses of childhood have on teachers' practice of PwC. When analysing the starting points for enquiry that teachers reported or that we observed in practice, there was a bias towards stimuli that led children towards topics such as bullying or unkind or selfish behaviour, which are part of the Personal and Social Education (PSE) curriculum in England and Wales. Teachers justified such choices as 'good for moral education'. Often the resources had very clear, unambiguous messages that did not invite critical or contested thinking – they were seen to help children to 'be good' rather than enabling them to explore what it might mean to lead a good life. Where this was happening, observation of enquiries saw practice that resembled circle time (Mosley, 1996), where children are invited to share their thoughts in the group rather than submit their ideas to enquiry. Visits to schools that had been practising PwC for some time, where teachers felt it was embedded in their practice, often revealed that teachers focused on the development of caring and collaborative thinking rather than critical and creative challenge, as revealed in the stimuli chosen for enquiries linked to the PSE curriculum.

The PwC child

When addressing the 'C' in PwC, there is a growing body of writing we can draw on to construct an alternative discourse of the child. Wall (2010) calls on us to see the child as a full human being who inhabits and creates fully meaningful worlds for themselves, who has thoughts and theories worth listening to. Similarly, Stables (2008) presents us with the semiotic child as an agent in their own right and calls on us all to respect the integrity of the child's world. Educationalists influenced by post-structuralism also contribute to changing the adult gaze by arguing that the child should be seen for what they can do and for what they know – a being, not a becoming (Davies, 2014). Drawing on the model of the child as social actor, children's insights and perspectives on the world can improve adult understanding of children (MacNaughton *et al.*, 2007). These ideas build on the idea of children as rights-bearing citizens entitled to be treated as social actors, able to act on their own behalf and with a participatory right to be consulted and heard in matters affecting them.

This model has clear implications for practice and it is not surprising to find a focus on listening as a premise of the learning relationship (Rinaldi, 2005). Haynes (2014) calls for teachers to prioritise listening to children. Dahlberg and Moss (2005) want a pedagogy of listening so that teachers can make meaning *with* children and leave behind preconceptions of what they are capable of. Davies (2014) wants teachers to practise listening as an ethical response based on respect for difference and the other.

This implies a shift in knowledge-power relations from teachers' rights to shape curriculum towards children's participatory rights as citizens to shape the curriculum (MacNaughton and Smith, 2015). It implies that we cannot treat children as lesser mortals, not deserving the same rights and respect as adults: children are not 'incomplete human beings to be shaped into society's needs'; they have 'rights which must be respected' (Woodhead, 1996, p. 12).

The practice of PwC calls on teachers to start with the child's perspective, to seek their ideas as starting points for enquiry. PwC requires a democratic community to ensure that all voices are heard. Children as well as teachers have to take responsibility for listening to the multiple views of others and to respect diverse opinions. The four Cs of thinking – collaborative, caring, critical and creative – are at the heart of P4C practice. Pedagogy is dialogic, encapsulating both listening and speaking. This means that teachers have the major task of creating a classroom as a community of enquiry. We should not underestimate how hard this is to achieve in the light of dominant narratives of child/childhood.

Conclusion

Teacher conceptions of the child have emerged as central when trying to understand why some teachers successfully engage with PwC and others find this a challenge. Our findings suggest that if we want to ensure that PwC becomes embedded in schools then training should include the opportunity for teachers to identify and problematise the different discourses of childhood that act as either barriers or affordances to PwC. It is important not to underestimate the power of historically rooted models, alive in teachers' everyday 'doing' of practice, and their potential to influence the gaze some of them bring to bear upon children. This impacts upon the ways in which some teachers interpret PwC training.

However, our findings also suggest that the participatory practice of PwC has the power to shift teachers' views of childhood away from deficit narratives of 'immature', 'incompetent', 'innocent', 'unruly', 'blank slate' or 'developing' towards a competency model. Teachers who see children as social actors and participants generally find PwC a supportive pedagogic tool. Many teachers say that the actual process of implementing PwC in their classrooms has been a major factor in supporting a competency model of childhood. In interviews teachers spontaneously expressed their surprise and amazement at the capabilities of young children (Boyce, 2008). PwC therefore has the potential to shift the asymmetrical valuation of adults and children (Campbell, 2003) to create a more ethical space in which to practise enquiry. In practice PwC can be a powerful vehicle for challenging teacher perceptions, to problematise views of childhood and to act as a catalyst for attitudinal change.

In teacher education, it is important to help students and teachers to clarify the 'C' in PwC. I have found the writings of Matthews (1980, 1992, 1996), Kennedy (2001, 2006) and Wall (2010) particularly helpful. Matthews brings the philosophical voice of the child to life through his dialogues. Building on this, Wall (2010, p. 2) reminds us that 'neglecting children diminishes the humanity of us all' and regards children's moral thinking capabilities 'as complex and diverse as those of adults' (2010, p. 168). Kennedy (2006) recognises children's ability to disrupt, to bring fresh ways of looking at things.

The emerging 'philosopher's child' therefore provides support for P4C as a practice that seeks to promote children's democratic involvement in communities of enquiry as persons in their own right, not as adults-in-waiting. The task of decentring that will need to take place if teachers are to change their gaze presents a challenge to PwC trainers, as Kennedy (2006, p. 167) points out:

> To change we need an emphasis on non-instrumental relations, implying a meticulous respect for and attention to the perceptions, interests, and goals of childhood and of individual children; a continuous attention to equitable relations of power, which implies political autonomy and self-governance, both within the school – which includes the classroom itself – and in the school's relation to larger associations of which it may be a part.

I conclude that a model of child as person needs to be articulated to challenge the binary adult/child and to bring about the changes necessary if PwC is to be accepted as a practice with the power to shift teacher/child relationships and promote more enabling discourses of childhood. This is an ethical challenge. John (2003, p. 19) calls on us to treat children 'as if they are people, powerful people, not as people in the making'. Ethics in the light of childhood challenges us to listen to our interlocutors; it means trying to hear that which cannot be said but which tries to make itself heard (Davies, 2014).

PwC is about opening up the not-yet-known through dialogue which is of benefit not only to children but also to adults:

> adult psychological development through dialogue with children is crucial to the developmental advance of human culture, because parents who grow through dialogue with their children tend to produce adults who reap the fruits of that growth, and are positioned to grow even further through dialogue with their own children, and so on. When dialogue becomes normalized as an aspect of child-rearing, the human world changes.
>
> *(Kennedy, 2001, p. 5)*

For Kennedy, seeing the child as a 'fully-fledged interlocutor' is the basis for an ethics of the adult–child relation.

If teachers are to see children as social actors and participants whose opinions are valid and important, they need to be aware of research that presents a model of young children as complex, socially constructed beings (Kehily, 2015; Stables, 2008; MacNaughton *et al.*, 2007; James, 2007; Kennedy, 2006; Webb, 2014). These writers can help teachers identify and then question their own working models of childhood in order to create an 'environment of greater respect for children's authority as creators of knowledge' (Haynes and Murris, 2009). In order to succeed we need to take as a focus 'not the children's needs and deficits' but 'their hopes and aspirations, their dreams, their visions and their untrammelled imaginings – *as if* these things mattered. Doing so will treat children and represent them as if they are people, powerful people, not as people in the making' (John, 2003, p. 19).

References

Alderson, P. (2000) *Young Children's Rights: Exploring beliefs, principles and practice*. London: Jessica Kingsley.

Beah, I. (2007) *A Long Way Gone*. London: Harper Perennial.

Bluebond-Langner, M. (1978) *The Private Worlds of Children Dying*. Princeton, NJ: Princeton University Press.

Boyce, K. (2008) A study of the perceived impact of dialogic teaching, using the P4C model, on children's engagement in learning. Unpublished research report. Swansea Metropolitan University.

Burman, E. (1994) *Deconstructing Developmental Psychology*. London: Routledge.

Campbell, E. (2003) *The Ethical Teacher*. Maidenhead: Open University Press.

Cannella, G. S. and Viruru, R. (2004) *Childhood and Postcolonization: Power, education and contemporary practice*. London: Routledge Falmer.

Dahlberg, G. and Moss, P. (2005) *Ethics and Politics in Early Childhood Education*. London: Routledge.

Davies, B. (2014) *Listening to Children: Being and becoming*. London: Routledge.

Eggers, D. (2006) *What is the What: The autobiography of Valentina Achak Deng*. London: Penguin.

Haynes, J. (2014) Already equal and able to speak. In S. Robson and S. F. Quinn (eds) *Routledge International Handbook of Young Children's Thinking and Understanding*. Abingdon: Routledge.

Haynes, J. and Murris, K. (2009) Opening up space for children's thinking and dialogue. *Farhang*, 69 (Spring), 175–88.

James, A. (2007) Giving voice to children's voices: Practices and problems, pitfalls and potentials. *American Anthropologist*, 109(2), 261–72.

James, A., Jenks, C. and Prout, A. (1998) *Theorizing Childhood*. Oxford: Polity Press.

John, M. (2003) *Children's Rights and Power: Charging up for a new century*. London: Jessica Kingsley.

Kehily, M. J. (2015) Understanding childhood: An introduction to some key themes and issues. In M. J. Kehily (ed.) *An Introduction to Childhood Studies*, 3rd edn (pp. 1–15). Maidenhead: Open University Press.

Kennedy, D. (2001) Parent, child, alterity, dialogue, *Philosophy Today*, 45(1), 33.

Kennedy, D. (2006) *The Well of Being: Childhood, subjectivity, and education*. Albany, NY: State University of New York Press.

Lyle, S. (2008) Dialogic teaching: Discussing theoretical contexts and reviewing evidence from classroom practice. *Language and Education*, 22(3), 222–40.

Lyle, S. (2013) The implications of research into the successful implementation of P4C for the development of theory and practice. Paper presented at ICPIC Conference, *Critical Thinking, Enquiry-based learning and Philosophy with Children*, University of Cape Town, South Africa.

Lyle, S. (2014) Embracing the UNCRC in Wales (UK): Policy, pedagogy and prejudices. *Educational Studies*, 40(2), 215–32.

MacNaughton, G. (2005) *Doing Foucault in Early Childhood Studies: Applying post-structural ideas*. London: Routledge.

MacNaughton, G. and Smith, K. (2015) The young child: From social actor to rights-bearing citizen. In M. J. Kehily (ed.) *An Introduction to Childhood Studies*, 3rd edn (pp. 120–34). Maidenhead: Open University Press.

MacNaughton, G., Hughes, P. and Smith, K. (2007) Rethinking approaches to working with children who challenge: Action learning for emancipatory practice. *International Journal of Early Childhood*, 39(1), 39–57.

Mosley, J. (1996) *Quality Circle Time in the Primary Classroom: Your essential guide to enhancing self-esteem, self-discipline and positive relationships*. London: IDA.

Matthews, G. (1980) *Philosophy and the Young Child*. Cambridge, MA: Harvard University Press.

Matthews, G. (1992) *Dialogues with Children*. Cambridge. MA: Harvard University Press.

Matthews, G. (1996) *The Philosophy of Childhood*. Cambridge, MA: Harvard University Press.

Murris, K. (2013) The epistemic challenge of hearing child's voice. *Studies in Philosophy and Education*, 32, 245–59.

Palmer, S. (2006) *Toxic Childhood: How the modern world is damaging our children and what we can do about it*. Oxford: Oxford University Press.

Rinaldi, C. (2005) *In Dialogue with Reggio Emilia: Listening, researching and learning*. London: Routledge Falmer.

Stables, A. (2008) *Childhood and the Philosophy of Education: An anti-Aristotelian perspective*. London: Continuum.

Stainton-Rogers, R. and Stainton-Rogers, W. (1992) *Stories of Childhood: Shifting stories of child concern*. London: Harvester-Wheatsheaf.

Stainton-Rogers, W. (2015) Promoting better childhoods. In M. J. Kehily (ed.) *An Introduction to Childhood Studies*, 3rd edn (pp. 101–19). Maidenhead: Open University Press.

United Nations General Assembly (1989) United Nations Convention on the Rights of the Child. Online at: www.unicef.org.uk/Documents/Publication-pdfs/crcsummary.pdf (accessed October 2010).

UNICEF (2007) *Child Poverty in Perspective: An overview of child well-being in rich countries*, Innocenti Report Card 7. Florence: UNICEG Innocenti Research Centre.

Walkerdine, V. (1984) Developmental psychology and the child-centred pedagogy: The insertion of Piaget into early education. In J. Henriques, W. Hollway, C. Urwin, C. Venn and V. Walkerdine (eds) *Changing the Subject: Psychology, social regulation and subjectivity* (pp. 153–202). London: Methuen.

Wall, J. (2010) *Ethics in the Light of Childhood*. Washington, DC: Georgetown University Press.

Webb, R. (2014) Doing the rights thing: An ethnography of a dominant discourse of rights in a primary school in England. Doctoral thesis. Online at: http://sro.sussex.ac.uk/50800/.

Welsh Government (2011) Children and Young Persons (Wales) Rights Measure. Online at: http://wales.gov.uk/topics/childrenyoungpeople/rights/?lang=en (accessed 3 March 2013).

Woodhead, M. (1996) *In Search of the Rainbow: Pathways to quality in large-scale programmes for young disadvantaged children*. The Hague: Bernard Leer Foundation.

Ying Ying Fry and Klatzkin, A. (2001) *Kids Like Me in China*. St Paul, MN: Yeong and Yeong.

Yousafzai, M. and Lamb, C. (2013) *I am Malala: The girl who stood up for education and was shot by the Taliban*. London: Weidenfeld & Nicolson.

4

PEDAGOGICAL JUDGEMENT

Darren Garside

Introduction

Teachers make judgements all the time. They also make and take decisions, issue instructions, negotiate, react, respond and listen. Often they are doing these things in rapid succession over a long period of time and that is why teaching can be so exhausting but also exhilarating. To be caught up in the flow with young children and adults who are learning with excitement is an endorphin-packed ride.

Research about these activities comes from a variety of perspectives. Sometimes a sociological perspective can reveal issues about the structure and dynamics of classroom spaces, such as the hidden but pernicious influence of class, gender and race on the lived experience of those participants in this form of social life, and classrooms are quite curious places when viewed anthropologically. Psychologists may be more concerned with individual functioning such as the role of character or theories of learning; particularly fashionable at the moment is the growth of educational neuropsychology – theories of learning that emphasise the role of the brain. Where philosophers differ from these types of empirical researcher – that is, research that emphasises the role of observational evidence in constructing arguments – is that philosophers are also concerned with the normative.

Normative argument is prescriptive rather than descriptive; it concerns what we ought to do rather than merely describe what it is that we do. The philosopher David Hume identified that the gap between what is the case and what ought to be the case is not straightforward. For example, we know from evidence that there are different outcomes in the schooling system depending on what type of school you attend. Those attending private schools tend to go on to have very different types of career and life experiences from those attending state schools. This is a statement of what is the case. What ought we do about it? Well, we could advocate for the common school or we might adopt an academisation programme, such as that recently embarked upon by Education Secretary Michael Gove and the UK Conservative Government of 2010–15. What we ought to do does not proceed automatically from what is the case.

In this chapter I examine three philosophical paradigms of what may count as 'good' judgement. The implication is that we ought to aspire to making these types of judgement as often or as well we can. I go on to show how each of these forms of judgement can be recognised in good P4C practice but that there are tensions between the forms. It is simply not possible to be like this all the time, and sometimes different forms may work against one another. In the same way that tackling inequality in the school system comes down to competing value systems worked out in the political arena, so the professional teacher must reconcile different values – of herself, her children, her school and wider context – and this will influence what types of judgement at which she tries to arrive. Having conscious choice that there is more than one way might be liberating, and this chapter provides a framework for reflective and reflexive deliberation and scope for further reading.

The first model, 'judgement as wise action', draws on the philosophy of Aristotle and practitioners will recognise the description of the practically wise teacher-as-judge. Kant informs the second model, 'judgement as truth', where we focus on how truth in the form of truthful statements or propositions underpin much of what is valued in educational research and policy discourses. Here we also understand the value placed upon so-called 'objective measurements' such as school attainment league tables. Dewey is a controversial figure in education, often wrongly identified with the 'progressivism', and the section on 'judgement as inquiry' describes Dewey's belief in the value of inquiry in underpinning good educational action. If we do not teach according to the children's interests, then why should we expect them to be interested in their and our world?

The final section of the chapter considers the relationship between these three models and the critical difficulties this might throw up for the practitioner. I draw on recent developments in philosophy that are controversial and still being actively worked out by philosophers. However, when we turn to 'judgement as negotiation/exploration', then we are invited to consider a radically revised understanding of our ethical relationship to children as beings and how we might facilitate their encounter with the world and each other. Here the assumption is that we live in a world of plurality and difference, and helping children navigate that is the best thing we can do as teachers. I conclude by addressing how each of these models can be found in P4C practice and theoretical literature and future directions for the interested reader to consider.

Judgement as wise action

The model of the wise teacher has its roots in the ancient Greek philosopher, Aristotle (*c.*384–322 BC). Of course, other wisdom traditions trace their sages back far further than these dates, but for our purposes Aristotle is a key figure. Aristotle not only taught across the field of human endeavour known at the time, for example as tutor to the young aristocrat who would become Alexander the Great, he also developed a vast body of knowledge that includes philosophy that still has considerable influence on our thought today.

To understand Aristotle we need to focus on two key ideas: that his work is teleological and empirical. By teleology I mean that for Aristotle everything unfolds or develops or is caused according to its proper function or reason for being. Aristotle is trying to provide explanations based on the observable facts using empirical data or observation, upon which he then inductively builds a more abstract philosophy. For example, he draws on empirical work in what we now call physics, astronomy and biology to develop a metaphysical theory of causation. The relevance of this is that Aristotle sees everything unfolding according to rules and laws and necessity. Children must become adults because that is their potential, and education will help bring them to that state (Stables, 2008). This also applies to knowledge and understanding in what Aristotle called the practical arts. One can have theoretical knowledge of the world, *theoria*, for example through mathematics (think Pythagoras' theorem); one can also have technical knowledge or technique, called *techne*, if one has a determinate object such as a vase or a poem that one wishes to construct or make; however, there is a third class of knowledge called *phronesis* or practical wisdom. Some fields such as politics require more than a technical knowledge of how to arrive at a determined end; they also require the wise practitioner to reflect on the ends themselves; thus to act well or virtuously the practitioner must consider what they are working towards as well as how they are accomplishing it.

It has been argued by philosophers of education that much contemporary professional educational practice overemphasises technical concerns at the expense of deliberative and considered practical wisdom. David Carr, for example, argued that educational professionalism that is based on technical efficiency (we might consider teaching to the exam to be such an example) is a reductive or restricted idea of what it means to be a professional teacher (Carr, 2000). Dunne (1993) argued in *Back to the Rough Ground* that phronesis is characterised by an immediate and specific understanding of what is the case here and now. Technical and theoretical knowledge is meant to apply universally (Smith, 1995) but practical wisdom pays attention to the specific case at hand. Practical wisdom requires a particular sensitivity or understanding that goes beyond the theoretical. It explains why an experienced teacher may choose not to apply a rule that a novice teacher might enforce rigidly. When an experienced teacher hears a classroom noise that their student of initial teacher education (ITE) ignores, maybe because the latter does not yet know how to respond through lack of experience, the former may peer over their glasses and quietly enquire, 'Everything OK, Abbie? What do you need to help you concentrate?' Simply put, the wise judge of Aristotle's philosophy sees more, reflects, considers and deliberates more, and therefore acts better as a result of their unique type of judgement.

There is a normative element to this as well. Judgement that is of the type recognisable as phronesis is a desirable quality; we should prefer that our teachers are capable of exercising this type of judgement as much as is deemed appropriate by the phronimos themselves. At the end of the chapter I will consider how much P4C practice encourages the development of phronesis in the facilitator.

Judgement as truth

Aristotle's impact on the ancient European and, via Rome, the subsequent medieval worldview, cannot be overestimated. Apart from doctrinally significant borrowings from Plato, such as the realm of forms standing outside of the world, Aristotle's systematic philosophical worldview is allied with medieval Christian doctrine and used to explain how the world is. This worldview is able to sit comfortably for a while with the growth of scientific methods of understanding and explanation. Scientific knowledge, however, based on evidence, method, procedure and reasoning comes to provide an increasing challenge to some of the fundamental assumptions in the Catholic understanding of the cosmos.

One of the biggest challenges is the shift from a geocentric to a heliocentric conception of the solar system. Whereas in Aristotle's philosophy the world is the starting point and all other things are understood in relationship to this reference point, in the heliocentric model the Sun sits at the centre and around it all things revolve. This shift in worldview is known as the Copernican revolution and it lies at the heart of a corresponding revolution in philosophical thought. In the second of his three monumental critiques, Kant wrote: 'Two things fill the mind with ever-increasing wonder and awe, the more often and the more intensely the mind of thought is drawn to them: the starry heavens above me and the moral law within me' (Kant, 1999b, p. 269). The philosophical problem that Kant is setting out to resolve, and he refers to his solution as a 'Copernican revolution' in philosophy, is reconciling knowledge and belief (understanding according to our reason) to sensible experience; and then additionally reconciling these understandings with the idea of our free will and necessity to act according to our conscience rather than someone else's idea of what is right, that is 'received wisdom'.

Before Kant, metaphysics is concerned with essence and knowledge of things-in-themselves, but the Western Enlightenment undermines Aristotelian/Catholic metaphysics. This undermining occurs in three forms: Hume's scepticism, Locke's empiricism and what Kant terms 'indifferentism' (towards the necessity of metaphysics). Kant is therefore concerned to create a form of metaphysics that acknowledges both scientific inquiry and knowledge, and subjective moral law. In Kant's philosophy, judgement is the creation of a unified understanding of the world that blends our intuitive appraisal of the world with the underlying conceptual structure of understanding consciousness. Most famously this is expressed in the first critique thus: 'Thoughts without intuitions are empty, intuitions without concepts are blind' (Kant, 1999a, p. 75). For Kant, the world outside of us is fundamentally unknowable in itself; we can never know the noumenal realm. Instead we come to understand the phenomenal world, the world as it appears to us. Our representations of the world then are bound up in our conceptual understanding, and this propositional representation can be ascertained as more as less true. We can and must put our truths to the test and the demand of the Enlightenment is that no one should ever take anything at face value – hence the slogan, *sapere aude*, 'Dare to know'.

When teachers are assessing a child's understanding, they are engaged in making judgements of truth; when league tables of school assessment performance are compiled, they are presented as representations of the world that are a truthful picture; when agents of accountability, such as the regulatory body OFSTED in the UK, make pronouncements ostensibly against criteria, then judgements of truth are being made. Philosophers of education make the argument that this form of rationality is so pervasive in Western public that it is hard to perceive that it is only one form of judgement among many and does not deserve its pre-eminence. However, like a fish asked, 'How's the water?' who replies, 'What is water?', we may not perceive the tides of rationality in which we as individuals and teachers are swimming. This form of judgement might then be said to be so strongly normative that we do not notice its prevalence in our classrooms and our everyday interactions with one another in schools and classrooms.

Judgement as inquiry

The third type of judgement I would like to consider is based on the philosophy of the American John Dewey (1859–1952). Both Aristotle and Kant share a basic philosophical assumption about the world. This assumption is dualist: that there is fundamental distinction between the self and the world. We have subjective selves and we have objective worlds. Philosophy, among other traditions of thought, concerns itself with the relationships between these two binary aspects. Dewey was concerned to develop a non-dualistic philosophy where a self and its environment were seen to be an integrated whole, not two separate parts that are interrelated. In this non-dualistic philosophy the self and its environment are seen to be continuous with one another. The habits or customs of thought are seen as adaptations and responses to the person's experience of their environment. On the one hand this can be useful, as it allows us to take cognitive short cuts by using concepts and habits that have proved to be effective before in similar situations. However, a person can also get into habitual or fixed interactions or responses with their world that become stereotypes and a poor response to the actual exigencies of the situation.

At the heart of Dewey's philosophy is his 1938 work *Logic: The Theory of Inquiry*. Dewey's theory of judgement is highly technical and so I present here a sketch of the salient core concepts. As with any sketch this can only give an impression of this work, which is deserving of greater attention than can be provided here. The first aspect to consider is how judgement resolves an indeterminate situation into a determinate one. When something becomes problematic for an organism in its environment then this is a state of indeterminacy. This can be met by one of two responses. The first is habitual, stereotypical and rule-bound action – if the mindset of this response were voiced it might be something like: 'This is what I do here', or 'This is what this situation/person/place is like', or 'This is what ought/must/should be done here'. The other response is to engage in inquiry, which is much more of an active investigation of what is the situation or case, here and now, and that inquiry eventually resolves into a new judgement or determinate conclusion. This judgement settles the matter for now so that the inquiry is no longer ongoing' although it might become reawakened at some later time. There is an important implication of this conceptualisation of judgement, namely that judgement is constructed and that it is active.

Dewey regards previous work on philosophy as suffering from 'the spectator theory of knowledge'. For example, in the previous section on Kant we saw how in his philosophy knowledge is a representation or picture of the world and a good judgement is the same as a true understanding of the world. This propositional understanding is fundamentally flawed as far as Dewey is concerned because there is nothing in the picture that we hold of the world that compels us to act on that understanding. We may believe that poverty is evil and should be eradicated, yet a spectator view means we that observe this truth without feeling motivated to act upon it. For Dewey this observation or hypothesis or picture about the world is not yet a full judgement. A full judgement is actually evaluative as well as cognitive or epistemological. It is a position towards the world that reflects some scale of values and implies that in some way the world must or will change according to the judgement that we have arrived at.

This distinction is at the heart of pragmatist philosophy. A truth's veracity is established by the quality of the process by which it is constructed – that is, how well justified it is. The meaning of the truth is how well it plays out in action. If I claim that the world is fair, as a pragmatist I am not making a claim that is like a photograph of the world: 'Here is a picture. Let us judge against criteria. Is it fair or not (judgement of kind)? To what extent is it fair (judgement of degree)?' The pragmatist's truth is more like an unfolding video. If I believe the world is fair, what happens as a result of me acting as if that were true? How well justified is that judgement about truth I have arrived at? Hence, for Dewey, our lives are fundamentally deliberative. Some concepts such as truth, beauty and justice may be at the heart of a lifelong inquiry. For example, I write this chapter in a café in an Italian town, and I am appraising what for me as a person is: 'What constitutes the practically good life in a time of change?' The philosophical dictum 'know thyself' is part of this attitude or orientation that characterises pragmatism. It is an openness to inquiry and judgement as a way of life.

Dewey can be claimed to be one of the most influential philosophers on educational thought and practice and as such his legacy is bitterly contested. He is often and erroneously associated with 'educational progressivism', long a term of abuse among certain critics. Over recent years Richard Pring in the UK has done much to carefully excavate the authentic Dewey from the caricature portrayed by his critics. Working carefully to expose the binary or dualistic thinking that Dewey was at pains to combat, Pring (2005) offers insights into how Dewey can help us consider the tension between different functions or purposes of schooling, as does Fesmire (2003). In America Jim Garrison's work is of similar stature (Garrison *et al.*, 2012).

Plurality of judgement in P4C

Metajudgement: judgements about judgement.

Given the variety of ways of judging, how do we judge what type of judgement might be good to use? Might this be a process of infinite regression – that is, in order how to judge how to judge, do we then need to know how to judge how to judge how to judge? It is, to use a technical philosophical phrase, turtles all the way down. We encounter similar problems with other educational verbs such as 'to learn': we ask at what point we might have learned how to learn how to learn to …

How as a teacher or educational leader do I judge that my judgement is a good one here? At this point an appeal is often made to some metaprinciple or process in educational literature such as 'reflective judgement' (Schön, 1983; Pollard, 2002). On examination we find that principles such as these can be identified with a particular philosophical tradition. Schön's categories of reflection-in-action and reflection-on-action very much presuppose a Kantian consciousness. Models of action inquiry, such as those utilised by Kemmis (2010) and McNiff and Whitehead (2009), can trace their philosophical roots to Deweyan modes of inquiry.

It is at this point I challenge a premise hitherto not made explicit: that we must have firm ground upon which to stand when we make judgements. I will argue in the rest of the chapter that teaching is the type of professional activity where we can never be absolutely certain of ourselves and that a fundamental aspect of being a teacher is living with uncertainty and contingency – the latter term meaning that whatever we choose to do, we could also have chosen otherwise. P4C then might be seen as a useful tool for helping understand how judgements are made, what underpins judgements, such as evidence and facts, explanations of how the facts justify the claim, how alternative explanations ought be rejected, and how our claims are scoped (i.e. do not always apply across all times and spaces but apply to particular contexts). These last criteria are drawn from a particular model of argumentation from Stephen Toulmin (2003), from the Deweyan tradition, about how arguments can be understood as a function of their justification. In Lipman's original materials, the focus is much more on Aristotle's logic as the basis for sound argumentation, even though the process for forming sound arguments is then based on a Deweyan mode of inquiry. Different traditions of P4C inquiry can be critically understood against these philosophical traditions.

Judgement as dialogue, relating and cartography

The traditions of thought of three classic philosophers can give rise to different modes of judgement but it might be more helpful to consider a body of work, rather than a specific philosopher, that dwells on P4C as a process for arriving at sound judgements. What weaves these thinkers together is a motif of judgement as a dialogue, and/or a radically open-ended negotiation. The first three modes of judgement are recognisable as types of judgements that teachers may do in the classroom or while engaged in their practice. Here I want to consider judgement as social processes involving pluralities and multiplicities of people, sites, contexts and relationships.

David Kennedy's work *The Well of Being* (2006) marked an important turning point in the P4C literature. It was the first full-scale treatment of postmodern themes such as inter-subjectivity in the context of philosophising with children. Postmodernism was and is an intellectual movement that by its very nature is hard to define since it fundamentally rejects the idea that meaning and definitions can be fixed – or, in other words, that we can get to the essence of things. Opponents of postmodernism often accuse it of philosophical relativism, the idea that ideas are in some way a product of their time, place and location; whereas post-modernists do not find this accusation troubling but instead see it as a good place from which to start inquiry. Jean-Francois Lyotard (2013) famously said of postmodernism that it marked 'the end of grand narrative' – all-encompassing systems of ideas that aim at explaining every-thing, such as Marxism, Kantian philosophy or any other -ism such as empiricism.

For postmodernists it is the process of knowledge production, and the conditions that give rise to the possibility of socially recognised knowledge, that matter more perhaps than the substance of what is said. Kennedy's work is important therefore for recognising that the his-torical child–adult relationship, stretching in the West back to the Aristotelian deficit model, and enshrined in Piagetian psychology, fundamentally limited the possibilities of children. Schooling further perpetuated such restrictive and limiting relationships. Kennedy returned to the work of Dewey and read into him postmodern themes that were latent in Dewey's work. Kennedy concluded that inter-subjectivity, the idea that there was a unique space cre-ated between individuals that afforded rich philosophical meaning-making and that this was at least as important as individual meaning-making if not more so.

The theme of relating is an important one in philosophy of education. One of the most trenchant criticisms of contemporary schooling is that it has borrowed a wholly inappropriate vocabulary from the practices and language of business management and set of beliefs about the relationship between children, teachers and the subject matter of learning. The 'Taylorist' model of factory production focuses on productivity, inputs and outputs and the whole system of production in order to focus on the most important business value of efficiency. Respected critics such Biesta (2013) have argued strongly against the appropriateness of such business models for considering relationships of teaching and learning. For example, he tackles what he calls 'learnification' culture where a child's 'learning' is commodified, treated as a discrete quan-tity, and can somehow be poured or placed into children. Learning cannot be separated from teaching, however, and when learning is referred to without mention of teaching this isolates the learner, and relegates to the margins the relationships that are at the heart of the educational process. These relationships are reduced to a technical management process, what we referred to earlier in the Aristotelian account as *techne* rather than full, wise judgement. These business models can have a tragic impact on a teacher's career as vocation, and Higgins (2011) has writ-ten on the dangers of the professional who either burns in or burns out of their profession rather than maintaining their vocation as a living and vital inquiry over their working life-course.

As a final speculation I would like to consider how a variety of ideas can be brought to bear on the idea of educational judgement. Rosa Braidotti writes about radical feminism from a post-human perspective using the idea of nomadic subjectivity. Hers is an enormously rich and complex philosophy and at first glance not entirely relevant to education and professional judgement. However, certain of her ideas might be translated into our concerns in this chapter. For example, she claims that she writes 'cartographies' (2011, p. 46), intellectual landscape gardening that provides horizons or frames of reference that allow her to navigate while never actually belonging anywhere but merely visiting. How would pedagogical judgement look that was based on nomadic cartography? Would a teacher be charged with understanding the terrain created and inhabited by children? Would their professional training address questions such as how to visit such terrains sustainably, without wrecking invasive and permanent damage, like oil-drillers in the Arctic? These are philosophical questions about ethics and would require a completely different sensibility and orientation, including a radically different professional toolkit, from the ones currently being promoted in initial teacher education.

In another example, Braidotti talks about identity very differently from how we are used to in everyday language. For her identity is something we construct after the event, rather than being the thing that creates the event or causes the action; we look back afterwards and say, 'There I was', rather than, 'I am here', as it is a 'retrospective notion' (2011, p. 40). What might judgement be like for a teacher whose professional identity is radically uncertain and always under doubt and examination? I think we would need very different types of school, if not society. And that is the gift of philosophy: to be concerned not with what is the case but with how things ought or should be.

Conclusion

In this chapter I have introduced three traditions of philosophical thinking that understand judgement very differently from one another. I relate these forms to educational and P4C practice before going on to discuss the difficulty in making judgements when each position offers a stance to critique one's practice no matter how well justified one's judgement is. I argue that there is no place that one can stand that allows an objective judgement and that good practitioners come to live with this contingency and build this into their practice by being sensitive to negotiation and relationship and by being an educational 'visitor' to the pedagogical encounter.

References

Biesta, G. J. J. (2013) *The Beautiful Risk of Education*. Boulder, CO: Paradigm.

Braidotti, R. (2011) *Nomadic Subjects: Embodiment and sexual difference in contemporary feminist theory*. New York: Columbia University Press.

Carr, D. (2000) *Professionalism and Ethics in Teaching*. Abingdon: Routledge.

Dewey, J. (1938) *Logic: The theory of inquiry*. New York: Henry Holt.

Dunne, J. (1993) *Back to the Rough Ground: 'Phronesis' and 'techne' in modern philosophy and in Aristotle*. Notre Dame, IN: University of Notre Dame Press.

Fesmire, S. (2003) *John Dewey and Moral Imagination*. Bloomington: Indiana University Press.

Garrison, J., Neubert, S. and Reich, K. (2012) *John Dewey's Philosophy of Education: An introduction and recontextualization for our times*. New York: Palgrave Macmillan.

Higgins, C. (2011) *The Good Life of Teaching: An ethics of professional practice*. Oxford: Wiley-Blackwell.

Kant, I. (1999a) *Critique of Pure Reason* (ed. and trans. P. Guyer and A. W. Wood). Cambridge: Cambridge University Press.

Kant, I. (1999b) *Practical Philosophy* (ed. and trans. M. J. Gregor). Cambridge: Cambridge University Press.

Kemmis, S. (2010). What is to be done? The place of action research. *Educational Action Research*, 18(4), 417–27.

Kennedy, D. (2006) *The Well of Being: Childhood, subjectivity, and education*. Albany, NY: State University of New York Press.

McNiff, J. and Whitehead, J. (2009) *Doing and Writing Action Research*. London: Sage.

Pollard. A. (2002) *Reflective Teaching*. London: Continuum.

Pring, R. (2005) *Philosophy of Education: Aims, theory, common sense and research*. New York: Continuum.

Schön, D. A. (1983) *The Reflective Practitioner: How professionals think in action*. New York: Basic Books.

Smith, R. (1995) The rationality of practice. *Pedagogy, Culture and Society*, 3(2), 209–15.

Stables, A. (2008) *Childhood and the Philosophy of Education: An anti-Aristotelian perspective*. London: Continuum.

Toulmin, S. E. (2003) *The Uses of Argument*. Cambridge: Cambridge University Press.

5

NEGOTIATING MEANING IN CLASSROOMS

P4C as an exemplar of dialogic pedagogy

John Smith

L: Can I just say something that I … think of …

JS: Fine, fine.

L: This is what I … well, it can't be like have an illness, it can't have a cold.

D: It can have a virus [*general laughter*].

Introduction

At first sight, the exchange transcribed above seems to make little sense. The words of the speakers are difficult to interpret and the laughter, which ensues, seems incongruous. However, a little context might radically transform this view. L and D are among the 12 Year 6 children (10 and 11 year olds) taking part in a P4C discussion led by myself, JS. The question being considered is whether there is anything that a human being can do that a computer or robot could not do. L raises the intriguing example of illness, which seems to fall into this category, saying that the computer or robot 'can't have a cold'. Quick as a flash, D retorts that it could have a virus, and his witty response gives rise to the laughter referred to. This brief extract from a longer discussion, which will be returned to later in this chapter, captures much that can be achieved by practitioners using P4C and other similar approaches. The nature of the talk here seems to be the kind sometimes referred to as 'exploratory talk' in which children unpick and reconnect their ideas in a search for deeper understanding. Exploratory talk is one of the outcomes of a kind of teaching known as 'dialogic teaching' (Wegerif, 1996).

This chapter explores some of the relationships between P4C and dialogic teaching. There have been separate but overlapping issues to do with these matters within primary and secondary schools during the last few decades, but for the sake of simplicity this chapter is largely concerned with developments in primary schools. I begin by identifying some key points in the development of dialogic approaches to teaching in UK classrooms from the 1960s through to the present day. I then consider the similarities between dialogic teaching and the pedagogy of P4C. Common sources of inspiration underpin both of these approaches and the stated aims of each are very similar in some crucial respects, with many observers suggesting that P4C can be viewed as one of the most effective exemplars of dialogic teaching.

Following this examination of the two models, I return to the case study of P4C featured above before concluding with an argument that study of dialogic teaching and P4C should be viewed as a vital part of both ITE (initial teacher education) and teachers' CPD (continuing professional development).

Teacher and pupil talk

Research into the talk, which takes place in both British and American classrooms, has suggested that typically teachers dominate talk and that opportunities for pupils to engage in high-level, extended talk are limited. Evidence to support this conclusion has emerged consistently over many decades, with Alexander (2008) summarising this research. One feature that has been commonly observed in classrooms is a three-part communicative exchange between teachers and pupils, often described as 'initiation-response-feedback' or IRF, after it was first described as such by British linguists Sinclair and Coulthard (1975). In IRF, the first and third moves are made by the teacher, while the pupil makes a constrained move between these two. A simple example might be:

> *Teacher:* What is the capital of Spain?
> *Child:* Madrid.
> *Teacher:* Well done.

There have been many attempts to enhance oracy in British classrooms. These have included national initiatives such as the curriculum development initiated by the Bullock Report in the 1970s (DES, 1975), the work of the National Oracy Project in the late 1980s and early 1990s, and a range of projects sponsored by the former Schools Council, such as Tough (1977), and other bodies. The Cambridge Primary Review (Alexander, 2010) and the Independent Review of the Primary Curriculum (more commonly referred to as the Rose Review: DCSF, 2009) both urged primary schools to place greater emphasis on oracy (often referred to in a largely synonymous way as 'speaking and listening'); the recommendations of the Rose Review were due to have formed the basis of a new primary curriculum beginning in 2010. This development was brought to an abrupt halt when the new government elected in May 2010 scrapped the plans of its predecessor. The current National Curriculum (DfE, 2013) for primary children, which eventually emerged in its place, contains a single page of statutory requirements related to spoken language covering school Years 1 to 6.

Over the last few decades, a large number of smaller-scale initiatives have been introduced in the UK, in attempts to create better conditions for oracy in the classroom. One very important recent movement, which seeks to identify and promote classroom talk, is the approach known as 'dialogic teaching', deriving in particular from the work of Robin Alexander (2008). Alexander argues that UK classroom talk has too often been characterised by teacher monologue. His recommendation is that schools should move towards forms of talk that represent a genuine dialogue between pupils and teachers and between pupils themselves, and he uses the name 'dialogic teaching' as an umbrella term to describe such approaches. Like many others in this field, Alexander is strongly influenced by the ideas of Vygotsky and other thinkers, which stress the importance of communication and social context in the learning process (Vygotsky, 1962, 1978).

Alexander's aim is not to promote a single model of classroom talk but to identify the features that are likely to be found in an effective style. He suggests that teaching of this kind has five defining characteristics: it is 'collective', 'reciprocal', 'supportive', 'cumulative' and 'purposeful' (2008, p. 28). Drawing upon extensive international research, he claims that there are potentially five types of spoken communication between teachers and pupils. The first three he calls 'rote', 'recitation' and 'instruction/exposition'. These are the forms commonly found in many classrooms in the UK and elsewhere (2008, p. 30) and they include the IRF structure described above. The crucial feature of dialogic teaching however, is that it incorporates two further types of communication, which Alexander terms 'discussion' and 'dialogue'. These, he argues, are less evident in UK classrooms but can be found more commonly in the classrooms of some other countries (2008, p. 30).

The ideas and practices of dialogic teaching are gaining greater currency in UK classrooms and are being implemented by many teachers and schools. The theoretical and practical work of Neil Mercer and others is favourably viewed by Alexander. This work is also strongly influenced by Vygotsky's notion of thinking as both an individual and a social activity (Mercer *et al.*, 1999; Mercer, 2000). It is influenced too by the ideas of earlier classroom researchers, notably Douglas Barnes, from whose work emerged the notion of exploratory talk, mentioned above (Mercer and Littleton, 2007). It is evident, therefore, that although the term dialogic teaching is comparatively recent in this context, it is an approach that draws upon a highly respected body of ideas and practices stretching back many decades.

P4C and the social exploration of ideas

P4C is an inherently dialogic approach, and its originator, Matthew Lipman, took account of some of the same influences cited by Alexander and others, in particular the work of Vygotsky (1978). It will be useful at this point to examine some areas of overlap between P4C and dialogic teaching. Some of these similarities can be seen most clearly if we compare the ways in which the two approaches have been described by their main proponents, Lipman and Alexander. As noted earlier, Alexander describes dialogic teaching as 'collective', 'reciprocal', 'supportive', 'cumulative' and 'purposeful' (2008, p. 28). In a P4C community of enquiry, the following features are commended by Lipman: 'inclusiveness', 'shared cognition', 'feelings of social solidarity', 'deliberation' and 'the quest for meaning' (2003, pp. 95–6). Although these descriptions are by no means identical (and the descriptors of P4C are taken in any case from a longer list offered by Lipman), it is clear that the two approaches have a great deal in common.

Close study of P4C and related approaches also brings into question the 'dualistic' model of cognition, which has dominated Western thought since at least the time of Descartes. This view suggests that the boundaries of individual thinking are clearly delineated and that individuals think entirely in 'their own minds', even though they exchange their thinking with others through speech and writing. The boundaries between the 'private thoughts' of individuals and the thoughts of others seem less clear on closer inspection however, than they do at first sight. Commentators such as Mercer and Littleton suggest that the human brain may be, figuratively speaking, hard-wired to 'interthink', that is, to work in concert with the brains (or minds) of others (Mercer and Littleton, 2013). The 'social brain' (see, for example, Torrance and MacLure, 2010) is another term which has emerged to describe this capacity, while Goleman uses the term 'social intelligence' (Goleman, 2007) to describe what appear to be similar phenomena. P4C enquiries regularly produce dialogue which appear to be the result of subtle collaboration – what Lipman refers to as 'shared cognition' – and one possible example of this will be examined in the following section.

Thinking through language: a case study

The transcribed section which opened this chapter appears again within the longer transcript below. As mentioned earlier, 12 Year 6 children, equally split by gender, are engaged in a philosophical discussion, led by myself (JS). University philosophers might describe this discussion as being in the area of philosophy known as the 'Philosophy of Mind'. The children's discussion, though, has been provoked by a story about a boy who has a computer/robot as a friend and they are considering the differences between such a 'friend' and a human being. Immediately before this group discussion, the children have discussed the question in pairs.

JS: If I go to a computer and I put in a really difficult maths problem, it could work it out very quickly; isn't that thinking?

M: No, it's not, because when you tell it to do that it isn't actually doing that [*another child is saying similar things in the background*], it's not actually doing that, it doesn't have a brain to think about that, it just comes out like a calculator.

JS: OK, so, another really good, this is really good thinking this afternoon … F.

F: It's a bit like M said, well …

JS: Well done for making that link.

F: You just command what, what it has to talk about, it can't just say what it wants to or that's everything, everything …

JS: OK, OK, thank you, F … B.

B: I don't immediately think that a robot, it's a bit like K's, it could never have emotions that affects a human because robotic crying, it wouldn't affect you because you'd know that was programmed … I don't think it would affect me like, you know, like if your friend cries or just feels upset because of something you've done, you'd feel a bit bad but I don't think if you did that with a computer you'd feel the same.

JS: We'll maybe come back to, there are number of these we might come back to in a minute, but thank you for that one B … C, C can you just speak on behalf of your pair perhaps for the moment.

C: Well, me and G [*inaudible*] well, it kind of links to M's which is basically the [*background noise*] … you would never get to state an opinion because it's like programmed, just to [*inaudible*], to say things it's programmed to say, it would never have its own opinion.

JS: L, then I'd like a go myself, if that's OK, so, L …

L: Erm …

JS: Did you already have a go before? D, do you want to speak on behalf of your pair?

L: Can I just say something that I … think of …

JS: Fine, fine.

L: This is what I … well, it can't be like have an illness, it can't have a cold.

D: It can have a virus [*general laughter*].

JS: (*laughing*) Very clever, D, very clever, it can have a virus all right but it can't have a cold in a human sense. OK, really clever ideas, really clever ideas, now let me just put a couple of them back to you. OK, I can imagine a computer, if we haven't got them already, that if people were ill they could get in touch with that computer, they could, you know, either speak or type things in whatever way the computer was taking input, and they could describe their symptoms, say, they got the flu or something, I can imagine a computer that could say, 'Please tell me your symptoms', and if, say, 'Got a temperature, got aches and pains I've, er, got sniffles and sneezes, it's lasted for four or five days,' the computer could come back and say, 'I think [*voice in background*], I think you've got flu,' or maybe even, 'Yes, it sounds definitely as if you've got the flu, please, please stay warm, get lots of rest, drink lots of liquids.' It could actually tell me what a doctor might tell me or a nurse might tell me, now how is that different, isn't the computer, isn't there an argument for saying that the computer is doing some of the things you said, it's got an opinion, it has an opinion that I've got the flu, based on what I've told it, er, isn't it thinking? I'm not saying I agree with this, I'm just putting these back to you to think about, isn't it thinking in a way that M said it couldn't think? Whether it's got emotions, whether it feels anything about me having the flu is another question, but we can leave that aside for the moment. What do people feel? Isn't it doing some sort of thinking and holding opinions and so on? Erm, D …

D: Well, first of, computers don't have brains and they can't think so that's one thing that proves you wrong and the other one is, how would they think anyway?

JS: Do you want to explain a bit more what why [*D speaks in background*] what that question means … you maybe need to say what you understand by thinking … what thinking is.

D: Well, thinking is like your own private chat-room … it gives you, you can think to yourself, whereas robotic things … they run on electricity … we have electricity inside us but we don't run on electricity and they don't have organs and things.

What seems to emerge from the discussion is that, following my prompts, the children have collaborated to create shared understandings of a number of linked ideas. Immediately prior to the transcribed section, H had asserted that computers cannot think. I then offer H and the group the counter-example of a computer producing answers to maths problems but M appears confident that performing this task does not involve thinking. As he says, 'it's not actually doing that, it doesn't have a brain to think about that, it just comes out (like) a calculator'. Of particular interest is F's contribution soon afterwards. F makes clear that he intends his remarks to build upon those of M. He makes this explicit when he says 'it's a bit like M said' and he goes on to say, 'you just command what it has to talk about, it can't just say what it wants to'. This small sequence is worth dwelling upon a little longer. We cannot know whether F would have offered his own view if M had not paved the way for this insight. It seems clear, though, that the point has been refined through the collaboration of the two speakers.

The next contributor, after my intervention, is B, who reminds the group of K's contribution some time earlier. She makes the point that 'robotic crying, it wouldn't affect you because you'd know that was programmed'. Although B introduces another element here – the notion of robots and computers having feelings, which is one she takes issue with – she also builds upon the contributions of M and F. The chain of reasoning seems to go something like this:

1. M introduces the general idea that a computer/robot is not thinking when it replicates human output but he does not introduce any specialist vocabulary to support this idea.
2. F extends this idea and introduces the word 'command' to suggest human agency in enabling the computer/robot to function.
3. B extends the idea further by using the word 'programmed'. This subsumes 'command' and generalises the idea.

As observed earlier, D's witty remark about the virus caused much hilarity. At the risk of destroying the joke by overanalysis, D's skill lay in his ability to recognise and articulate the double meaning in the word 'virus' as it is used for humans and computers. As with many good jokes, the effect of D's remark was to introduce an unexpected connection between a new lexical item – a word or a phrase – and the topic under discussion. Words and phrases like 'off the wall', 'outside the box' and so on, go some way towards capturing this deliberately engineered incongruity, and it seems a very good example of the 'creative thinking' that is often observed and encouraged within P4C. It is worth noting, however, that the success within the group of D's joke depends upon the group *as a whole* being alert to possible reinterpretations of the words being used. D required particular skill in articulating the joke as rapidly as he did and his timing was crucial. However, the joke would have fallen flat without his audience – the rest of the group – being *tuned in* to the humour.

D then makes another significant contribution to the discussion. After I have made a lengthy contribution to try and refocus the discussion, presenting another challenge to the idea that computers could not think, I end my turn by asking, 'Isn't it [a computer pro- grammed to assess medical symptoms] doing some sort of thinking and holding opinions and so on?' D responds quickly, claiming that I am wrong because computers do not have brains, and he follows this by asking, 'How would they think anyway?' When asked to say more about what his question meant, he gives a fascinating answer: 'Well, thinking is like your own private chat-room … it gives you, you can think to yourself, whereas robotic things … they run on electricity … we have electricity inside us but we don't run on electricity and they don't have organs and things.'

I believe that this extract from a P4C discussion shows a number of features, which are typical. These include features identified by Lipman, such as 'shared cognition', 'feelings of social solidarity' and 'the quest for meaning'. It also exemplifies the criteria, which Alexander sees as central to dialogic teaching – in particular it seems 'supportive', 'cumulative' and 'pur- poseful'. The children are critical of one another's suggestions and my own but they express this critical thinking in ways that respect and attend to one another's contributions – 'caring ways', as they are often described in P4C. It is an inherently collaborative process. The ideas that emerge cannot easily be reduced to the individual contributions of the participants; instead they seem to incorporate socially negotiated or co-created ideas.

Oracy, teacher development and P4C

In this concluding section I briefly discuss the shifting approach to dialogic teaching that has emerged in British classrooms and teacher training in the last few years, before ending with some thoughts about the importance of P4C. As noted earlier in this chapter, the current National Curriculum does include a section that highlights the importance of speaking and listening, but there is a strong sense that it is seen as playing a role that is very much subordinated to the development of literacy skills. The crucial point is that these two objectives should not be seen as conflicting with one another. The document that laid the foundations for the abandoned curriculum of 2010 presented a more holistic picture, with speaking and listening forming an essential element of the whole: '"If they can't say it they can't write it" has become something of a cliché which nevertheless captures the nature of the interdependencies of speaking, listening, reading and writing' (DCSF, 2009, p. 59).

If dialogic approaches are to flourish in schools, including P4C as a very prominent example, then these will need to be embedded more fully within ITE and CPD so that teachers are properly trained to teach in these ways. It is not easy to achieve this, however, as ITE providers must always reconcile the professional judgements and expertise of their staff with the agendas set by central government. While ITE practitioners in higher education institutions (HEIs) do what they can to encourage oracy and dialogic teaching, with quite a number developing highly innovative practice in this area, such development is inevitably limited by the need to remain within the remit defined for them by central government. In the last six years, the development of oracy within schools has not been greatly encouraged by the governments of the day, in contrast to the stance of the government that lost office in 2010. Ministerial statements over this period have often claimed that high standards are likely to result from a return to classroom practice of the past or to selected practice from other countries, practice in which oracy is seen as having a limited and subsidiary role in the process of learning.

Schools have in some ways had greater freedom than HEIs over this same period to challenge the trends set by central government, given a repeated commitment to school-led, curricular innovations. Schools too, however, have had to take care that they remain sufficiently close to central directives to gain and retain the required ratings from OFSTED. There is considerable anecdotal evidence, though, to suggest that OFSTED has not looked unfavourably upon schools that have shown significant use of oracy-based teaching approaches, such as P4C. On the contrary, it has in quite a number of cases praised this practice, where teaching and learning have been judged to be up to standard.

There is a great diversity of voices and influences upon school practice, including central government and many others. I do not believe that there is currently any clear consensus about the importance of dialogic approaches, such as P4C. Few would dispute their importance, but opinions differ about the priority they should be given in the classroom. It is also important to note that no single approach to teaching will suit all children and all situations in any event. Susan Cain (2013), for example, has strongly challenged the notion that every child enjoys learning through dialogue, while Phil Scott (2008), whose work supports the principles of dialogic teaching, has provided a persuasive model of the blending of talk styles that a teacher should encourage and use within the classroom if their lessons are to achieve maximum impact. As the old adage has it, a good golfer does not play well with a single club. The present chapter and others in this book are predicated on the belief that teaching that aims to use and develop children's oracy skills is an indispensable element of good classroom practice and that P4C is an invaluable approach for teachers wishing to teach in this way.

For true embeddedness of oracy to take place within schools, there would need to be a paradigmatic shift of the kind proposed by Robin Alexander and others in their promotion of dialogic teaching. The subtitle of Alexander's book (2008) is *Re-thinking classroom talk*. These words capture the seismic shift in classroom practice that he envisages, a shift that echoes much in the vision of Matthew Lipman, which first emerged several decades earlier. In 2014, I interviewed Neil Mercer, one of the leading authorities in the area of dialogic teaching in this country, and in that interview he suggested some useful areas for teacher development.

> JS: What sorts of things can the busy teacher, primary or secondary, do to make his or her classroom more dialogic?

NM: One of the first things is that they should become more aware themselves of how they use talk and what they are trying to get it to do. They should critically examine whether they are using it to the best effect. The second thing would be to help children become more aware of what talk is for and the value of it. One reason that children don't always get the most out of talk in class is because they sometimes don't think talking is important in class … If they can be helped to see that talk is learning and you can learn through talk then they will participate in it more wholeheartedly. Beyond that it's a case of teachers looking at what dialogic techniques other teachers have been using that they are not using yet and they could try them out.

(Smith, 2014, p. 9)

As Mercer makes clear, it should not be a case of seeking *either* success in literacy and other academic areas *or* success in promoting oracy, but rather of seeking the first *through* the second. Governmental support for dialogic approaches of the kind offered in 2009 would be extremely beneficial if it came again and it would probably be the single most useful boost to their development. However, as this chapter and others in this book make clear, there are already sufficient supporters of such approaches – including the very substantial programmes of CPD and growing amounts of ITE led by SAPERE – to allow P4C to thrive. We should also remember the importance of what we might term 'classroom-led change', where teachers share dialogic techniques, as Mercer advises. P4C is likely to emerge very well from such a process since it exemplifies and enacts the most important features of dialogical pedagogy and yields enormous benefits to children.

References

Alexander, R. (2008) *Towards Dialogic Teaching*, 4th edn. York: Dialogos.

Alexander, R. (ed.) (2010) *Children, their World, their Education: Final report and recommendations of the Cambridge Primary Review.* Abingdon: Routledge.

Cain, S. (2013) *Quiet: The power of introverts in a world that can't stop talking.* London: Penguin.

DCSF (2009) *Independent Review of the Primary Curriculum: Final Report* (The Rose Report). Nottingham: DCFS.

DES (1975) *A Language for Life* (The Bullock Report). London: HMSO.

DfE (2013) *The National Curriculum in England. Key Stages 1 and 2 framework document.* Crown copyright.

Goleman, D. (2007) *Social Intelligence: The new science of human relationships.* New York: Random House.

Lipman, M. (2003) *Thinking in Education*, 2nd edn. New York: Cambridge University Press.

Mercer, N. (2000) *Words and Minds: How we use language to think together.* Abingdon: Routledge.

Mercer, N. and Littleton, K. (2007) *Dialogue and the Development of Children's Thinking: A sociocultural approach.* Abingdon: Routledge.

Mercer, N. and Littleton, K. (2013) *Interthinking: Putting talk to work.* Abingdon: Routledge.

Mercer, N., Wegerif, R. and Dawes, L. (1999) Children's talk and the development of reasoning in the classroom. *British Educational Research Journal*, 25(1), 95–111.

Scott, P. (2008) Talking as a way to understanding in science classrooms. In N. Mercer and S. Hodgkinson (eds) *Exploring Talk in School.* London: Sage.

Sinclair, J. and Coulthard, M. (1975) *Towards an Analysis of Discourse: The English used by teachers and pupils.* London: Oxford University Press.

Smith, J. (2014) Walking the talk. In *DLP: Developing Learning Partnerships*, Autumn, Issue 1. Manchester Metropolitan University Faculty of Education.

Torrance, H. and MacLure, M. (2010) 'The social brain and the curriculum' and 'The curriculum and the agency of young people'. An interpretative report. RSA Projects: Education.

Tough, J. (1977) *Talking and Learning: A guide to fostering communication in nursery and infant schools.* London: Ward Lock.

Vygotsky, L. S. (1962) *Thought and Language.* Cambridge, MA: MIT Press.

Vygotsky, L. S. (1978) *Mind in Society: The development of higher psychological processes.* Cambridge, MA: Harvard University Press.

Wegerif, R. (1996) Using computers to help encourage exploratory talk across the curriculum. *Computers and Education*, 2(1–3), 51–60.

PART 3

P4C in school

6

P4C IN EARLY CHILDHOOD EDUCATION

Fufy Demissie

Recent research findings have fuelled the growing momentum that philosophical enquiry improves children's cognitive capacities and performance on national tests in English and Maths (Gorard *et al.*, 2015). For early childhood educators, despite concerns about philosophy's relevance for young children, the growing interest in philosophical enquiry has led them to consider its appropriateness for the early childhood context. In this chapter I examine the extent to which the pedagogy of P4C overlaps with early childhood education pedagogies and, with specific reference to the English Early Years Foundation Stage (EYFS) (DfE, 2014), how philosophical enquiry in the early childhood classroom could help teachers address curriculum aims and goals. The chapter concludes by arguing that while tensions remain between the educational goals of P4C and early childhood education programmes, there is sufficient overlap between the two to warrant its use in the early childhood context.

Key themes in early childhood education

The nature, content and priorities of early childhood education programmes understandably vary depending on government aims and policies, together with historical and current philosophical influences. For example, curricula can differ in terms of what counts as sound preparation for school. In New Zealand's Te Whariki curriculum (Lee *et al.*, 2013), school readiness is mainly seen in terms of children's dispositions for learning, such as motivation and engagement, while in the English EYFS school readiness encompasses the academic, physical and social/emotional aspects as well as the their learning characteristics (DfE, 2014). Curricula approaches and policies can also differ in terms of how they conceptualise children's developmental stages, exemplified in contrasting expectations of the age at which children can start formal schooling, which range from 4 years old (England and Ireland) to 7 (Scandinavia) (OECD, 2012). Nonetheless, despite differences about the nature, content and priorities of early childhood education, there is a widely held consensus that children in the early years (however this is defined) have different needs and ways of learning and that this distinctive educational phase requires distinctive practices and approaches.

Elements of consensus in early childhood education (ECE)

This consensus that young children have different needs and ways of learning is immediately obvious from the way the learning environments are constructed. A key influence was Jean Piaget (1966), who argued, based on his detailed observations, that curiosity and exploration were defining characters of the young child, who is driven by the need to make sense of their environment using their senses. Thus, it is not uncommon to find some or all of the following in varied early education traditions: areas for exploration and investigation (such as sand and water), jigsaws, play dough and plasticine and small world play items, as well as well-designed outdoor spaces that include elements of the natural world (such as sensory gardens, woodland), and larger versions of indoor resources such as sand and water.

The provision of these environments is in line with the widespread agreement that there are distinctive ways of learning that best suit young children. For example, the English EYFS (DfE, 2014) clearly states that there are certain characteristics of learning (playing and exploring, active learning, and creating and thinking critically) that underpin effective learning. For this purpose, it encourages adults to provide first-hand experiences, ensure that children have time to be involved deeply in activities and encourage open-ended thinking. The notion of 'holistic learning' is also implicit in many early childhood programmes, evidenced in Reggio Emilia's project-based work approach, where topics or problems identified by the children or the teacher become the focus for learning (Thornton and Brunton, 2014). This perspective stems from the belief that young children do not learn in compartmentalised ways, so the learning experiences presented should develop more than one aspect of their learning, as in Te Whariki discussed above. Thus, sand play can help children to consolidate and extend their understanding of scientific concepts and associated language, while at the same time catering to their personal and social development as they negotiate, take turns and discuss their ideas with their peers.

Play

The centrality of play is another widely shared consensus among different early education programmes. It is supported by research in various disciplines that shows that play appears to be the principal or leading way in which children explore and make sense of experiences (Moylett, 2014). Its importance stems from emerging views of the child from the seventeenth century, where play is seen as the natural expression of young children, leading to Froebel's first curriculum, which was based on play and planned to promote children's growth and development. More recently, the nature, purpose and process of play have been further refined to encompass different ideas about types of play, such as role play, games play, schemas, child-led play, adult-led play and the characteristics of playful learning – exploration, creativity, risk-taking, involvement and flow. In the EYFS, for example, play is seen, among other things, as a 'key opportunity for children to think creatively and flexibly, solve problems and link ideas', with a recommendation that educators 'establish the enabling conditions for rich play: space, time, flexible resources, choice, control, warm and supportive relationships' (DfE, 2014).

Play as a process also features strongly in the Te Whariki curriculum. Play is more than an activity; it is also a catalyst for creativity. Play's ubiquity might suggest that there is universal agreement about what play means and how it should be promoted, but it remains a problematic concept. Debates continue about the importance and relevance of different types of play experiences, such as adult- versus child-initiated play for young children's growth and development. Despite the differences, however, most early childhood curricula incorporate the idea to different degrees that children play and explore naturally and that play is an important context for learning and development (Moylett, 2014).

The role of the adult

The status of the adult or the teacher in the early childhood classroom also illustrates the philosophy that teaching and learning in the early childhood classroom is distinctive. In Montessori classrooms, for example, the teacher is a facilitator of the learning environment; they carefully select the resources that are designed to address particular learning and development needs. In Reggio Emilia and the EYFS, however, the teacher's role illustrates a Vygotskian perspective (Vygotsky, 1978). The teacher is also a facilitator of the learning environment, but they facilitate children's learning and thinking through interactions, questions, discussions and through building close and meaningful relationships. Thus, in contrast to teachers in other in subsequent phases, most programmes share the view that young children need someone who facilitates their learning through positive relationships, who provides appropriate resources through respectful and empowering interactions. Without these attributes, it is unlikely that children can access the environment through first-hand experience and appropriate resources, which are necessary for further growth and development.

In summary, although ECE curricula are designed to reflect different aims, values and cultures, there is a common thread that early childhood is a distinctive phase that reflects young children's needs and interests, and supports their capacity to think and reason and make sense of their environment with adults who can provide learning environments that facilitate and nurture their innate capacity.

Philosophy for Children and the early childhood education context

The essence of the Philosophy for Children programme is the improvement of thinking and its most important dimensions: the 'critical, the creative and the caring' dimensions of thinking (Lipman, 2003, p. 197). In contrast to other programmes, however, Lipman chose to use philosophy and the pedagogy of the community of enquiry, in which thinking could be improved.

Philosophy as a context

A popular view of philosophy is of an abstract, dogmatic and esoteric body of knowledge that is only accessible and understandable by a few (Fisher, 1995). In the context of this, it is perhaps unsurprising that Lipman's use of philosophy in the context of primary education was and continues to be controversial. But Lipman is careful to make a distinction between the 'academic' tradition of philosophy and the Socratic tradition from which P4C has emerged. Philosophy in the Socratic tradition is of philosophy as 'practised' rather than as 'known' or 'applied ... a form of life ... something that any of us can emulate' (2003, p. 12). In other words, philosophy is a part of our everyday interactions and experiences through concepts such as fairness, justice or beauty. There are parallels between this perspective and the pedagogy of early childhood education, where teachers provide familiar contexts (such as role play) to promote meaningful learning. Similarly, Murris (2001, p. 46) argues that adults can use children's concrete experiences to draw out the underlying concepts to facilitate genuine exploration of ideas that matter to them. For example, in one enquiry with a group of 4 and 5 year olds, Maurice Sendak's *Where the Wild Things Are* provoked discussions about what makes something real, something that many young children often wonder about. However, without this familiar context, it seems unlikely that they would be interested or able to listen to each other and contribute their ideas.

The view of the child

The faith that Lipman put in children's capacities for participating in philosophical enquiry signals a view of the young child as competent and capable. On one level at least, this perspective echoes some of the underlying themes in some of the early childhood curricula encountered earlier of the young child as capable and full of potential. A distinguishing characteristic of this programme therefore is that the child's role is critical for its success. Children are responsible for asking the questions, voting for the questions, contributing their thoughts, asking for reasons and challenging their own and others' claims to knowledge.

The philosophy of childhood in P4C is more radical, but there are echoes of it in the principles of ECE curricula. In Reggio Emilia, for example, the curriculum is based on a recognition that all children have preparedness, potential and curiosity (Thornton and Brunton, 2014), and in the EYFS (DfE, 2014), the 'unique child' is one of the overriding principles, where every child is seen as one 'who is constantly learning and can be resilient, capable, confident and self-assured'. This echoes Donaldson's (1986) view that young children are capable of much more complex reasoning if the right environment is provided.

But the concept of the child and their capabilities is hotly debated and used by critics of P4C, who question children's capacity for discussions, their ability to engage with abstract concepts and their preference for active hands-on learning. In response, others have not only questioned the tenability of maturity-based child development theories, but also refer to Donaldson's (1986) critique of Piaget's stage of intellectual development of the importance of context in judging young children's capacities. There is also evidence from the large-scale study Researching Effective Practice in Early Years (REPEY), which found that when adults act as co-enquirers, children are capable of taking part in deep and meaningful acts of 'shared sustained thinking' (SST) (Siraj-Blatchford *et al.*, 2002). Aside from these debates, there is also an underlying tension between this view of the child and the one that informs early childhood education curricula where the deficit model of childhood dominates.

Learning processes

Certain assumptions about the learning process are visible in philosophical enquiry activities. Lipman's motivation for designing the P4C programme was that existing curricula programmes did not sufficiently address the process of learning. In P4C, the process of learning, and in particular the thinking process, is the basis of the programme. When children are engaged in dialogue within a community of enquiry, it is not necessarily the outcome of the dialogue that is significant, but rather the process of thinking, such as their ability to state a claim, question its soundness and relevance, build on each other's ideas and engage in reflective thinking. Reflective thinking, according to Lipman, is 'prepared to recognise the factors that make for bias, prejudice and self-deception. It involves thinking about its procedures at the same time as it involves thinking about is subject matters' (2003, p. 26). In other words, the process is equally as important as the outcome of the thinking. The assumptions about the learning process also echo important ECE principles of characteristics of effective learning (DfE, 2014), the exploration strand of Te Whariki's principle of empowerment, and High/Scope's (Wiltshire, 2012) principle of plan-do-review.

The role of the adult

In philosophical enquiry, while it is the children who drive the enquiry and dialogue, nevertheless the adult or facilitator role is also critical. Facilitators set up the learning context, for example by establishing ground rules and providing the stimuli for discussion; they also have an important role in ensuring that the community of enquiry pays attention to inconsistencies, contradictions and missing reasons, in addition to ensuring that the dialogue is cumulative and that it takes place in a caring and collaborative context. Good facilitators are responsive and attuned to individual children's and the groups' responses, through questions and interventions such as, 'Do you agree with X says?', and mindful that participants treat each other with care. Thus, much like the adult in curricula such as EYFS, Te Whariki, Reggio Emilia and High/Scope, the teacher/facilitator is a guide who must create an enabling environment, building and sustaining relationships between the children and with the children, and who models the thinking processes and approaches that children need to take part in deep and meaningful dialogue.

Summary

This section has attempted to address the question of what if any overlaps there are between early childhood curricula and the pedagogy of philosophical enquiry. In most cases, first-hand experiences and familiar contexts and the role of the adult seem paramount. Moreover, there also seems to be common ground between the early childhood curricula and pedagogy of philosophical enquiry that draw on the ideas of key thinkers such as Vygotsky and Piaget. The implication of this is that there is a rationale to consider philosophical enquiry's relevance for the early childhood context. In the following sections, I examine what affordances philosophical enquiry might have, particularly in relation to the English EYFS (which has drawn heavily from a range of early childhood traditions such as Te Whariki, Reggio Emilia and High/Scope), before outlining some of the approaches they might take to incorporate philosophical enquiry into their practice.

P4C in the specific context of the Early Years Foundation Stage (EYFS)

The EYFS is England's statutory document that covers the 0 to 5 years age range; it evolved from two separate curricula, for 0 to 3 years and 3 to 5 years. It focuses on the key themes of the unique child, learning and development, relationships and the learning environment and the associated principles for each of the themes. For example, the theme of 'unique child' is expressed in the principle that 'each child is a unique learner that is capable'; positive relationships as 'children learn through responsive relationships'; enabling environments as 'the importance of the learning environment and learning'; and 'learning and development' specifies the curriculum content for each area of learning (language and communication, personal and social emotional development, mathematical development, understanding of the world) and the process of learning (active learning, playing and exploring and creativity).

The prime areas of EYFS

In the EYFS, three areas of learning are considered to be the 'prime' areas of learning (in other words, the foundations necessary for literacy and reading, mathematics, etc.). This distinction between areas of learning is perhaps unsurprising. Increasingly, research evidence is showing how personal and emotional development is the basis for learning, and how starting school with poorly developed language and communication skills affects young children's educational outcomes. The language and communication area of learning includes listening and attention, expressing oneself, understanding and speaking, and by the end of the foundation stage (before the start of formal schooling), children are expected to communicate effectively, showing awareness of each other's needs and listen attentively.

Language and communication

There are several reasons why philosophical enquiry can complement existing strategies for promoting language and communication. Echoing Neil Mercer's (2000) research into the conditions for effective talk, philosophical enquiry provides an ideal context that can nurture listening skills, paying attention and self-expression. In their attempts to come to a shared understanding of a concept, children actively listen and construct a dialogue that is based on important communication skills such as stating a viewpoint, asking for clarification, disagreeing or agreeing, thus providing a model of what communication looks like in practice. When children are using these skills and attributes, they are doing so in ways that reflect the characteristics of effective learning (such as exploring, being actively engaged and thinking critically and creatively) in early childhood. Therefore the early childhood educator can, in the processes of doing philosophical enquiry, introduce, consolidate or extend the skills (as the context requires), understanding and attributes required to develop effective language and communication.

Personal social and emotional development

Another important prime area is personal and social development, which includes forming relationships, taking turns and (by the end of non-statutory schooling) expects children to demonstrate an understanding of their place in the world and awareness of others. Once again, a community of enquiry, through its emphasis on the caring and collaborative dimensions of thinking and the teacher's active promotion of this (without which the philosophical enquiry project cannot work), can be a highly suitable context for consolidating their understanding of relationships, awareness of others and interdependence. By combining the affective and cognitive dimensions the teacher can begin to introduce the knowledge, skills and understanding necessary to be a member of a group and of society.

P4C and early childhood practice

Having established the pedagogical overlaps of philosophical enquiry and early childhood education curricula, and highlighted some of the ways philosophical enquiry can help to meet important curriculum goals on language and learning and personal and social development, in this section I give a brief overview of the different ways in which teachers can begin to integrate this into their practice.

Many teachers commonly encounter philosophical enquiry in the form of Philosophy for Children (P4C) methodology, when introduced as part of whole school training. But early childhood educators often see the 7-step structure of P4C as unsuitable to children between the ages of 3 and 5. In this structure, the class sits in a circle, the teacher presents the stimuli, questions are raised and written down, before the class votes for one question and the dialogue begins. This is a process that can take up to one hour, too long perhaps even for older children. The unease is understandable as on the surface at least P4C seems to be in direct contrast to the pedagogy of early childhood education, where young children are seen to learn best from actively doing in the context of potentially short attention spans.

The P4C structure and ECE

However, there is some anecdotal evidence that even young children (under 4 and 5) can concentrate for much longer periods of time, respond to stimuli, ask questions, express preferences and make meaningful contributions. Karen Murris (2001), a highly experienced P4C practitioner and philosopher, attributes this to the particular context of P4C, where children are in charge and following their own interests.

In one enquiry conducted by the author, involving ten children aged 4 and 5, attending a school in a highly deprived socio-economic area, similar things were observed. Supported by two adults, even the most reluctant speakers took part in a full P4C enquiry that lasted approximately 40 minutes. The stimuli was Maurice Sendak's *Where the Wild Things Are*, and the question they voted for was 'Was Max's bedroom real?' In a rich and in–depth discussion, they showed respect for each other and collaborated to answer their question. For example, in one instance, one child stated that Max's (the main character) bedroom cannot be real because it had 'trees growing on the wall'. In the discussion that followed, they considered examples of real and not real things and when the facilitator asked if the forest was 'real' (as it too had trees growing in it) another child disagreed, stating that 'trees grow in forests but not inside the house'. This example illustrates how even very young children can take part in a structured philosophical enquiry, and when they do they can reason collaboratively and communicate their ideas to their peers. It is therefore a type of learning experience that can support early childhood educators to introduce and consolidate the learning goals that relate to making relationships, listening and attention, and expressing themselves and showing awareness of others (DfE, 2014).

Philosophical thinking – an integrated approach

As stated above, early childhood curricula increasingly prioritise the development of children's language, thinking and reasoning skills, and there is considerable overlap with the aims and processes of philosophical enquiry. But the standard P4C structured approach to developing these skills and attributes may not be suitable for all young children. Philosophical enquiry, however, does not necessarily require, or some might say need, this formal structure. Educators can find more developmentally appropriate approaches in Paley's (1992) inspiring accounts of her classroom (where she used children's stories as a context for exploring moral questions that arose in the classrooms), and more recently Stanley's work (2012) on promoting critical and creative thinking using children's play.

In both cases, the educator creates a culture of enquiry and exploration where 'independent thinking becomes the norm' (2012, p. 2). Stanley's approach is based on the principle that play is a rich source for philosophical thinking and exploration, which can be exploited by adults to develop their language, reasoning and thinking. Thus, through play scenarios and picture books, she shows how the everyday context can be used to develop children's capacities for giving reasons for their views about characters and stories, to challenge each other about the implications of their views, explore concepts and imagine possibilities. It is a challenging approach, because it lacks the security of a formal structure, which means that teachers who take up this approach need to be good listeners, sensitive to problematic issues and concepts in children's play and stories, and adept at asking questions that promote thinking.

Games and skills

There is another approach to philosophical enquiry that some teachers might prefer to explore, at least in the early stages. Effective and meaningful participation for enquiry and dialogue requires a wide range of skills and dispositions, such as knowledge of different types of questions, the difference between a question and statement, ability to take turns, listen, give reasons and express oneself. The skill-building approach may be one way of starting the philosophical journey using ideas such as pair and group work, challenges and problem-solving activities. Similarly, everyday activities such as 'Grandmother's footsteps' and shared whispers can also be used to develop listening, taking turns, building on ideas and developing awareness of others.

However, there are also now many examples of skill-building activities that have a philosophical emphasis. Once more, Stanley (2012) provides a wealth of ideas, such as the 'always/sometimes/never' game that can be used to help children to develop more precise thinking. Children are given various scenarios and asked to say whether they are always, sometimes or never a good thing (e.g. birthdays every day), and encouraged to give reasons for their position. This type of experience can provide the building blocks of philosophical enquiry, such as stating a viewpoint, seeking evidence, challenging evidence and justifying choices. As many early childhood curricula aims include the development of critical and creative thinking capacities, these approaches can be a way of introducing and consolidating young children's skills.

Tensions and contradictions in philosophical enquiry and ECE

Nonetheless, despite the broad overlaps between the pedagogies of P4C and early childhood, tensions and contradictions remain. For instance, there are differences between the Deweyan principles of education (Dewey, 1933) as a process that underpins philosophical enquiry and the utilitarian views of formal education as preparation for adulthood with a focus on education as the acquisition of knowledge. Thus, in philosophical enquiry the role of the teacher is as a co-enquirer, whereas in non-philosophical contexts the role of the teacher is that of an authority figure, who imparts the common core of essential knowledge.

However, this is not to say that Lipman (2003) disregarded the importance of knowledge. On the contrary, he often showed how philosophical enquiry strengthened children's capacity to think in maths, science and the arts. But his main contention is that the acquisition of knowledge has been exaggerated at the expense of thinking and the cultivation of judgement. Early childhood contexts are perhaps somewhat fortunate, as in the case of the EYFS the fundamentals of learning (language and communication and personal and social emotional development) are closer to Lipman's vision of why young children should do philosophy. Despite these tensions, even if Lipman's goals cannot be fully realised, adopting a philosophical approach still has the potential to foster and promote some of the skills and attitudes that underpin many early child education programme goals.

Conclusion

Recent research studies show the benefits of philosophical enquiry for primary children's learning and development. Despite the lack of studies in the EC context, it is an approach that early childhood educators can explore with children as young as 3. This is because with the increased emphasis on language and reasoning and personal and social emotional development, educators need to extend their repertoire of strategies. Philosophical enquiry offers one way of doing this. Its pedagogy has close parallels with important early childhood pedagogical principles (such as the role of the adult, the view of the child and of learning as exploration and inquiry) and it gives educators a framework for fostering critical, creative and caring thinking.

References

DfE (2014) *The Early Years Foundation Stage* (EYFS). London: Department for Education.

Dewey, J. (1933) *How We Think: A restatement of the relation of reflective thinking to the educative process*. New York: Heath and Co.

Donaldson, M. (1986) *Children's Minds*. London: Fontana.

Fisher, R. (1995) Socratic education: A new paradigm for philosophical enquiry? *Creative and Critical Thinking*, 4(1).

Gorard, S., Siddiqui, N. and See, B. H. (2015) *Philosophy for Children: SAPERE, Evaluation Report and Executive Summary*. London: Education Endowment Foundation.

Lee, W., Carr, M., Soutar, B. and Mitchell, L. (2013) *Understanding the Te Whariki Approach*. London: Routledge.

Lipman, M. (2003) *Thinking in Education*, 2nd edn. Cambridge: Cambridge University Press.

Mercer, N. (2000) *Words and Minds: How we use language to think together*. Abingdon: Routledge.

Moylett, H. (ed.) (2014) *Characteristics of Effective Learning: Helping young children become learners for life*. Buckingham: Open University Press.

Murris, K. (2001) Can children be philosophical? *Theory and Practice: Children's philosophy*. London: Teaching Thinking.

OECD (2012) *Starting Strong III – A quality toolbox for Early Childhood Education and Care*. Paris: OECD.

Paley, V. G. (1992) *You Can't Say You Can't Play*. Cambridge, MA: Harvard University Press.

Piaget, J. and Inhelder, B. (1966) *The Psychology of the Child*. London: Routledge and Kegan Paul.

Stanley, S. (2012) *Why Think? Philosophical play from 3–11*. London: Continuum.

Siraj-Blatchford, I., Sylva, K., Muttock, S., Gilden, R. and Bell, D. (2002) *Researching Effective Pedagogy in the Early Years*. Research Report 356. London: DCSF.

Thornton, L. and Brunton, P. (2014) *Bringing the Reggio Approach to your Early Years Practice*, 3rd edn. Abingdon: Routledge.

Vygotsky, L. (1978) *Mind in Society*. Cambridge, MA: Harvard University Press.

Wiltshire, M. (ed.) (2012) *Understanding the High/Scope approach*. London: Routledge.

7

P4C IN THE PRIMARY SCHOOL

Kathy Stokell, Diane Swift and Babs Anderson

The primary context

Philosophy for Children in the primary school is an approach that has been adopted by increasing numbers of primary schools in the UK since its inception. It can act as an antidote to prescriptive national curricula, which can be seen as increasingly divorced from the reality of the lived experiences of the children, their own pressing concerns and engagement with the world around them. It also foregrounds disciplined thinking, creating opportunities for learning from a more knowledgeable other (Vygotsky, 1978), so that the ideas of others may support the development of concept formulation for the whole community, in either agreeing with or challenging the original position expressed. The theoretical position of social constructivism as proposed by Vygotsky (1978) and Bruner (1960) among others is one that has gained much interest in its application to educational pedagogical theory in the UK and elsewhere. Nevertheless the true extent to which this is realised in practice is debatable. Much of the group work within primary schools may be viewed as work in parallel rather than true collaboration with the integration of ideas from all the group members. The sheer physicality of sitting in a group situation does not mean in itself that the individuals are working together, resulting in a cumulative synthesis of ideas, more extensive than the original individual contributions. Instead the children may be all working on the same topic with little sharing of ideas or insights.

P4C as a community of practice offers an explicit means to examine conceptual understanding within a group situation for children in primary school. It enables this to be embedded within their own interests, and their desire to know about the world around them.

> If you are going to be a decision-making citizen, you need to know how to make sense and how to recognise when someone else is making sense ... You need to know how to share forms of argumentation. When people don't have methods of argument in common, they can't have intelligent disagreement, they have a fight ... Education is a training in what you can trust and what you can share ...
>
> *(Williams, 2008, cited in Higton, 2012, p. 136)*

In the UK, the most common structure is that cohorts of children stay together as a class group for the majority of their primary years, from the ages of 5 to 11. Setting may occur in Key Stage 2 for specific subjects, but the home class base remains stable. Although the individual teaching staff may vary from year to year, the cohort of children constitutes an entity throughout their primary school career. They have no choice in their classmates, so a primary class may be seen as a microcosm of their community, reflecting this through the arbitrary date of birth of the class members. Schools therefore must take into account that while their primary task is that of an institution tasked with the education of the young of the population, this is within a specific demographic and socio-cultural context. P4C can provide an opportunity for children to consider a wide range of perspectives from their peers and teachers, so that the children are able to reflect on their own opinions and beliefs as products of their experiences rather than the 'whole story'. This is also true for teachers:

> … to be reflective about our practices, to avoid inconsistencies in our belief, to be aware of what we are committed to as a consequence of holding the principles we claim to hold, and to expand the horizon of possibilities by considering alternative goals and ideas that might not have occurred to us …
>
> *(Phillips, 2010, p. 18)*

If primary teachers are to act as role models for learners, they must also engage with learning at a profound level. This includes the establishment of an ethos of sharing and engaging with others as the foundations of learning.

Pedagogy for the primary classroom

Alexander (2010, p. 7) defines pedagogy as

> … the act of teaching together with its attendant discourse of educational theories, values, evidence and justifications. It is what one needs to know, and the skills one needs to command, in order to make and justify the many different kinds of decisions of which teaching is constituted.

The teacher makes choices as to how to engage with the children and the types of interactions they encourage. Alexander suggests: 'It is the principles by which productive teaching is underpinned, which should first command teachers' attention' (2010, p. 7).

P4C offers a means of examining these principles as key concepts related to this notion of productive teaching. These include scholarship and love of learning, which are related to the teachers' standards as designated by the UK government. Other key concepts may be viewed in terms of cognitive outcomes, such as judgement, interpretation, reasonableness, authenticity, disciplined thinking, compliance and engagement. Others in the affective domain include trust, relational thinking and risk-taking.

Within the field of education as a forum for social justice, Young (2007, p. 17) suggests:

> The sociology of knowledge is an important set of conceptual tools for preventing us from becoming immersed in the minutiae of specific policies, and for reminding us that

the big questions about how promoting greater equality is not separate from the structuring of knowledge and the conditions for its acquisition still need to be asked.

It is these conditions that P4C actively seeks to promote, in examining concept formation, the community context for this and the content of the curriculum. A case study in one primary school is examined below as an example of this in practice.

Case study: A primary teacher's reflection on using P4C in the classroom

As the personal social and health education (PSHE) lead in school, I had always been interested in integrating PSHE fully into the school curriculum to allow children to explore their own and other people's health and emotional well-being. As part of my senior management role, which also included the role of SENCO, I was becoming increasingly aware of the number of children in school who were suffering from anxiety and low self-esteem, and knew that this needed to be addressed if we were to help children to develop strategies to keep themselves heathy and safe.

Circle time had always commandeered a regular slot on my timetable but it was becoming increasingly apparent that this wasn't enough. I knew that teaching pupils about mental health and emotional well-being as part of a developmental PSHE education curriculum was essential but felt that the children had come to view this regular circle time slot as a way to just contribute in the way that they thought was acceptable to the teacher. The format didn't necessarily allow the pupils to explore their own and other people's thoughts and beliefs in any depth. However, as the PSHE Association acknowledges, there are potential and significant challenges for teachers, when teaching about mental health and emotional wellbeing (PSHE Association 2015), so this wasn't just about pupils being unable to talk about sensitive issues but about teachers too.

It was apparent that in order for teachers to be able to address the more sensitive and challenging areas of mental health and well-being, it was imperative that they were adequately trained and had the confidence to work with children in areas that may not always feel comfortable and predictable. Therefore it became evident it was necessary to introduce a strategy or intervention in school that would allow children to feel more confident to express their ideas and thoughts in a non-threatening atmosphere of inquiry and talk. In order for teachers to tackle the more sensitive and challenging areas of mental health and well-being, it was important that they were adequately trained and had the confidence to work with children in addressing these issues. They needed a means by which they could develop the confidence to foster critical, creative and caring thinking, not only in children but also in themselves. They needed to have the time and space to talk, which would help to allay some of the stresses and anxieties they were feeling, when discussing these types of issues.

A colleague advocated P4C as a way of helping children to understand the more complex issues involved in teaching about global issues and felt that it did allow children to think more freely, allowing them to question and explore contentious issues.

In my position, being a teacher of a Year 6 class as the final year of primary school meant that there were high stakes in terms of National Curriculum Assessments (commonly known as SATs) results in mathematics and English. As a junior school, there were targets to meet in order to show aspirational and expected progress from Key Stage 1. The school had a two-form entry and both Y6 teachers were given the opportunity to attend Level 1 P4C training.

The opportunity to teach in a more creative way was welcomed but, as in many Y6 classes, we had become used to focusing on maths and English with little room for creativity. In her training sessions in schools, Joanna Haynes comments that teachers often complain that they do not have time for exploratory and open-ended talk with children, even though in theory they do believe in the value and worth of this type of interaction as a way of enabling 'pupil voice' and individual expression (Haynes, 2007). In addition to this, there was also the worry that this was going to be another short-term initiative, requiring effort and planning, which had additional time requirements on an already overladen curriculum.

However, despite the above reservations, we did decide to embark on the training and see how this would impact our teaching and learning and most importantly the learning and development of the children. There was a desire to become more creative in our teaching and allow our children to step out of the 'passive learner' mode, which we had created in an attempt to prepare them for the end of Key Stage 2 SATs. Dweck (2007) has undertaken seminal research into the importance of mindsets in teachers and learners and stresses the importance of teachers not only having a growth mindset for themselves but the ability to develop this within the children they teach. Fixed mindsets can stifle creativity in both the learner and teacher and it was this 'fixed mindset' that had led to a narrow curriculum, in turn leading to a restricted range of teaching and learning strategies in Year 6. There was also the worry that this was having an impact on the children's emotional health and well-being.

Following the training and now equipped with the new knowledge and skills of how to facilitate philosophical enquiries, it was decided to implement this as a regular slot on the weekly Year 6 timetable before introducing the idea of P4C to the rest of the staff. We felt that we had been well prepared, and although inexperienced in facilitating P4C we were so inspired by the training that we were enthusiastic, yet curious to see how this would work within our own classrooms. Denby (2012) highlights the link between subject knowledge and confidence, stressing that teachers who are secure in their subject knowledge are more likely to take risks in their teaching and adopt more creative strategies for their learners. This gives them the confidence to teach creatively, which should then help them to provide a more enabling environment, allowing creativity to flourish in their learners.

P4C seemed a way of developing creative teaching in the classroom. Creativity requires the teacher to create an environment that encourages questioning and possibility thinking, so developing a community of enquiry. One of the key ways for children to develop their thinking is through dialogue in a space where they feel safe enough to express themselves openly through a mutual exchange of ideas. Hopefully this had always been the case within my classroom; however, in reality it must be acknowledged that this wasn't always apparent. The rushed nature of lessons and the constant pressure of targets and attainment in Year 6 meant that the children had little time to explore ideas in any depth. One of the key statutory requirements of the Spoken Language strand in the 2014 National Curriculum stresses the importance of using 'spoken language to develop understanding through speculating, hypothesising, imagining and exploring ideas' (DfE, 2014), yet the classroom environment does not necessarily give children the time, opportunity or support to do this.

The first philosophical enquiry within the class was part of a lesson on PSHE. The class had been looking at different types of families during their Sex and Relationships lessons, and as Mother's Day was approaching this led to a discussion about what it meant to be a mother. Although the P4C session was a success in terms of pupil engagement and enjoyment, it was apparent that we had only just begun, and both teacher and children would need much more practice. Time is needed for creative thinking and dialogue to be effective, so if this is to become part of the ethos within the classroom, it is essential to give value to this type of learning. Fisher suggests that 'Creative dialogue cannot be left to chance, it must be valued, encouraged and expected – and seen as essential to good teaching and learning' (2013, p. 41).

Four types of thinking are identified by SAPERE as being developed through P4C if it is to be used effectively within the classroom, these being caring, collaborative, creative and critical. Children within the class were not necessarily thinking in this way, although there was no doubt they had the capacity to do so. Although it was already March and moving towards the 'dreaded' SATs, a commitment was made to ensure that the class would undertake an enquiry every week until the end of the school year. By this stage there was no choice; the children were already 'hooked' and were constantly asking when the next session of P4C would be.

As the weeks progressed, the children became more confident. Initially I had expected those children on the Gifted and Talented register to be more involved. P4C focuses on higher-order thinking, and Robson and Moseley (2005) argue that gifted students need environments that encourage autonomy and focus on critical, creative, caring thinking in order to nurture personal talent. However, this was not the case to begin with and one boy in particular was extremely quiet during the first few enquiries. In contrast, those children who were usually very quiet, one of whom had a social and communication difficulty, were in fact very vocal. When J was asked why he liked P4C so much, he replied, 'I really like the way people listen to each other. Usually everybody ignores me and I feel stupid but in P4C people like what I say and they are nice to me.' It was at this point that some of the four Cs were actually becoming visible within the class. The children were collaborating, they were being critical and creative, and most importantly were beginning to really care about each other. This transcended all areas and it became apparent that the children were in the process of becoming critical thinkers.

On a personal note, I hadn't appreciated the impact that this would have in all areas of the curriculum, such as pupils' confidence to speak, patience when listening to others, and self-esteem. P4C also seemed to have a positive impact on general classroom engagement and resulted in some pupils asking more questions across all lessons. This was particularly noticeable in our history lessons. Rather than just learning about refugees and evacuation during World War Two, the children themselves were researching the link between this and asylum seekers today and one child brought a newspaper article as a stimulus. They were beginning to question everything we did, and reading comprehension sessions, which had in the past seemed dull and uninspiring, became a vehicle for children to ask more questions. They were using inference and deduction skills without needing to be taught. These were mere observations at the time but recent research funded by the Education Endowment Foundation, and independently evaluated by a team at Durham University, found that teaching P4C to Years 4 and 5 had a positive impact on learning throughout the curriculum.

The primary goal of this evaluation was to assess whether a year of P4C engagement for pupils in Years 4 and 5 would lead to higher academic attainment in terms of maths, reading and writing. The project also assessed whether P4C instruction had an impact on Cognitive Abilities Test results. Interestingly, although both Year 6 teachers at the school had attended P4C training, only one of the two teachers committed to facilitating a P4C enquiry every week. It was that class which subsequently scored higher in the Key Stage 2 Reading SAT, despite having lower targets. As the classes weren't subjected to a research trial, this is merely an observation so no real conclusions regarding the value of P4C on academic achievement can be drawn from it.

An initial interest in implementing P4C had been stimulated in order to address the emotional health and well-being of the children in school. What it did achieve was an opportunity to allow children to talk more openly and freely about topics that interested them. The school community provides a meaningful context for children's first introduction to public life not only for learning but also for personal and social development, while respecting them as individuals with ideas worthy of contribution and consideration (Haynes, 2007).

Following the introduction of P4C in the Year 6 class and the resulting visible and tangible improvements in children's academic and personal and social development, it was decided to implement this throughout the school. This was following an INSET day in school in which all teaching staff members were trained to facilitate P4C within their classrooms. P4C has now become part of the weekly timetable.

References

Alexander, R. (ed.) (2010) *Children, their World, their Education: Final report of the Cambridge Primary Review*. Abingdon: Routledge.

Bruner, J. S. (1960) *The Process of Education*. Cambridge, MA: Harvard University Press.

Denby, N. (ed.) (2012) *Training to Teach: A guide for students,* 2nd edn. London: Sage.

DfE (2014) *The New National Curriculum for England*. London: Department for Education.

Dweck, C. S. (2007) *Mindset: The new psychology of success*. New York: Ballantine.

Fisher, R. (2013) *Teaching Thinking*, 4th edn. London: Bloomsbury.

Haynes, J. (2007) Freedom and the urge to think in philosophy with children. *Gifted Education International*, 22(2/3), 229–37.

Higton, M. (2012) *A Theology of Higher Education*. Oxford: Oxford University Press.

Phillips, D. C. (2010) What is philosophy of education? In R. Bailey, R. Barrow, D. Carr and C. McCarthy (eds) *The Sage Handbook of Philosophy of Education*. London: Sage.

Prescott, G. (2015) Creative thinking and dialogue: P4C and the community of enquiry. In S. Elton-Chalcraft (ed.) *Teaching Religious Education Creatively*. Abingdon: Routledge.

PSHE Association (2015) Teacher Guidance: Preparing to teach about mental health and emotional well-being.

Robson, S. and Moseley, D. (2005) An integrated framework for thinking about learning. *Gifted Education International*, 20(1), 36–50.

Vygotsky, L. (1978) *Mind in Society*. Cambridge, MA: Harvard University Press.

Young, M. (2007) *Bringing Knowledge Back In: From social constructivism to social realism*. Abingdon: Routledge.

8

P4C IN SCIENCE EDUCATION

Lynda Dunlop

Introduction

In many nations, scientific literacy has been identified as a key aim of science education. This recognises that while science is an important feature of contemporary culture and society, only a proportion of young people will follow careers in science and that during the years of compulsory science education, preparation of future scientists cannot be justified as the main aim of science education because it puts the needs of a minority above those of the majority.

Scientific literacy evades an agreed definition, with some definitions paying attention to introducing young people to the world of scientists (and particularly the laboratory) through the development of an understanding of scientific explanations of phenomena and the ability to express an opinion on social and ethical issues with which they will be confronted (Millar and Osborne, 1998). However, other perspectives focus on scientific literacy as a property of communities (rather than individuals) that enables people to use science (and other ways of knowing) in meaningful ways to create more socially just conditions for living.

What draws these different conceptions of scientific literacy together is that they involve engaging young people with philosophical issues in relation to science. Questions about the nature, purpose and ethics of science cannot be answered using scientific methods, and to address these questions suggests the need for an approach more in line with the teaching of philosophy (in which few beginning science teachers will have participated themselves) in order to challenge science, and the conditions under which scientific knowledge is created and used. Philosophy for Children (P4C) is one such approach that opens a space for questioning and critique in relation to science and lived experiences.

The purpose of this chapter is to argue for the inclusion of Philosophy for Children in initial (science) teacher education. Reflecting on work with beginning and in-service teachers in relation to the aim of science education for scientific literacy, this chapter considers how P4C in science education can contribute to scientific literacy as conceived as a way of educating through science (rather than for science) and identifies some of the challenges associated with approaching these issues with beginning teachers.

Science education and scientific literacy

As recognised above, scientific literacy has been interpreted in different ways, some with greater emphasis on individuals and serving science, and others with an emphasis on science as one dimension of knowledge that can serve communities in political action. Each conception has implications for the way in which science is taught, and the ways in which beginning teachers are prepared. This section considers Holbrook and Rannikmäe's (2007) vision of scientific literacy as 'education through science' and the implications of this for practice.

Holbrook and Rannikmäe (2007) argue that all subjects must contribute to general educational goals for students. This means that rather than serving science ('science through education'), there is a need to move towards 'education through science', in which the nature of science is but one domain of science education, the others being the personal and the social. This implies that science education will serve the broader goals of education, and will attend to the personal and social. In this model, socio-scientific issues, rather than 'big ideas' in science, are seen as the starting point for science learning. This shift in emphasis has the consequence that no idea is seen as fundamental to the teaching of science, but rather the scientific content is necessarily dependent upon the situation (social and cultural) of the learner: it relates to 'need to know' knowledge, which enables an individual to function in society.

Holbrook and Rannikmäe identify their vision of scientific literacy as 'society-focused, socio-scientific issues-led education through science where science is merely the vehicle for learning' (2007, p. 1357). Taking the education through science approach to the development of scientific literacy implies being attentive to learners, understanding their experiences and their social context, enabling them to access the knowledge that is of value to them, and enabling them to develop an understanding of how scientific knowledge is created, and how to engage with social and ethical issues without an assumption of pro-scientific attitudes. The following section considers the implications of starting from a consideration of socio-ethical issues in science, and examines the place of the teacher, pedagogy and the curriculum in relation to the intersection between philosophy and science, before exploring the value of P4C in this context.

Teaching philosophy in/of science

One of the challenges in relation to addressing philosophical issues in science relates to the preparation of science teachers to do so. Most science teachers in the UK have very limited experience with philosophy. There is no requirement to study philosophy at pre-university level (university admission requirements for science courses mitigate against this), and very little philosophy of science makes its way into undergraduate science or postgraduate teacher education programmes. As a result, some researchers (Monk and Osborne, 1997; Abd-El-Khalick and Lederman, 2000; Bryce, 2010) have questioned whether science teachers have the capacity to teach about the nature of science, given the extent to which it is covered in undergraduate science degrees and postgraduate teaching qualifications.

In addition to the formal preparation of science teachers in philosophy, teachers' attitudes towards such issues can present a barrier to addressing philosophical (particularly ethical) issues in science. This juxtaposition of science and ethics can be particularly uncomfortable for teachers who define science in terms of objectivity (Sadler *et al.*, 2006). Teachers need to be given opportunities as part of their initial teacher education to become accustomed to talking about these issues, and to have an opportunity to reflect on their views about science as it relates to social and ethical issues so that they can do so comfortably in a classroom with children.

These challenges are not relevant only to beginning science teachers. Even teachers who have experience in dealing with values in science education have experienced difficulties and discomfort in doing so (Ratcliffe, 2007), and many teachers have been found to be reluctant to deal with issues that may be sensitive or controversial (CCEA, 2005), even though these are directly relevant to the science content that is presented in many national curricula, for example in relation to sex, genes, the environment and space exploration. Engaging with situations that require choices to be made between better and worse alternatives allows a richer understanding of science as well as ethics to develop (Rogers, 2008). Furthemore, it has been argued beyond the science context (Haynes and Murris, 2012) that a sanitised curriculum is neither realistic nor desirable, noting that children discuss challenging issues out of a desire to know, and that this can be achieved without causing harm or distress using structured and tactful facilitation. Indeed, they argue that it is up to adults to create opportunities to listen to children and support their discussion of difficult issues in educational settings, and this includes the science classroom.

In some cases, teachers lack the confidence and expertise to address social and ethical issues, perceiving their job is to 'teach the facts', with social, moral and ethical issues addressed as a bolt-on (Levinson and Turner, 2001). This approach to 'science through education' (Holbrook and Rannikmae, 2007) does not see the place for incorporating values into science education (although this in itself is a statement of values), and denies young people the opportunity to develop an awareness of ethical issues, improve their knowledge of ethics and their ethical judgement, through which they may become better people (Reiss, 1999, 2007, 2008). Furthermore, if such discussions are absent from science classrooms, there exists a danger that students will ignore the scientific evidence behind problems and perceive it as unconnected to contemporary societal issues (Ratcliffe, 2007), which is inconsistent with scientific literacy.

The pedagogy associated with addressing these issues also presents a challenge to 'traditional' science teaching, which has been described as presenting science as a 'rhetoric of conclusions' (Schwab, 1962), compounded by teaching techniques that value the transmission of knowledge from the teacher 'authority' to student 'novices'. For example, the dialogue patters that typically dominate in science include authoritative teacher talk (Mortimer and Scott, 2003), with student input largely in response to teacher-initiated questions (Duschl and Osborne, 2002). Although active learning strategies are more commonplace in contemporary science classrooms, the extent to which these challenge the transmission model is debatable, particularly where teachers feel pressure to 'deliver' a content-heavy curriculum. It has been argued that science teachers lack the time and skills to address philosophical issues in science and therefore there is a limit to the extent to which meaningful learning may result (Davson-Galle, 2008). However, such a science education based on facts rather than processes is known to disengage learners (UNESCO, 2010) and to be detrimental to students' interest in science and their understanding of what science is and how it contributes to their lives. Indeed, McLaren (in Calabrese-Barton, 2001, p. 853) has argued that 'the corporate approach to science in our classrooms has failed to raise questions dealing with what knowledge counts most, for whom, and for what purposes'. Providing opportunities for students to *raise* questions, and to challenge scientific knowledge and the uses to which this is put, is important not only to create connections between science, society and individuals' lives, but also to create opportunities for students to become aware of issues relating to social justice in relation to doing and applying science.

Recent developments in relation to interdisciplinary approaches to education have highlighted the importance of taking seriously perspectives from other disciplines in science. For example, Erduran and Mugaloglu (2013) provide suggestions for taking knowledge of economics seriously in the teaching of science. If philosophy (and in particular epistemology and ethics) is to be an essential component of science education, it is important also to take seriously pedagogical issues related to the teaching and learning of philosophy, and to address philosophical issues in a way that is consistent with the teaching of philosophy.

In an attempt to introduce science teachers to philosophical issues, this work has involved developing an approach to developing communities of enquiry from SAPERE's Philosophy for Children (P4C) model in working with beginning and in-service science teachers to develop communities of enquiry founded on scientific stimuli. The purpose of this work has been to engage teachers with social and ethical issues associated with science for their own sake, to explore teachers' experiences and perceptions of P4C and to consider the implications of philosophy of science, and of doing P4C, for science teaching.

Philosophy for children in science education

This section outlines the approach to Philosophy for Children adopted in this work, and identifies the place for this in science education, the evidence in support of the approach, and the nature of the stimulus and questions in supporting scientific literacy to support 'education through science'.

Some of the elements common to philosophical and scientific enquiry include generating questions, suggesting hypotheses, giving reasons and examples, making distinctions and connections, analysing implications, devising and using criteria and developing clear, coherent and consistent arguments. Reasons for doing Philosophy for Children are not limited to desired development of thinking skills. Doing philosophy with children in science helps students to clarify concepts and create meaning, enabling them to link scientific ideas with other ideas, to promote understanding of the nature of knowledge (including science knowledge); it permits them to explore socio-ethical issues and it can give them access to philosophy as a discipline (Sprod, 2001). Further benefits in the context of science are that Philosophy for Children and the associated creation of a community of enquiry embraces the spirit of science by encouraging a critical temper of mind and the promotion of the questioning of facts (Lipman *et al.*, 1980). Underpinning this work is the experience of being in a community of enquiry, learning with and from others who bring different perspectives, examples and ideas to bear on the issues at stake. This contrasts with the banking approach to education (Giroux, 2011) that is more common in science classrooms.

The approach to developing communities of enquiry taken with science teachers here is developed from SAPERE's approach to P4C, which puts children's questions and ideas at the centre of learning (Lipman, 2003). It advocates teaching children to ask and select their own philosophical questions in response to a stimulus, and exploring a selected question through dialogue. The central idea of the community of enquiry is to provide a group learning environment in which students cooperate to test, share and improve on their thinking together (Splitter and Sharp, 1995). The teacher facilitates the enquiry, supporting children to develop reasons and create meaning together, primarily through questions that are attentive to the child, community and the question. This approach is participatory: that is, curricular needs are not all defined in advance of interacting with learners (although some may be anticipated), and it is recognised that multiple perspectives, opinions and active engagement contribute to the final context of the learner experience (Siemens, 2008 in Simmons *et al.*, 2011). It is characterised by open questions, attentiveness to the group and creating spaces in which exploration is encouraged. This invites the members of the group, whether teachers or children, to decide what they think is important to discuss based on the stimulus provided. It prioritises their thinking, and it is recognised that the community may not reach a consensus view. What is of value is the process, and the new knowledge and understanding that participants gain from belonging to the community of enquiry.

There exists significant empirical evidence from studies involving philosophical enquiry with children, whether using the original materials and philosophical novels developed by Matthew Lipman, which provide opportunities to engage with philosophy of science (e.g. Lipman, 1974) or teacher-selected stimuli that demonstrate its ability to improve outcomes for students (Gorard *et al.*, 2015), their cognitive abilities including reasoning (Sprod, 1999; Thwaites, 2005; Trickey and Topping, 2004, 2007), as well as their self-esteem and confidence (Trickey and Topping, 2004, 2007) and motivation in science (Bartley, 2004). In the context of this work, the stimuli and associated warm-up games were developed specifically to problematise advances in contemporary science, particularly those with pronounced social and ethical implications.

Problematising science: stimulating philosophical enquiry with teachers

Consistent with Lipman's (2010) conception of education as starting with the student's awareness of the problematicity of the subject matter, the materials used as warm-up games and stimuli for enquiry in a socio-scientific context (Dunlop, 2012a) have been produced to problematise subject matter, and to relate this to and beyond the lived experiences of participants in an participatory space where teachers (or students) reflect on and critique their world. This was attempted by adopting an approach analogous to Freire's (2003) codification in adult literacy work in which images both illustrated the words that students were trying to read and represented problematic social conditions that could be challenged through collective dialogue (Burbules and Beck, 1999). In this work, images, cartoons, videos and texts were produced to illustrate science of high school level (e.g. genetic engineering, transmission of infections, and cloning) but that also represented problematic social conditions that could become the focus of dialogue that involves interpretation of the world and considering the possibilities for change. For example, a stimulus that presented intensive farming practices, including the use of selective breeding programmes, fertilisers and pesticides, and genetic engineering through the story of the Cavendish banana, allowed for the possibility of questions about nutrition, monoculture, the ethics of genetic engineering and pesticide use, and discussion of the precautionary principle. The social and political context of decision-making in science and agriculture was also examined.

This stimulus, used with experienced teachers in Northern Ireland, designed with the intention to shed light on problematic applications of science, also raised questions about government, land ownership, food production and distribution and the Great Famine in the nineteenth century, enabling teachers to reflect on their own position, and at the same time, develop ways of talking about highly sensitive subjects to people with a range of different perspectives. In this way, beginning with the socio-scientific context can support Holbrook and Rakkinmae's education through science, in which the needs of the community are given priority over covering particular curriculum topics.

Likewise, an experiential stimulus relating to food production invited participants to sample some insects prepared as food while listening to a '60 second idea to change the world' (BBC, 2007) arguing that people should eat insects rather than meat from mammals to reduce their carbon footprint. With children, this stimulus raised questions about greenhouse gases, food chains and webs, food safety, intensive farming, animal rights, vegetarianism, culture, and the nature of disgust. This direct experience problematises how food arrives on the plate and makes connections between the local and the global that enable participants to reflect on their own lives and taken-for-granted assumptions and behaviours.

The importance of focusing on matters of importance to young people has been highlighted through a number of research studies in science education. One of the key findings of the Relevance Of Science Education (ROSE) project involving young people in over 40 countries (Sjøberg and Schreiner, 2010) was that the issues that young people perceive as meaningful are dependent upon the culture and material conditions in the country in which they live, with students in less developed nations generally viewing a career in science and technology as more meaningful than those in more developed nations, and students (particularly girls) generally considering school science less interesting than other subjects. Schreiner and Sjøberg (2007) caution that it is not appropriate to design the science curriculum entirely based on the interests of young people. What can be achieved through Philosophy for Children is a way of engaging with school science that enables young people to be critical and that is more attentive to the interests, values and concerns of young people, and allows them to consider scientific ideas in a context that applies to their lived experiences.

Developing a community of enquiry represents a different way of engaging students with science, and of including their voices in the science classroom. Work with experienced teachers (Dunlop, 2012b) highlighted that these teachers consider this approach to science to be 'more personal', more student-led and student-centred, with questioning and dialogue taking students' ideas (not just about science, but the way in which science is taught) as important. It allowed the group the freedom to address ideas that were 'annoying' them, although the tension between the needs of the community of enquiry and the demands of the curriculum was recognised as a challenge in contemporary classrooms. Teachers expressed discomfort that students left classrooms with more questions than they arrived with, feeling that there were unresolved issues. However, this reflects how decisions about and involving science have to be made outside school, where risks have to be calculated, and other (e.g. political, health and economic) factors carry significant weight.

Beginning teachers, in their PGCE year, however, are in a different place from experienced teachers, particularly in the current climate of measurement in initial teacher education, where beginning teachers are expected to demonstrate that they have met 'standards' for qualified teacher status. Stevens has argued that this (the 'standards' culture) favours habit, compliant obedience and mastery of knowledge and skills over experimentation, risk-taking and responsiveness, autonomy of the teacher and of problematising pedagogical situations, observing that: 'There is an interesting (and all too often debilitating) parallel between transmission models of teaching and learning in the classroom and competence-led practices in teacher education/training' (2010, p. 194). For beginning teachers, Philosophy for Children could open up a space for problematising pedagogical situations more generally, for example in relation to government initiatives, as well as in the teaching of science. The following section focuses on the latter, discussing beginning teachers' perspectives of the approach to philosophy for children outlined above, beginning with stimuli devised to problematise socio-scientific issues.

Beginning teachers' perspectives

In order to explore beginning teachers' perspectives, a group of beginning teachers enrolled in a postgraduate certificate of education in secondary science programme participated in community of enquiry. The aim was not to prepare these teachers to do P4C with their students, but rather to engage teachers in philosophical issues, give them experience of socio-scientific enquiry for its own sake and to explore teachers' experiences and perceptions of P4C in science.

One of the stimuli used with beginning teachers featured a cartoon of a couple presented with a decision to make. They had been unable to conceive naturally and had completed their family using in vitro fertilisation (IVF), and were faced with the decision of what to do with their remaining embryos. This is an issue that many couples face: the Human Fertilisation and Embryology Authority estimates that one in seven couples have difficulty in conceiving, and over 5 million babies have been born worldwide as a result of IVF, and as a result this is an authentic situation for many people. Engaging with the difficult decisions that have to be made requires sensitivity and space to test out possibilities. For example, questions raised in relation to this stimulus included those asking when a human life begins, the ethics of abortion, ownership of embryos and consent for use of embryos produced during IVF, and the distribution of NHS resources. In one enquiry, the question selected related to whether or not it should be necessary to obtain the couple's consent to use remaining embryos in scientific research. The idea of 'resources' was pronounced, not only in terms of financial and healthcare resources, but also the idea of embryos as a 'resource' for scientific research, and as a commodity that could be owned and exchanged between interested parties. Although there was some discussion about these ideas, only one teacher challenged the source of the couple's dilemma: the way in which IVF was carried out, suggesting that a less problematic approach would be to produce fewer embryos. In doing so, the problems associated with egg removal and IVF success rates were identified. These teachers also explored the distinction between what is allowed in law, and different ethical standpoints.

Following this enquiry, the teachers were asked to reflect on what they had learned, how they had learned it, and what would have helped them more. Although some identified learning relating to substantive science content of the enquiry (IVF) and many highlighted getting to know their peers' views on this (and as a result getting to know each other better), teachers mainly identified learning in terms of pedagogy: in particular, how to engage young people with science, how to get their own students thinking, how to manage group work and class discussion (including dealing with challenges), how to address ethical issues, and how to develop questioning and analysis skills. One teacher also said that they had learned about the importance of getting to know their class. Although these teachers were positive about what they had learned from this enquiry, the extent to which this will inform their practice or views about science teaching can be questioned. Many student teachers focused on the practical, and how they could develop their own teaching practice rather than on their own enquiry and their meaning of associated concepts. The predominance of pro-scientific and pro-research attitudes left many assumptions unquestioned, suggesting that involving teachers from other discipline areas might be valuable in bringing a broader range of perspectives to the enquiry, particularly those that may be more critical of science.

Beginning science teachers also reported feeling uncomfortable in relation to objectives and intended learning outcomes, and in relinquishing 'control' over the question selection to the group. Some were concerned about the extent to which they could trust children to make decisions about the direction of the enquiry through the generation and selection of questions, but these concerns are rarely borne out in practice with young people, who find enquiries based on socio-scientific stimuli engaging, relevant to their lives, and the starting point for discussion that continues beyond the classroom (Dunlop *et al.*, 2011). Nevertheless, scientific literacy as education through science allows for the possibility of addressing science as relating to the needs of the community rather than as predetermined by the teacher.

These teachers also discussed feeling uncomfortable that they could not determine the content and focus of the enquiry in advance, and felt that this was in conflict with expectations. This is perhaps unsurprising, given the pressure that novice teachers are under to 'deliver' the curriculum, and the accountability culture that encourages a focus on defining specific learning outcomes in advance and the concomitant measures of progress within the space of a lesson. Furthermore, challenging dominant discourse practices (and therefore existing power relationships) and engaging in those that empower young people beyond the bounds of a school subject implies a challenge to the social order they represent (Rocha-Schmid, 2010), and in initial teacher education teachers are unlikely to see the gain in challenging the community into which they are trying to enter, at least in the short term. However, raising awareness at an early stage of teachers' careers allows for the possibility of developing practices that are critical and participatory, and allow for meaningful connections between science and the experiences and interests of learners, to which beginning teachers may turn as they gain confidence in context.

Conclusion

Charles Sanders Peirce, to whom Lipman attributes the original idea of a community of enquiry, states that science

> does not consist so much in knowing, nor even in 'organised knowledge', as it does in diligent inquiry into truth for truth's sake, without any sort of axe to grind, nor for the sake of the delight of contemplating it, but from an impulse to penetrate into the reason of things.
>
> *(Peirce, 1960, p. 19)*

One interpretation of an education for scientific literacy takes the approach of beginning with social and ethical issues and students' individual experiences to develop scientific knowledge and understanding that is grounded in the context of learners' lives, and responsive to their needs. To achieve this, both scientific and philosophical enquiry are necessary in the secondary science classroom, and indeed the seminar rooms of a PGCE course. One practice that allows for this 'education through science' is Philosophy for Children based on socio-scientific stimuli.

It is perhaps unrealistic, as Matthews (1994) argues in his defence of modest goals in teaching about the nature of science, that teachers should be philosophers of science, or indeed for them to develop confidence and enthusiasm for addressing issues that are complex and controversial over a limited period of time. However, as Rogers argues:

> consider[ing] matters honestly, openly considering alternative views, taking responsibility for our choices, questioning our assumptions and presuppositions, criticising our prejudices and deeply held beliefs, and changing as a result of this examination, then – in the deepest philosophical sense – we are open to being members of a genuine democracy.
>
> *(2008, p. 200)*

Creating a space in which teachers are encouraged to experience the challenge of addressing socio-scientific issues, and the value of learning from others' experiences, and of thinking about science from alternative perspectives has the potential to support teachers to explore controversial and socio-ethical issues with the young people they teach in support of the aim of scientific literacy for all.

References

Abd-El-Khalick, F. and Lederman, N. G. (2000) Improving science teachers' conceptions of nature of science: A critical review of the literature. *International Journal of Science Education*, 22(7), 665–701.

Bartley, C. F. F. (2004) Teaching about genetically modified crops – a different approach. *School Science Review*, 86(315), 95–6.

BBC (2007) Rafael Lozano-Hemmer suggests we should eat more insects. Online at: www.bbc.co.uk/worldservice/specials/1435_60_second_ideas/page2.shtml.

Bryce, T. G. C. (2010) Sardonic science? The resistance to more humanistic forms of science education. *Cultural Studies of Science Education*, 5(3), 591–612.

Burbules, N. C. and Beck, R. (1999) Critical thinking and critical pedagogy: Relations, differences and limits. In T. S. Popkewitz and L. Fendler (eds) *Critical Theories in Education: Changing terrains of knowledge and politics*. London: Routledge.

Calabrese-Barton, A. (2001) Capitalism, critical pedagogy and urban science education: An interview with Peter McLaren. *Journal of Research in Science Teaching*, 38(8), 847–59.

CCEA (Council for the Curriculum, Examinations and Assessment), 2005. *The Impact of Statutory Curriculum and Assessment Change from 2006 on Teacher Education and Training in Northern Ireland*. Online at: www.deni.gov.uk/walker_report.pdf (accessed 1 July 2012).

Davson-Galle, P. (2008) Why compulsory science education should not include philosophy of science. *Science & Education*, 17, 677–716.

Dunlop, L. (2012a) P4C in science. In N. Chandley and L. Lewis (eds) *Philosophy for Children through the Secondary Curriculum*. London: Continuum.

Dunlop, L. (2012b) Engaging young people with science through communities of scientific enquiry: A mixed methods evaluation. Doctoral dissertation, University of Ulster.

Dunlop, L., Humes, G., Clarke, L. and McKelvey-Martin, V. (2011) Developing communities of enquiry: Dealing with social and ethical issues in science at key stage 3. *School Science Review*, 93(342), 113–20.

Duschl, R. A. and Osborne, J. (2002) Supporting and promoting argumentation discourse in science education. *Studies in Science Education*, 31(8), 39–72.

Erduran, S. and Mugaloglu, E. (2013) Interactions of economics of science and science education: Investigating the implications for science teaching and learning. *Science & Education*, 22(10), 2405–25.

Freire, P. (2003) *Education for Critical Consciousness*. London: Bloomsbury.

Gilbert, J. K. (2010) Supporting the development of effective science teachers. In J. Osborne and J. Dillon (eds) *Good Practice in Science Teaching: What research has to say*, 2nd edn. Maidenhead: McGraw-Hill.

Giroux, H. A. (2011) *On Critical Pedagogy*. London: Continuum.

Gorard, S., Siddiqui, N. and See, B. H. (2015) *Philosophy for Children: SAPERE, Evaluation Report and Executive Summary*. London: Education Endowment Foundation.

Haynes, J. and Murris, K. (2012) *Picturebooks, Pedagogy, and Philosophy*. London: Routledge.

Holbrook, J. and Rannikmae, M. (2007) The nature of science education for enhancing scientific literacy. *International Journal of Science Education*, 29(11), 1347–62.

Levinson, R. and Turner, S. (2001) *Valuable Lessons*. London: Wellcome Trust.

Lipman, M. (1974) *Harry Stottlemeier's Discovery*. Montclair, NJ: Montclair State University.

Lipman, M. (2003) *Thinking in Education*, 2nd edn. Cambridge: Cambridge University Press.

Lipman, M. (2010) Philosophy for Children: Some assumptions and implications. *Ethics in Progress Quarterly*, 2(1). Online at: http://ethicsinprogress.org/?p=437.

Lipman, M., Sharp, A. M. and Oscanyan, F. S. (1980) *Philosophy in the Classroom*, 2nd edn. Philadelphia: Temple University Press.

Matthews, M. R. (1994) *Science Teaching*. London: Routledge.

Millar, R. and Osborne, J. (eds) (1998) *Beyond 2000: Science education for the future*. London: King's College London.

Monk, M. and Osborne, J. (1997) Placing the history and philosophy of science in the curriculum: A model for the development of pedagogy. *Science Education*, 81(4), 405–24.

Mortimer, E. F. and Scott, P. H. (2003). *Making Meaning in Secondary Science Classrooms*. Maidenhead: Open University Press.

Peirce, C. S. (1960) Lessons from the history of science: The scientific attitude. In C. Hartshorne and P. Weiss (eds) *Collected Papers of Charles Sanders Peirce, Volumes I and II: Principles of Philosophy and Elements of Logic Charles Sanders Peirce*. Cambridge, MA: Harvard University Press.

Ratcliffe, M. (2007) Values in the science classroom – the 'enacted' curriculum. In D. Corrigan, J. Dillon and R. Gunstone (eds) *The Re-Emergence of Values in Science Education*. Rotterdam: Sense.

Reiss, M. (1999) *Teaching Secondary Biology*. London: John Murray.

Reiss, M. (2007) What should be the aim(s) of school science education? In D. Corrigan, J. Dillon and R. Gunstone (eds) *The Re-Emergence of Values in Science Education*. Rotterdam: Sense.

Reiss, M. (2008) The use of ethical frameworks by students following a new science course for 16–18 year olds. *Science and Education*, 17(8–9), 889–902.

Rocha-Schmid, E. (2010) Participatory pedagogy for empowerment: A critical discourse analysis of teacher–parents' interactions in a family literacy course in London. *International Journal of Lifelong Education*, 29(3), 343–58.

Rogers, K. (2008) *Participatory Democracy, Science and Technology [electronic resource]: An exploration in the philosophy of science*. Basingstoke: Palgrave Macmillan.

Sadler, T. D., Amirschokoohi, A., Kazempour, M. and Allspaw, K. M. (2006) Socioscience and ethics in science classrooms: Teacher perspectives and strategies. *Journal of Research in Science Teaching*, 43(4), 353–76.

Schreiner, C. and Sjøberg, S. (2007) Science education and youth's identity construction – two incompatible projects? In D. Corrigan, J. Dillon and R. Gunstone (eds) *The Re-Emergence of Values in Science Education*. Rotterdam: Sense.

Schwab, J. J. (1962) The teaching of science as enquiry. In J. Schwab and P. Brandwein (eds) *The Teaching of Science*. Cambridge, MA: Harvard University Press.

Simmons, N., Barnard, M. and Fennema, W. (2011) Participatory pedagogy: A compass for transformative learning. Online at: http://celt.uwindsor.ca/ojs/leddy/index.php/CELT/article/view/3278/2657.

Sjøberg, S. and Schreiner, S. (2010) *The ROSE project. Overview and key findings*. Online at: http://roseproject.no/network/countries/norway/eng/nor-Sjoberg-Schreiner-overview-2010.pdf (accessed 1 July 2012).

Splitter, L. and Sharp, A. M. (1995) *Teaching for Better Thinking*. Melbourne: ACER.

Sprod, T. (1999) 'I can change your opinion on that': Social constructivist whole class discussions and their effect on scientific reasoning. *Research in Science Education*, 28(4), 463–80.

Sprod, T. (2001) Building scientific thinking via philosophical discussion. *Teaching Thinking*, Autumn, 14–18.

Stevens, D. (2010). A Freirean critique of the competence model of teacher education, focusing on the standards for qualified teacher status in England. *Journal of Education for Teaching*, 36(2), 187–96.

Thwaites, H. (2005) Can 'philosophy for children' improve teaching and learning within attainment target 2 of religious education? *Education 3–13*, 33(3), 4–8.

Trickey, S. and Topping, K. J. (2004) Philosophy for Children: A systematic review. *Research Papers in Education*, 19(3), 365–80.

Trickey, S. and Topping, K. J. (2007) Collaborative philosophical inquiry for schoolchildren: Cognitive gains at 2-year follow-up. *British Journal of Educational Psychology*, 77(4), 787–96.

UNESCO (2010) *Current Challenges in Basic Science Education*. Paris: UNESCO. Online at: http://unesdoc.unesco.org/images/0019/001914/191425e.pdf (accessed 8 March 2012).

9

AN EVALUATION OF P4C

Sarah Meir and Julie McCann

This chapter summarises the findings of a pilot programme evaluation for a whole school approach to P4C in Liverpool schools. In 2012, Liverpool Primary Care Trust (PCT) had identified a need for supporting well-being and mental health in schools to complement the mental health provision being commissioned. As a partnership between organisations, such as Sustainability, Child and Adolescent Mental Health Services (CAMHS) and School Improvement Liverpool, a pilot programme introducing Philosophy for Children as a whole schools approach was established to enable schools to become a catalyst for pupils, teachers and school communities to develop skills for improving well-being and increasing community resilience.

While Philosophy for Children training had proved immensely popular with individual teachers, wider benefits were believed to be possible from a whole schools approach. The intention was to explore and evaluate whether a whole schools approach to philosophical enquiry could provide young people and the wider school community with enhanced skills for health and well-being. All schools in Liverpool were invited to participate in the pilot and four schools (three primary and one secondary) were selected, reflecting different learning potential. The pilot programme commenced in September 2012, when first training sessions were held, and ran until early July 2013.

The evaluation's brief was to monitor and report on the awareness, perceptions and expectations of outcomes to P4C, prior to teacher training and immediately post-training, ahead of application. Then, at the mid-point and end stages of the academic year the outcomes of the application on pupils, teachers and schools would be measured and evaluated. In particular, the pilot's intention was to explore and evaluate how a whole school/year group approach could provide pupils and the school community with enhanced skills for health and well-being. These included increased and improved critical, creative, caring and collaborative thinking, reasoning and problem-solving, communications and inquiry skills, engagement and collaborative working, capacity for rational analysis, educational attainment, capacity for personal relations, self-esteem and well-being, and resilience across the life-course.

A mixed methodology of qualitative and quantitative evaluation techniques and measures was agreed, based on the requirement to address a diverse audience of teachers, pupils (primary and secondary), and parents/carers. In addition to teacher, pupil and parent interviews and surveys, information to support the evaluation would come from whole school data, and pupil and teacher logs/scrapbooks. A tailored evaluation methodology was agreed with each school, using an evaluation template, with specific measures dependent upon each school's individual circumstances.

Julie McCann delivered SAPERE (Society for the Advancement of Philosophical Enquiry and Reflection in Education) Level 1 training in Philosophy for Children to colleagues from each of the participating schools, and provided follow-up support tailored to the needs of that particular school.

Pre-pilot phase

Teachers were interviewed before training to evaluate their awareness and perceptions of P4C, ahead of the whole school approach commencing. Experience or awareness of P4C varied, with some having already had some involvement or observed previously.

A number of themes for teachers' hopes before training emerged, including:

- They would have more time to listen to children.
- Children would develop skills to think about and cope with life situations.
- Confidence levels and better behaviour would increase.
- Children would understand that it is fine to disagree.

All were keen to get started with P4C straight after the training, so as to maximise on the skills while fresh. However, this did mean that they also hoped to be given adequate resources and support to do this. Some were unsure what to expect and concerned about whether they would take to P4C and be able to facilitate easily.

Pre-training concerns included the time required to run philosophical enquiries properly, and teachers felt that there were practical issues about fitting P4C into the curriculum, as

TABLE 9.1 Breakdown of methodological approaches used in the evaluation against sample sizes

Phase	Methodology	Sample size
Pre-pilot phase	Pre-training teacher critical reflection interviews	12
	Post-training teacher critical reflection interviews	11
	Pupil observational feedback group sessions	6
	Teacher and pupil well-being surveys	508
Mid-point interim report		
Post-pilot phase	Teacher critical reflection interviews	11
	Pupil observational feedback group sessions (8–10 pupils per session across Years 3–7)	7
	Parent/carer feedback group	1
	Teacher and pupil well-being surveys	212
	Analysis of whole school data and scrapbooks	

well as logistical issues about classroom space. They had concerns about how much time was needed, or allowed, for planning P4C sessions, and were keen that they could do this with colleagues, so they could develop skills and resources together. Additionally, there were queries about the optimum time to run P4C classes in the school day, in order to maximise benefits, as well as how frequently. Another aspect of time constraints was that some felt that they might only manage to implement P4C strategies within the class subject. This was observed particularly in secondary teachers, such as using PSHE/English/RE lessons, and with primary teachers, who suggested that literacy sessions might be a suitable vehicle for P4C activities and approaches. Finally, some teachers of very young children, in Early Years Foundation Stage or Key Stage 1, expressed concerns about the practicalities of P4C in the age group; however, they reasoned that more ideas or a 'practical toolkit' would help.

Following training, teachers were interviewed again and pupil observational feedback sessions were held to evaluate initial implementation perceptions, experiences and anticipated benefits. Most pupils saw a real benefit to having P4C introduced to their school, and were particularly keen about the concept of there being no single 'right' answer – rather that a number of possible 'good' answers might exist. Pupils valued that their opinion was valid, listened to and respected by others. Many children reported immediate positive changes in the behaviour of classmates and themselves, and some even found that lessons had started to help them cope with problems both inside and outside school.

Initial implementation concerns and barriers were explored, with some teachers perceiving that having time for P4C sessions in their entirety was potentially limited by school demands and the curriculum. There were some mixed views as to the practical logistics of running 'stand-alone' philosophical enquiries in an already 'packed curriculum' (especially in secondary schools, with pressures on exams, and achieving levels of progress and targets). Therefore some felt that they would be more likely to use P4C as a strategy to support teaching other subjects, such as PSHE, or within literacy topics. Teachers were also anxious about time for planning for a new teaching strategy like P4C, and felt that they also needed adequate time and investment in resources, to build and develop a suite of activities for their school/year groups. Views on the appropriate regularity of P4C classes varied.

In terms of positive outcomes, early reports from teachers noted examples of increased confidence, improved communications skills and behaviour, particularly where challenging behaviour existed, such as with some Nurture groups. Improved behaviour in and out of the classroom was observed, including additional improvements in language, writing and the maturity of responses in pupils. Teachers said that they were pleasantly surprised by some of the actions and reactions of pupils. Teachers reported already seeing real benefits to a whole school/year group approach and that sharing and developing ideas and approaches with their colleagues was a vital requirement to the process, particularly where adopting P4C had brought together teachers from infant and junior schools.

The detailed feedback from teachers on their initial experiences of trying out P4C highlighted how their own confidence was growing and that using P4C was stimulating and enriching their own teaching. They found it both challenging and effective to be taking more of a back seat and controlling classes less. One said, 'It makes me confident to try different things … we learn how much children teach us – we learn from them … It has stimulated my teaching.'

Teachers saw a number of positive outcomes on well-being in the children and the way they interacted with one another, in particular the increased confidence to participate of normally less dominant children, the respect paid to one another, and the fact that pupils were listening and talking to one another more. A number of examples of seeing reduced disruption with children normally displaying challenging or selfish behaviour were given. Some said it was as beneficial outside the classroom as it was in it, and that P4C had had a positive impact on children's personal issues. One teacher described this: 'Children realise their issues are not the only issues in the world … it makes them feel better about themselves and they are more confident and happier.'

One teacher who was already running P4C weekly, particularly with children with learning or behavioural challenges, reported many tangible and positive benefits. She said that children were 'given a voice … they listen and there's no aggression, and conflicts of opinion are peaceful'. She had noted clear differences in behaviour in class and in the playground, and gave examples of children known to self-harm or from difficult home circumstances who were behaving noticeably better.

Teachers reported, and admitted to being pleasantly surprised by, the maturity of children's responses and the level of intellect displayed, when choosing and discussing philosophical questions that teachers considered quite 'deep', for example, 'Is it ever right to steal?' The maturity of response and intellect had also manifested itself into other lessons, with teachers reporting improvements in other classes, such as producing better written work in English and in their use of language. Children who had previously struggled to articulate themselves were described as 'using lots of different stuff I wouldn't have expected.'

Others reported being surprised by how well groups behaved, particularly mixed or lower ability groups. One teacher said that she had expected it to be a bit 'chaotic' in one of the first sessions, but the children took one another's hands quietly for the activity. She commented, 'It was nice to see that my preconceived ideas [about pupil behaviour] were not borne out by the children,' and another admitted, 'They didn't behave as I expected them to … they stepped up.'

Teachers said that these sometimes surprising outcomes and successes would give them the extra motivation and confidence they needed to deliver more P4C sessions. One said that this would give her the confidence to do a stand-alone philosophy class, rather than simply incorporate the activities or strategies into other lessons, which she felt she was otherwise more likely to do, because, she said, it's 'a whole new way to teach'.

End of pilot phase

A mid-point report reflected on key areas of focus for the end of pilot phase, with additional feedback from well-being surveys informing interviews and focus groups with teachers, parents/carers and pupils. Three key well-being themes emerged alongside the whole school approach were specifically explored in the final phase: behavioural (behaviour for learning), academic benefits and social skills. Most teachers agreed that the skills being developed in P4C supported and facilitated these attributes.

The overall experience reported by teachers was of philosophy having a positive influence on themselves and on their teaching, particularly highlighting how it had encouraged them to allow more 'thinking time' for pupils. Teachers and pupils clearly enjoyed and benefited from being part of a community of enquiry, with pupils widely reporting that it was 'different' and something to look forward to. Other key well-being themes emerging, when talking to pupils, included feelings of reassurance and safety, increased confidence to take part, feelings of inclusion, fairness and equality, as well as an increased respect for one another, and improved and new relationships with classmates.

Behavioural outcomes

Teachers reported a wide range of positive behavioural outcomes on pupils and classes, largely within the P4C session setting, but often in the classroom and beyond that into wider school life. While improved behaviour was not consistently extended beyond the session, there was circumstantial evidence, for example with Nurture groups, where greatly improved playground and home-setting behaviour was reported. Limited school data available showed a slightly improved absence rate trend since the introduction of P4C.

All teachers saw improved behaviour in P4C sessions and an excellent response to the code of conduct and approach of P4C. Teachers found that the code of conduct particularly facilitated the need to respect one another and not to judge, and they found that those behaviours then started to embed in the culture of the class and outside. Teachers said that the benefits materialised because the children looked forward to the sessions and were in the right mood or frame of mind to learn and behave. Some teachers reported evidence that P4C had stopped fighting, shouting and negative behaviour and that children who were sometimes 'moody' or who could be 'nasty' to others often behaved completely differently in P4C sessions. Teachers evidenced examples of:

- increased reflection
- respect for others
- wider contribution and engagement from often quieter or reserved pupils
- increased enthusiasm to participate, confidence and self-esteem
- ability to manage conflict.

Academic outcomes

While not all teachers agreed that sustained or tangible academic benefits could be attributed at this early stage, many reported a number of areas of improvement that they felt had a direct relation to P4C, and agreed that potential academic benefits would become evident over a longer period of time. Tracking more longitudinally would be needed, as many had only been delivering P4C sessions for approximately six months.

In two of the schools, where P4C was being used with Nurture groups, teachers perceived that pupils' reading levels had much improved and that P4C was supporting and promoting Behaviour for Learning – that is, fostering and encouraging the optimum skills for a positive and effective learning environment.

Key academic outcomes teachers reported included increases in or evidence of:

- persuasive language and techniques
- improved vocabulary and literacy

- independence in learning
- reasoning skills
- working more sensibly and an increased maturity, which facilitated learning
- deeper thinking skills
- more developed and utilised listening skills
- reflection skills
- wider consideration
- debating skills in older children (one Year 5 teacher likened her class's increased skills to being 'superior to a group of children I saw on a programme about Mensa')
- collaborative working
- developed imagination
- observation skills
- inference skills.

Those pupils demonstrating academic improvements tended to be either in lower ability classes or groups (including Nurture groups), or in higher performing children, which teachers attributed to the opportunity to explore topics and stretch and challenge thinking further. In the middle ability groups, to date, there was less tangible evidence of significant improvements. Whole school data reviewed (where available) evidenced some positive increases in SATs scores between 2012 and 2013 results, in literacy and mathematics. Most agreed that longer-term monitoring of academic measures was needed in order to demonstrate a clear link between educational attainment and P4C. However, what was clear was that P4C facilitated Behaviour for Learning: the confidence and skills the pupils displayed and developed were perceived to be supporting the learning of other skills, such as literacy and numeracy.

Social outcomes

Most teachers agreed that social skills were being developed by the application of P4C and that it was being taken beyond the classroom, out to families, friends and communities, and that P4C was giving children tangible life skills. Communications skills were being widely developed, from articulation, improved vocabulary and listening skills, through to where new or alternative forms of communication were being encouraged, such as non-verbal. Children were responding particularly well to those activities where body language and non-verbal communication were required, and the children themselves described how language was not a barrier, for example with children whose English was less developed (whether academically or a second language).

This increased equality within the classroom was felt to facilitate and promote the development of other skills and increased the confidence of children who felt better equipped to communicate equally and without judgement. This promoted positive relationships in the classroom (and beyond), as some children mixed with others they would not normally engage with readily. New friendships were forming and classroom/playground conflicts were reportedly being resolved. Teachers felt that the communications skills gave the children a social 'conversation' that for many was becoming less common in their home environments, due to increased use of computer games, fewer shared family mealtimes or opportunities to converse, changing family dynamics, etc.

Other social/life skills and benefits that teachers either attributed to P4C or agreed were influenced by it included:

- following instructions such as the code of conduct
- problem-solving together
- decision-making skills and coming to consensus
- exploring feelings
- voting and democracy
- increased maturity and feeling 'grown up'
- increased feelings of inclusion: children realising they were not the only ones experiencing an issue
- reassurance of support and security
- increased cooperation
- new friends and boys and girls mixing more easily
- managing and resolving conflicts.

Whole school/year group approach

All teachers and those coordinating P4C agreed that a whole school/year group approach was essential for the successful application and embedding of P4C in their school, and that attempting to roll out P4C alone or in pockets would be isolating, with far fewer benefits and be less sustainable. It was considered vital to have senior management team leadership, support and commitment to ensure success longer term. Since the pilot, one school that embraced a whole school approach has increased its Ofsted rating to Good. However, in the case of the pilot school where a whole school approach had not been taken, issues of isolation were reported. Although teachers felt that they had done their best and were strong advocates of P4C, without the support and commitment to include P4C in the timetable, they felt that the embedding of the values, principles and culture of P4C would not develop, and too few pupils would experience P4C to materially change or influence behaviours, academic progress or school culture and well-being. As one of the trained staff was leaving, it was felt that it would be difficult to maintain momentum, as regularity and continuity of delivery would be harder to ensure.

The teachers' perspective

Teachers reported a number of positive benefits of P4C on them and their teaching. While difficult at first, the perceived lack of control or stepping back to let children lead the discussion, and concerns about managing timings/planning, teachers quickly realised the benefits of allowing children more 'thinking time' in P4C and in other lessons. A child who they might have previously jumped in to help answer a question now was allowed more time; however uncomfortable those 15 seconds were, the child was given the opportunity to think and respond successfully.

Teachers said they enjoyed P4C because it was new and different and enjoyable; one said: 'If we are enjoying it, this rubs off on the children.' Most reported using the tools and techniques of P4C in other lessons, particularly in subjects where debate and reasoning is involved, such as literacy, RE and history. Additionally, schools were developing self-observations of P4C and improving together in a non-judgemental way, ensuring successes and idea-sharing, with co-coaching and mentoring encouraged and developed. This was not only within the pilot schools but also partnering with other schools.

In terms of ongoing concerns, the challenge of delivering P4C within the busy curriculum and the impact this had on a full P4C session, was still considered demanding, and teachers worried about stimulus materials and getting the enquiry question 'right'. Some felt pressured to make the most of the enquiry, and that if the question 'went wrong' this would be viewed badly and they would be judged on that. However, those teachers of much younger children who had expressed concerns about how appropriate P4C was to the age group had all found that P4C worked well across the age groups. However, secondary teachers still had concerns about the application of P4C to some cohorts and how P4C should be fitted into the curriculum to ensure consistency of student experience. Teachers felt that their delivery and the experience of the pupils would improve and grow as they developed and gained experience. Regularity of enquiry and keeping P4C fresh was key. Teachers believed that a deeper and sustained cultural change would take longer than the pilot period to manifest, but that as pupils continued to do philosophy throughout their school lives the cultural and social benefits would embed longer term, in and outside of school life.

The parent/carer perspective

Most parents/carers confessed to knowing little or nothing about P4C, and indeed the pupils had reported that their parents/carers hadn't even believed that they were studying 'philosophy'. When sharing with other parents/carers, some realised that discussions they had had at home with their children were subsequent to their child's P4C session at school. They now recognised why their children were saying 'I agree with you because …', and why they were now expressing their opinions more fully. Parents/carers were keen to understand more and support their children in what they agreed was a significant enhancement to the curriculum.

The pupil perspective

Feedback sessions with pupils, alongside analysis of scrapbooks/teacher logbooks, demonstrated how children were consistently enthusiastic about P4C, reporting that they looked forward to the enjoyable sessions, that they felt supported and safe and able to express their opinions and feelings confidentially, without judgement. The maturity their teachers reported was evidenced in their comments and inquiry scrapbooks (see Figure 9.1).

Lessons from the pilot and the current position

The Liverpool CAMHS project had, and continues to have, implications for schools beyond those who participated in it. It enabled review and reflection of how to ensure that P4C is truly a whole school approach, as well as raising questions for further examination. Guaranteeing a whole school approach means going beyond the initial Level 1 Foundation training to ensure teachers that continue to increase their own philosophical skills and attitudes, as reflective practitioners and as facilitators of enquiry.

Schools that have done this most successfully have had a head teacher and P4C lead teacher who are committed to supporting ongoing development, progress and challenge. A structured action plan, which is a working document with clear outcomes, guides this process.

FIGURE 9.1   Pilot school scrapbooks

For this to be meaningful it should support existing whole school priorities. Examples may be the use of P4C to support conflict resolution and thus improve behaviour, or the use of P4C to explore mathematical concepts and support logic and reasoning, and thus increase attainment in mathematics.

Opportunities must be provided for teachers to continue to grapple with concepts and ideas intellectually, and to be challenged in their own thinking. Without this, P4C can become a process that is unthinkingly followed, rather than a habit of mind. Regular philosophical enquiries or activities foster a spirit of enquiry among colleagues and can be a useful method of addressing contentious issues objectively.

Investment in further training for lead P4C teachers empowers them to effectively lead, support and challenge colleagues to successfully facilitate and demand greater rigour in children's thinking. It is advisable that lead teachers collaborate closely with other team members so that there is additional capacity should they no longer be available to fulfil the role. Having just one particularly driven member of staff can result in over-reliance on that individual and a loss of momentum in their absence.

Well-planned philosophical activities and enquiries with increasing levels of challenge, allow progression through each year group; linking stimuli to the curriculum helps to deepen thinking about the wider issues and make learning more meaningful. This also provides justification, should it be required, for replacing a curriculum subject with P4C: for example, an enquiry into sustainability to replace a geography lesson or an enquiry into peace to replace a history lesson. Philosophical questions displayed around schools or on their websites, the provision of enquiries for the wider community, and philosophical homework all enrich a climate in which intellectual engagement is celebrated and ongoing, and questioning is encouraged.

Within Liverpool, schools increasingly value the intellectual rigour and focus on thinking skills provided through the practice of Philosophy for Children. Alongside this, schools identify the improvements in pupils' social and emotional well-being and greater openness to different ideas and experiences.

As of autumn term 2015, 21 Liverpool schools had adopted Philosophy for Children as a whole school approach, and a further 50 schools have had some members of staff trained. P4C has been cited positively in OFSTED reports and has supported schools in improving their OFSTED outcomes.

Note

While it was planned that all pilot schools would be applying P4C as a whole school/year group approach, one school did not implement this, and therefore results reflect that context.

10

P4C AND EDUCATION FOR DIVERSITY

Clive Belgeonne

Background to education for diversity

'Integration is a learned competence, like Maths or driving a car. It is not instinctive' (*Facing History Facing Ourselves*, 2009, p. 58). These words are from a speech by Trevor Phillips, then Chair of the Commission for Racial Equality, soon after the July 2005 London bombings. As the bombings were carried out by British-born people, this led to much discussion about issues of identity and belonging, and also about how our education system should respond.

Although Britain has been shaped by a history of invaders and migrants, and until the 1950s had the largest empire the world has ever seen (whose subjects were encouraged to see Britain as the 'mother country'), it was not until great numbers of migrants from Empire and Commonwealth countries began to arrive in the 1950s that issues of how to deal with difference began to be part of a national discussion. This was largely because although most migrants had been invited over to fill labour market shortages, they were mainly of a different skin colour and some of a different religion from most native-born Britons.

Educational initiatives in the UK which tried to deal with or address 'difference' started effectively in the 1960s, with the advent of migrant populations from former Empire and Commonwealth countries coming to urban centres around the UK. Official responses since that time have ranged from assimilation, integration, multiculturalism, anti-racism, race awareness and cultural diversity to 'community cohesion' (Chen and Belgeonne, 2010), and more recently the duties to promote 'British' values and prevent violent extremism.

Perhaps the most detailed investigations into how to educate for diversity came in the then Department for Education and Science sponsored responses to the July 2005 London bombings: a research review (Maylor and Read, 2007) and a curriculum review (Ajegbo *et al.*, 2007). Both found that most schools were failing to engage adequately with issues of diversity and identity.

Overall, the literature suggests that in order to effectively acknowledge diversity, the curriculum needs to provide discursive resources to promote 'collective identities' and to challenge ideologies that construct the nation and national identity in ways that exclude minority ethnic groups. Importantly, it should allow national identity and historical events to be 'retold' in order to demonstrate the contribution of minority ethnic groups (Maylor and Read, 2007, p. 6).

However, there was no clear guidance on what sort of pedagogies might help educate for diversity. In the section on 'Education for diversity in the curriculum', the curriculum review stated:

> Our vision defines one aspect of education for diversity as focusing on critical literacy, which allows pupils to reflect on their own cultural traditions and those of others. Pupils need to develop an understanding of how language constructs reality and the different perspectives they use to make sense of the world around them. It is crucial for education for diversity that pupils are given the skills to challenge their own assumptions and those of others. There needs first to be development and discussion about pedagogical approaches if such skills are to be developed so that education for diversity can be effective.
>
> *(Ajegbo et al., 2007, p. 46)*

It mentioned two possible methodologies, P4C (Philosophy for Children) and OSDE (Open Spaces for Dialogue and Enquiry), but did not explain in much detail how or why such methodologies would be effective.

The issue of effective teacher training was also raised: 'Research shows that there is insufficient effective training for teachers to feel confident with issues of identity, "race" and religion – either in initial teacher training, or through CPD for teachers throughout their career' (Ajegbo *et al.*, 2007, p. 67).

This lack of confidence in dealing with issues of diversity has been borne out by NQT surveys. 'Multiverse' was set up in 2003 in response to the annual newly qualified teacher (NQT) survey conducted by the then Teacher Training Agency. The TTA survey in 2003 suggested that 'NQTs did not feel confident that Initial Teacher Training (ITT) had prepared them well for teaching learners from minority backgrounds (ME) and pupils with English as an additional language (EAL)' (Multiverse, 2009).

By 2008 there had been a 'significant improvement', but six out of ten respondents still rated their training less than good. Multiverse noted that 'compared to their evaluation of other aspects of ITT training, there is room for further improvement'. This was borne out by the fact that the Multiverse website had an average of 1,500 users from the educational community accessing its website daily (Multiverse, 2009). However, funding for Multiverse ceased with the advent of the Coalition Conservative and Liberal Democrat government in 2010.

The latest figures from the National College for Teaching and Leadership (NCTL) NQT survey show an improved picture:

> When asked about their preparation to teach pupils from all ethnic backgrounds, 73% of 2,383 secondary-trained respondents rated their training as good (37%) and very good (36%). This is compared to the lower 66% of respondents in 2013, a statistically significant difference.
>
> *(Adewoye et al., 2014, p. 81)*

So this would appear to be an improvement on the 2008 figure, in that seven out of ten rate the training as good or above. The report notes: 'Notwithstanding these perceived improvements, this is still amongst the least positively rated aspects of training' (Adewoye *et al.*, 2014, p. 81). I would argue that this may indicate some improvement in NQTs feeling confident to teach pupils from all ethnic backgrounds – that is, teacher training may be getting better at addressing issues of inclusion, but it is less clear whether teachers are being adequately trained for education for diversity, in terms of some of the issues raised by Maylor and Read (2007) and Ajegbo *et al.*, (2007).

P4C as pedagogy for diversity

> Britain is both a community of citizens and a community of communities, both a liberal and a multicultural society, and needs to reconcile their sometimes conflicting requirements.
>
> *(Runnymede Trust, 2000)*

If Britain can be seen as a 'community of communities', where there is a need to reconcile a variety of community cultures, P4C is described by SAPERE as a community of enquiry process, which is defined as: 'A group of people used to thinking together with a view to increasing their understanding and appreciation of the world around them and each other' (SAPERE, 2015, p. 15).

The idea of developing understanding through dialogue is central to P4C. This need for dialogue, or as they termed it a 'national conversation', was suggested by the Church of England as part of their submission to the DfE's 'British values' consultation:

> The ways we, as communities and a nation, develop the language and practices of equality, diversity, community and the individual have changed rapidly in recent years and the proposed national conversation on values would be one way to build confidence and coherence in the wake of changes that have been unsettling for many and remain in many ways unresolved.
>
> *(National Society/Church of England, 2014)*

One means of addressing education for diversity mentioned in the *Curriculum Review: Diversity and Citizenship* (Ajegbo *et al.*, 2007) was school linking as a way of bringing together children from diverse cultures and backgrounds. The work of the Bradford School Linking project was mentioned. The final evaluation report found many beneficial effects, including an increased number of cross-cultural friendships and greater openness to mixing with peers from contrasting communities or cultures (Raw, 2005).

However, with regard to facilitating genuine dialogue around issues of diversity, the report identified some barriers:

> The context within each school, for example the degree of experience, amongst the children, in mixing with different communities and cultures, and any local or family politicisation regarding attitudes to different people; as well as the skills and confidence levels of teachers in facilitating such a complex debate, are key factors which have played a significant role in the limited success of the project itself in the area of openness of debate.
>
> *(Raw, 2005, p. 33)*

One Year 6 child commented that 'teachers had been too defensive' and did not allow 'any discussion of negative things'. The report adds: 'It is very important to find a way to make space for the debate children have told us they want to have' (Raw, 2005, p. 33). This requires teachers to have the skills and training to make such a space.

The Oldham Philosophy for Children Collaborative Evaluation Research Project was one of the first to use P4C to expressly address issues of diversity (develop positive regard for difference and other people and thus enhance community cohesion in its widest sense). However, this was only one of a six aims, and one for which there was the least evidence of impact. The report states that this issue:

> … was not directly addressed by many schools and the strongest evidence comes from the community groups. Community cohesion is an issue of significant scale and the P4C work is at an early stage. The signs are very promising but more evidence is needed. Few pupils had experienced P4C as an explicit method for addressing regard for others so they did not refer to it. In the one school that had, the pupils were very attuned to the issue of empathy.
>
> *(Leat and Thomas, 2008, p. 41)*

The report surmised that many schools had only 'reached a threshold in the deployment of P4C'. Although it was being used in most classes, 'only in a minority of schools is the pedagogy beginning to influence curriculum'. This is the challenge in terms of developing habits of dialogue and the 'safe space' to dig deeper. As the report recognises: 'To do this, at a whole school level, time and opportunity is required for staff to reflect and discuss together' (Leat and Thomas, 2008, pp. 41–2), and such time is not easily prioritised in most schools, as the evidence for the benefits is not sufficiently accepted.

So how might P4C be used as pedagogy for diversity? Hopefully an understanding of its underlying principles (building on the four types of thinking: caring, collaborative, critical and creative) gives an idea:

- Proper valuing of each person's interests and questions.
- Acknowledgement that each person's experience/story is unique.
- Recognition that no one is all-knowing or all-wise.
- Appreciation of different ways of interpreting and thinking. (SAPERE, 2015, p. 12)

These principles provide a framework for education for diversity:

> The process encourages all participants to share their ideas. It encourages participants to examine different perspectives and to think 'otherwise' – Is this always the case? How might it be viewed in a different culture/context? It allows participants to recognise that it is acceptable, even laudable, to change their mind in the light of dialogue and reflection. It is also important to recognise, value and learn from different perspectives and world-views.
>
> *(Belgeonne, in People in Need, 2005, p. 21)*

Such a process clearly needs a classroom environment where young people feel comfortable to engage in such a way. The creation of a 'safe space' for genuine dialogue is crucial, and this may take time for teachers to develop, as well as skills of listening, empathy and appreciation of diverse perspectives.

The Prevent Duty advice (DfE, 2015) has stated that schools must promote 'community cohesion', and that schools 'should be safe spaces in which children and young people can understand and discuss sensitive topics, including terrorism and the extremist ideas that are part of terrorist ideology, and learn how to challenge these ideas'.[1]

One of the challenges of P4C as a pedagogy of diversity is the role of the teacher themselves. Although the role is mainly one of a facilitator of dialogue, there are issues around what beliefs and assumptions the teacher is bringing into the room. It is usually the teacher who chooses the stimulus and can also guide the direction of the dialogue through interventions. At Level 1, for many teachers the two-day training may be taken as preparation to use another technique in the classroom, unless there is proper focus on the role of the facilitator in guiding dialogue around controversial and sensitive issues. They need to consider how to feel comfortable to 'let go' and allow the dialogue to develop, not to be 'too defensive … to make space for the debate children have told us they want to have' (Raw, 2005, p. 33).

Chetty (2014, p. 2) has warned of the danger of not including more critical perspectives of issues such as race 'amongst recommended starting points and training materials', which may lead to 'a form of "gate-keeping" of philosophical thought and thus whether the notion of "The Gated Community of Enquiry" might be illuminating'. It comes back again to the type of classroom environment the teacher is able to create, the 'safe space' to air and unpack difficult issues, and how they handle their role:

> Teachers need to be aware of differences in status and power within the group (including their own position) and think carefully about how and when to make interventions, in order to help students develop their own ideas in an inclusive and mutually supportive environment, yet one that accepts challenges to perspectives and perceptions.
>
> *(Belgeonne in People in Need, 2005, p. 22)*

I know from my own experience of teaching PSHE (personal, social and health education) in a secondary school the challenge of tackling racism in two one-hour sessions on the syllabus; on later reflection I realised that what the pupils had learned was 'We must not be racist'. This meant that they took care not to voice racist thoughts in the earshot of teachers. The pot had been stirred but they had not had space to really examine why the notion of difference was challenging. This was also picked up by the researchers in the Bradford Linking Project, who noted some pupils were using:

> … insults and sweeping personal declarations based on a rejection of particular differences, mostly religious or ethnic. Teachers were unaware of any of this kind of exchange between their pupils; this was a subculture, shared between children, out of the earshot of any adults.
>
> *(Raw, 2005, p. 35)*

I suspect that, like the pupils I taught, they had not really been given a safe space in dialogue to dig deeper and think: Where do these racist thoughts come from? Whose ideas are they? Do they stand up to analysis? What reasons can I give for them? Am I happy to voice them in public? Why might others think differently? Should I change my ideas in the light of examining different perspectives?

This is where the principles of the OSDE (Open Spaces for Dialogue and Enquiry) methodology are useful. It helps learners:

> a) to engage with complex local/global processes and diverse perspectives; b) to examine the origins and implications of their own and other people's assumptions; c) to negotiate change, to transform relationships, to think independently and to make responsible and conscious choices about their own lives and how they affect the lives of others; d) to live with and learn from difference and conflict and to prevent conflict from escalating to aggression and violence; e) to establish ethical, responsible and caring relationships beyond their identity groups.
>
> *(Andreotti* et al.*, 2006, p. 3)*

The Building Communities through Dialogue project: P4C as pedagogy for diversity

The Building Communities through Dialogue (BCtD) project was developed by DECSY (Development Education Centre, South Yorkshire), supported by the Paul Hamlyn Foundation. The main aims were for young people to have increased confidence and skills in speaking and listening, and increased ability to communicate constructively and build trust with people from different backgrounds from their own.

Building on the experiences of the Bradford School Linking project, the Oldham P4C project and a DECSY pilot project, 'Learning Together',[2] BCtD had similar aims to these projects in terms of relationship development and local linking, but was perhaps the first nationally to expressly use P4C and dialogic learning to achieve it, as well as additional benefits such as improved communication and critical thinking skills.

The aim of BCtD has been to provide children in the transition years of primary school the experience and ability to build trustful relationships with pupils from diverse backgrounds, focusing on Years 5 and 6. Areas of the city of Sheffield were identified where a secondary school had feeder primary schools that had contrasting social and ethnic make-up in their catchment area – that is, both monocultural, fairly affluent and suburban, and multicultural, fairly deprived, inner city areas. Usually the children from these different schools would meet for the first time in Year 7, at secondary school, by which time they would have formed a number of (not necessarily positive) assumptions about each other.

Primary schools from different sides of the catchment area were paired; the participating teachers were trained to Level 1 in P4C and to understand the aims of the project as well as the importance of the use of dialogic learning. One of the aims of the project was to facilitate the development of cross-cultural friendships, as was the case with the Bradford School Linking project, following Thomas Pettigrew's theory (1998, cited in Raw, 2005) that a key process for reducing prejudice is through the development of affective ties, or friendships. The teachers discussed how best to pair up the pupils as pen-pals, and they then began an exchange of letters. They then met at a neutral venue for half a day of ice-breakers and cooperative games.

Two different forms visited each other's schools and carried out P4C enquiries using stimuli that were likely to raise questions around diversity, difference and identity. Teachers worked hard to create a unique space for children to voice their opinions and listen to and engage with a range of different perspectives. The project also offered training to Year 7 (form/PSHE) teachers in the secondary school, so that they might continue the habit of dialogic learning around issues of diversity and identity when the pupils reached secondary school. Groups of sixth-formers were also given some basic training in dialogic learning and encouraged to attend P4C enquiries in the feeder primary schools. In the final term in Year 6, pupils did a P4C enquiry in mixed groups at the secondary school, with sixth-form students acting as hosts and taking part in the enquiries.

Getting pupils ready to take part in dialogic learning was a challenge for some of the groups of pupils. SAPERE (2012, p. 36) has suggested some key dispositions for dialogue, summed up in the SOCRATES acronym:

Seriousness (taking people and things seriously)
Open-mindedness
Consideration
Reasonableness
Amiability
Truthfulness
Empathy
Sense of humour (having fun!)

One primary school teacher had to work hard to develop the disposition of 'open-mindedness' in his pupils in order for them to be able to engage in dialogue. Although the school seems multicultural, the majority of pupils come from one ethnic minority group (Pakistani). In this Year 6 class, boys were in the majority, and though academically capable, several exhibited poor social and emotional intelligence.

After attending a Level 2 Philosophy for Children (P4C) course at DECSY, the teacher became interested in the idea of 'criticising the criticism'. With most of his class being Muslim and attending mosque each weekday, he felt that they needed to develop the ability to 'filter' and critically analyse all the sources that were giving them information. Though this may be true for all young people, he felt that identity was more of a mystery for children who enjoyed North American music, watched Indian films, lived in the UK and regularly visited Pakistan. It seemed easier for them to assume certain truths than to challenge them in a community where it was safe and encouraged. However, before the criticism can be criticised, the assumption has to be criticised and he felt that this skill should be the first that they looked at in their next enquiry.

Therefore he felt it was necessary to:

- Identify an assumption.
- Give the reasons for that assumption.
- Challenge that assumption.

He developed a series of lessons using images and texts, where he got pupils to become aware of their assumptions and how to challenge them. One stimulus was about a female Afghan boxer training to take part in the Olympic Games. This yielded the question: 'Why are some sports just for boys and not girls?' Importantly, what resulted was a clear discussion about assumptions and the reasons for them. The structure gave them a clear focus and enabled them to keep checking what the assumptions were and the reasons for them. All children made progress in the lesson and this was shown on a Venn diagram, something the teacher uses as his 'final thoughts' activity in most of their discussions (one circle represents 'Previously thought' – thought before today – and the other represents 'Discussed in enquiry', with the overlap in the middle).

At first there was little disagreement with the fact that girls should not be allowed to box (even from the girls), but then identifying reasons started to open up new thinking which challenged this. The difficulty was this idea of 'challenging assumptions' and this was something that continued to develop with the group. The baseline assessment carried out by the project showed some positive results:

- An increase in the number of pupils who believed that 'by talking about everyone's opinions, we can make progress together'.
- An increase in the number of pupils who believed that 'people pay attention to other people's feelings'.
- A decrease in the number of pupils who believed that 'listening to other people's feelings is a waste of time'.

Although the teacher felt that more work would need to be done with some of the boys, the classroom climate had changed, with quieter girls feeling that they now had a space and confidence to voice their ideas. The Bradford Linking Project noted that: 'Young children are less likely to have strongly held stereotypes about different groups than the adults' (Raw, 2005, p. 22), but that 'where prejudice was originally the strongest is where it has remained the strongest' (p. 37).

The recommendations from the Bradford Linking Project also noted the importance of setting up the sort of dialogic learning environment the teacher described above was aiming at:

> Teachers should ensure that they encourage ongoing open debate on issues of culture, and ethnic and religious differences, and how these issues affect everybody; ideally agreed ground rules of mutual respect, listening, and constructive comment should be used. A culture of such discussion and debating should be developed in the children's own classroom, then introduced into the link day plans, to involve children from both classes. Teachers will need to work hard to counter children's self-censorship in their presence.
>
> *(Raw, 2005, p. 62)*

The BCtD project was developed in one pyramid of schools – the 'Intervention' group (one secondary plus feeder primaries) – per year, with the next pyramid acting as the 'Control' group. The project managed to work with three pyramids of schools in total. It was externally evaluated by researchers at Sussex and Brighton universities, using both quantitative and qualitative measures. All pupils were given a baseline and follow-up questionnaire (483 primary, 340 secondary); from the 56 individual items in the baseline questionnaire, the researchers created eight composite measures: multiculturalism, acculturation, social exclusion, social inclusion, school climate, self-esteem, group working, intergroup anxiety. The Year 1 evaluation report found that six of the nine measures showed a significant shift over time, mostly in a 'positive' direction (i.e. more favourable from an intergroup relations perspective), and the Year 2 evaluation report (when the primary pupils had less direct contact than Year 1) showed a positive shift in five out of nine. The final evaluation report stated:

> The combination of quantitative and qualitative data provides rich insights into the DECSY Building Communities through Dialogue project. The new cohort of pupils from the three primary schools involved in the final year of the project showed a broadly positive pattern of change over the course of the school year, both in terms of intergroup attitudes and more general feelings about themselves and about their schools.
>
> *(Brown* et al*., 2015)*

The intended outcome, 'for young people to have increased confidence and skills in speaking and listening and increased ability to communicate constructively and build trust with people from different backgrounds from their own', was mainly achieved. Along with this several of the subsidiary aims were also achieved, such as developing teachers' skills (38 KS2 and 18 KS3 teachers were trained to P4C Level 1, and five KS2 teachers to Level 2; there was very positive feedback about the impact of P4C training – the researchers found that there was a significant impact on confidence with group work), building DECSY's capacity, raising the profile of dialogic teaching and learning related to diversity and transition; the aim of involving parents in parallel discussions, however, was achieved in only a few of the schools, as this proved challenging to organise.

The Bradford School Linking Project found little evidence to support the aim of 'Children demonstrating the confidence to take part in a debate about other people, and their values and points of view' (Raw, 2005, p. 52). The *Diversity and Citizenship in the Curriculum* research review concluded with this quote from a Year 5 pupil (white, female):

> I think it would be a really good opportunity to express ourselves to other people, so they know how you feel to be British and what it is like to come from different countries or look different, or sound different but be in this country.
>
> *(Maylor and Read, 2007, p. 112)*

The interviews and focus groups in the BCtD project found numerous examples of how P4C had helped to educate for diversity. I conclude with the views of four pupils from different schools:

> I think it's helped me to interact with children better as I wasn't good at it before.

> It has helped me to be more confident with different people and with people with different religions.

> It's easier to listen to people, we can agree or disagree with people, we can build on what people say.

> We now know that other people think differently and it's ok to think differently and others can listen to people's opinions.

Notes

1 A DFE research report (Bonnell *et al.*, 2011, pp.79–80) noted that P4C encouraged 'young people to question and interrogate ideas' and that its impacts 'have the potential to increase young people's resilience to extremism, by equipping them to think critically and independently'.
2 The pilot project showed some encouraging results about positive effects of linking and engaging with difference. For example, a white girl at one of the more affluent, monocultural schools said (before): '[Do] they think I'm odd the same way I think they are? What do you think is strange about me?' Then (after): 'They were Muslim and dark, I Christian and white. We are people and they're not strange like I thought' (Unwin, 2010, p. 37).

References

Adewoye, M. Porter, S. and Donnelly, L. (2014) *Newly Qualified Teachers: Annual Survey 2014 research report*. National College for Teaching and Leadership (NCTL). Online at: www.gov.uk/government/uploads/system/uploads/attachment_data/file/430783/Newly-Qualified-Teachers-Annual-Survey_2014.pdf (accessed 29 October 2015).

Ajegbo, K., Kiwan, D. and Sharma, S. (2007) *Curriculum Review: Diversity and citizenship*. London: DfES. Online at: http://resources.cohesioninstitute.org.uk/Publications/Documents/Document/Default.aspx?recordId=48 (accessed 29 October 2015).

Andreotti, V., Barker, L. and Newell-Jones, K. (2006) *Critical Literacy in Global Citizenship Education: Professional development resource pack*. Centre for the Study of Social and Global Justice, University of Nottingham/Global Education Derby. Online at: www.osdemethodology.org.uk/keydocs/pdresourcepack.pdf (accessed 29 October 2015).

Bonnell, J., Copestake, P., Kerr, D., Passy, R., Reed, C., Salter, R., Sarwar, S. and Sheikh, S. (2011) *Teaching Approaches that Help to Build Resilience to Extremism among Young People*, DfE Research Report 119. London: DfE. Online at: www.nfer.ac.uk/publications/OPXZ01/OPXZ01_home.cfm (accessed 29 October 2015).

Brown, R., Banerjee, R. and Robinson, C. (2015) Report on Year 3 of Building Communities through Dialogue School Evaluation Project (Development Education Centre, South Yorkshire), University of Sussex (unpublished).

Chen, L. and Belgeonne, C. (2010) Education for community cohesion: Lowest common denominator or daring to be different? *Critical Literacy: Theories and Practices* 2(1). Online at: http://criticalliteracy.freehostia.com/index.php?journal=criticalliteracy&page=article&op=viewFile&path[]=3&path[]=5 (accessed 29 October 2015).

Chetty, D. (2014) *The Elephant in the Room: Picturebooks, Philosophy for Children and Racism*. Institute of Education, University of London. Online at: http://dialnet.unirioja.es/descarga/articulo/5013911.pdf (accessed 29 October 2015).

DfE (2015) *The Prevent Duty Departmental Advice for Schools and Childcare Providers*. Online at: www.gov.uk/government/publications/prevent-duty-guidance.

Facing History Facing Ourselves (2009) *Identity and Belonging in Modern Britain*. London: Facing History Facing Ourselves. Online at: www.facinghistory.org/sites/default/files/publications/Identity_and_Belonging_0.pdf (accessed 29 October 2015).

Leat, D. and Thomas, U. (2008) *Oldham Philosophy for Children Collaborative Evaluation Research Project*. Newcastle: Newcastle University.

Maylor, U. and Read, B. (2007) *Diversity and Citizenship in the Curriculum: Research Review*. Institute for Policy Studies in Education, London Metropolitan University. Online at: http://webarchive.nationalarchives.gov.uk/20130401151715/https://www.education.gov.uk/publications/eorderingdownload/rr819.pdf (accessed 29 October 2015).

Multiverse (2009) *Submission to Parliamentary Select Committee: Training of Teachers – Children, Schools and Families Committee Contents*. Online at: www.publications.parliament.uk/pa/cm200910/cmselect/cmchilsch/275/275we13.htm (accessed 29 October 2015).

National Society/Church of England (2014) *Consultation Submission: Proposed New Independent Schools Standards*. Online at: https://staging.churchofengland.org/media/2112859/140730independentsch oolsbritishvaluesconsultationcofe.pdf (accessed 29 October 2015).

People in Need (2005) *Piecing the Puzzle Together: How to identify, understand and address global issues*. Prague: People in Need.

Raw, A. (2005) *Schools Linking Project 2005–06: Full final evaluation report*. Bradford: Education Bradford.

Runnymede Trust (2000) *The Future of Multi-Ethnic Britain* (The Parekh Report). Online (introduction) at: www.runnymedetrust.org/reportIntroduction.html (accessed 29 October 2015).

SAPERE (2012) *Communities of Enquiry: Level 2 Handbook*. Oxford: SAPERE.

SAPERE (2015) *SAPERE Handbook to Accompany the Level 1 P4C Foundation Course*, 4th edn. Dundee: Fairprint.

Unwin, R. (2010) How effective are reflexive activities for building more equal and ethical relationships in local school partnerships between children from UK primary schools serving multicultural and predominantly white communities? Online at: www.decsy.org.uk/projects/34 (accessed 29 October 2015).

PART 4

The higher education context

11

PHILOSOPHY FOR CHILDREN IN HIGHER EDUCATION

Lizzy Lewis and Grace Robinson

Founded by Professor Matthew Lipman in the 1970s, P4C has developed over 40 years and is practised in more than 60 countries. It conceives of philosophical enquiry first and foremost as a methodology, following a model of Socratic dialogue, in that rather than being taught philosophy didactically children are challenged to ask philosophical questions and develop their thinking about philosophical concepts through facilitated collaborative conversation. As pedagogy, P4C attends not only to the critical quality of individual contributions, but also to the social and emotional dynamics of the communal interaction – the development of what is called a 'community of enquiry'.

The P4C approach doesn't require familiarity with the history of ideas or to have read canonical texts prior to engaging with a philosophical question, meaning that – with the right support – it is possible to jump right in. Yet P4C supports significant philosophical learning over time. Regular practice engenders an appreciation of what is required to *do* philosophy. Those who participate in this kind of philosophical enquiry must develop a sensitivity to what makes questions intriguing, reasons convincing, examples illuminating, criticisms devastating and dialogue a success.

P4C originated in higher education, as Lipman observed among his students a lack of engagement with learning and thinking that prompted research into how children learn: particularly the work of Russian psychologist Lev Vygotsky. In recent years, Philosophy for Children (P4C) has returned to higher education in the UK, where it can be found in undergraduate and postgraduate programmes, initial teacher education and in the continuing professional development of school teachers and lecturers. In various contexts, where Lipman's P4C model is used with adults, P4C has been rephrased to mean Philosophy for Communities or Philosophy for Colleges; or a more general term is used, that of 'philosophical enquiry'. So P4C has come full circle: a pedagogy founded by an academic that has transformed school classrooms all over the world is now finding its way back into university education and philosophy departments.

> I attempt to show those who prepare teachers for the classroom that education without philosophy in the elementary school is just as deficient as education without philosophy would be in the undergraduate and graduate areas of education.
>
> *(Matthew Lipman, cited in Naji, 2013)*

Instrumental in this work is SAPERE, the UK charity that promotes Philosophy for Children, Communities and Colleges. It has developed a partnership model to support university teaching staff to introduce philosophical enquiry in undergraduate and postgraduate courses. In the next section we can see where we have reached in this journey and consider why the use of P4C is growing in adult education.

P4C in teacher education

P4C has played a role in the education of in-service teachers for some time. Approximately two-thirds of SAPERE's work in the UK involves delivering this kind of training in primary schools, and one-third with secondary schools. The form this training takes has evolved from a scenario where one or two teachers from a school would attend a P4C course, towards whole school P4C training. The whole school training may include teaching assistants, school governors, parents and administrative staff. Feedback collated by SAPERE suggests that this input has a significant impact on teachers' expectations of their children.

More recently there have been promising developments in pre-service teacher education, where a number of teacher educators have completed the SAPERE trainer pathway in order to offer training in their institutions. Here feedback reveals that student teachers who have had P4C training also reassess their expectations of what children are capable of, in particular their capacity to think, and that by practising P4C, trainee teachers can see for themselves that children are indeed able to articulate philosophical questions, to reason and to conceptualise. Student teachers are at a critical period in their development, where expectations are formed that can colour their classroom practice in the future. This kind of feedback suggests that P4C training might help to form expectations of children and of teaching that can effect some of the educational changes to which Lipman aspired.

Besides shedding light on what children are capable of, P4C training is also accompanied by a rich literature addressing theoretical matters of great importance. Among these issues are concerns about democracy (Dewey, 1916), reasonableness (Lipman, 1991) and childhood (Matthews, 1994) as well as the dimensions and dynamics of the child–adult relationship. The essay 'What is a child?' by Marie-Louise Friquegnon (1997) raises the kinds of questions that trainee teachers should be reflecting on in order to form their own theory of education. Friquegnon provides a helpful synopsis of how the concept of child has changed over time and she reflects that:

> balance is needed in education, between permissiveness and authority. Rousseau and James Mill represent the two extremes, the former overemphasizing appreciation and enjoyment of the intrinsic qualities of childhood, and the latter overemphasizing the importance of realizing the full potentialities of the individual child.

In thinking about childhood, student teachers need to consider their relationship with children: how they will negotiate decisions about rules, space, permission, authority, sanctions, behaviour, for example. All schools have guidelines about behaviour, and what is considered appropriate or acceptable. These guidelines reflect a position about the adult–child relationship; where the line is between permissiveness and authority and how children are perceived and valued.

The P4C programme also encourages trainee teachers not only to philosophise but also to see the philosophical potential of curriculum topics, such as science or history, and to develop ways to integrate philosophical enquiry across subject disciplines. We propose philosophical thinking about, and even 'within', the curriculum, and suggest that the curriculum should be both more philosophical in purpose (e.g. having more regard to the practical applications and ethical implications of learning) and more philosophical in its translation into teaching and learning (e.g. with greater emphasis on cognitive/conceptual development, and affective/attitudinal development).

P4C is not typically treated as a 'subject' within the school curriculum. Those promoting Philosophy for Children across the world tend to refer to it more often as a 'practice' – believing that treating it as a 'subject' encourages a certain way of thinking about 'philosophy', emphasising 'knowing that' rather than 'knowing how'. This is not to suggest that Philosophy for Children is pure method without any content. Although the movement does not prescribe particular content in the form of a set curriculum, each enquiry takes as its content philosophical questions and concepts. An appreciation of this helps trainees see how P4C can complement existing school subjects, all of which are conceptually rich. The role of P4C within schooling is to identify, investigate and interrogate these concepts, and where this happens effectively, learning across the curriculum is enriched. David Kennedy puts it this way:

> When formulated as community of philosophical inquiry in particular, [philosophy] offers the possibility of 'philosophising' the school curriculum in general, by extending the concept-work that doing philosophy entails to all of the disciplines.
>
> *(Kennedy and Kennedy, 2011, p. 265)*

Besides these curriculum possibilities, training in P4C also helps teachers identify other possibilities beyond the curriculum. For example, the values and methods of P4C lend themselves well to teacher/pupil bodies such as school councils, and for deliberative purposes with pupils about school projects.

Trainee teachers can also benefit from exploring philosophical questions *about* the curriculum most pressingly: what is its purpose, and who is it for? One of the required standards for teachers in the UK is secure knowledge and understanding of the school curriculum. Though this is not expressed as a 'philosophical understanding', we contend that it is necessary for trainee teachers to reflect critically on the curriculum and the way it is taught.

SAPERE's university partners report that P4C's emphasis on the intellectual, social and emotional dimensions of learning enhances student teachers' ability to conceptualise, analyse and communicate. They are better able to reflect on their own learning, and this deeper analysis has transferred to their essay writing. Though these are anecdotal reflections from students, there is good reason to believe that the skills practised within a dialogue – among them ordering one's thoughts, communicating them clearly, considering objections and revaluating one's position – also find employment in written tasks.

The value of P4C to teacher educators is that it enhances their students' repertoire of skills to use in classrooms, and contributes to the intellectual life of future teachers. But how does training and experience of philosophical enquiry help students become better thinkers, to be more reflective and have deeper understandings of childhood, and how children learn? For Floden and Buchmann (1989), philosophical enquiry for trainee teachers offers an opportunity to think about key educational concepts such as teaching, reflection, subject knowledge, argument and analysis. Philosophical enquiry can be used to address questions such as: 'What is teacher education?' 'What does it mean to be a teacher?' Its aim may be seen to support the examination of complex questions in an informal arena, using careful thinking, thoughtful reasoning, analysis of argument and sources of evidence.

In parallel with the aims of P4C in schools, P4C in universities can help improve students' ability to think for themselves by exploring philosophical questions through reasoning and collaborative dialogue. John Dewey, a key influence on Lipman, was writing about this at the turn of the last century (1904): 'The thing needful is improvement of education, not simply by turning out teachers who can do better the things that are now necessary to do, but rather by changing the conception of what constitutes education' (Dewey, 1965, p. 171).

An overall aim of P4C is, and should be, to enable ongoing dialogue between teachers and pupils to take place, so that teachers respond more thoughtfully and constructively to pupils' ideas, thereby encouraging pupils to develop their own reasoning and questioning further. Classrooms thus become places in which everyone reflects more deeply on conduct, concepts, knowledge, attitudes and values. With regular P4C practice, the following capacities are meant to progress over time: reasoning, recognising philosophical dimensions in experience (e.g. ethical and epistemological issues), and habits of reflecting on concepts that underlie thinking and conduct. At the heart of successful teaching is a positive engagement with the children and the ability to create and develop a safe but suitably challenging learning environment. These are precisely what practice in philosophical enquiry engenders, based as it is on the 4Cs of P4C: caring and collaborative thinking, balanced with critical and creative thinking.

It is particularly important that in the early years and the primary sector teachers of philosophical enquiry have a good grounding and experience of working with young children in developing their skills and dispositions for learning, so that they can gauge the level at which to plan and support working with key concept development across the curriculum.

Teachers should develop a good understanding of Vygotskian ways of learning, with particular regard to 'mediating' their journey into the 'zone of proximal development' – developing their intellectual capacity beyond that of the learner in isolation. The support of an adult and/or more capable peers in a 'learning dialogue' can make all the difference to the intellectual progress of the learner.

Daniel's (1991) research into the effects of P4C on experienced and pre-service teachers found that:

> the philosophical, far from repelling the trainees, corresponds to a need they experience: a need that manifests itself in the short term by a high level of interest among trainees and curiosity on their part about the concepts inherent in the philosophy of education. In the long run, the philosophical, being a significant means for the development of critical thinking, appears to be a solution to quality teaching that also provides teachers with a needed escape from routine.

Though a small-scale research project, the teachers expressed interest in philosophical concepts and, despite the pressures of the course, they made time for this work, which they valued. So, training in P4C coupled with experience of facilitation on teaching practice can prepare newly qualified teachers to be at the very least aware of the aims of philosophical enquiry and able to develop ways to teach philosophically. And, more importantly in taking part in philosophical enquiry with their peers, they will have had opportunities to analyse and reflect on key questions in the philosophy of education and their new role as a teacher.

Finally, students and their teachers felt that engagement with P4C had helped them to work more effectively with their peers. This has to do with the community of enquiry – the fact that as a group of learners, they were having a regular dialogue together, rather than sitting in lectures or doing 'group tasks'. In philosophical dialogue, they get to know one another in a more meaningful way.

Though the students and their lecturers report these positive outcomes and their interest in P4C, it is difficult for them to find the time and financial support from the university for this work. All learning institutions face enormous pressures of time and budget constraints, and in the face of this context it is difficult, to say the least, to make the case for doing philosophy. But growing evidence about the impact of P4C and the value it has in schools is helping. Several education departments have noted that head teachers are keen to recruit students with P4C training.

Philosophy courses

Work with university philosophy departments looks a little different but aims at similar ends, specifically the intellectual, social and emotional enrichment of university students, but also of the school children, teachers and academics that form part of the bigger picture. Among those involved in bringing together schools and universities is Thinking Space, a not-for-profit organisation whose practitioners include philosophy graduates, academics and teachers. This work began in 2012 with Leeds Philosophy Exchange as a result of collaboration between the University of Leeds and Thinking Space, established by Grace Robinson. The project brings together philosophy students and teachers in weekly philosophical enquiry with children from local primary schools. Integral to the ethos of the scheme is that this relationship between school and university is not a 'one-way street' whereby knowledge and skills from the philosophy department could somehow be transmitted to – or conferred upon – the school. Instead this project was conceived as an 'exchange' of knowledge, skills and experience that could *and should* benefit all parties.

In engineering this partnership, we recognised the knowledge, skills and experiences of student, graduate and academic philosophers, but noticed that this is rarely found in combination with an understanding of pedagogy, curriculum and the specific context of local schools and individual children. We also recognised that teachers, who know their children and their school intimately and are experts in pedagogy and curriculum, are often philosophical novices. Beyond this, we were convinced – on the basis of both personal experience and research – that children can benefit from the expertise of both teachers and philosophers, but also that adults can benefit enormously from philosophising with children.

The project at first attracted students and postgraduates as volunteers, but is now an accredited module for second-year undergraduate philosophy students with a lengthy period of compulsory training, a significant theoretical component and formal assessment with written, presentation and practical elements. There are several features of the project at Leeds that contribute to its success, several of which are outlined here.

At the beginning of each project cycle, care is taken to recruit only the most committed and competent students onto the course. Unlike most other modules, students are expected to attend a briefing, make a formal application and supply references in order to gain a place on the course, and the number of participants is capped. Students are made aware of the responsibilities they will assume if they are successful in their application and are encouraged to treat their placement as an opportunity that they ought to take seriously. For second-year students on a non-vocational course like philosophy, this is for many the first experience of work-like responsibilities and expectations they will have encountered.

Integral to the project is a strong partnership with the school. Shire Oak Primary School hosts the project in Leeds, where the head teacher Jane Devane is a Leeds philosophy alumnus. One consequence of an ongoing relationship with a supportive head teacher is that the school's teachers are enabled to grow philosophically alongside the students on placement. The staff at Shire Oak participate in regular staff–student meetings, attend twilight training throughout the year and exchange planning and resources with the students.

One of the benefits of working with philosophy undergraduate students is that they have a great deal of time to devote to training, practice, preparation and reflection. While in-service teachers might be spared for two days of training, undergraduates at Leeds are expected to take part in three hours of training a week over the first semester and three hours a week of preparation, classroom practice and reflection in their second semester. This luxury of time enables us to place students in schools who have something of value to offer to the school, something Devane acknowledges:

> They are properly trained in how to bring philosophy to schools. This isn't another placement for students to explore whether they might like to go into teaching, but rather a model of how to use their philosophical skills in different contexts. This step back is useful to the student in understanding how they might apply their degree to later working, but also genuinely useful to schools; we are absolutely inundated with volunteers and students who want to test out their teaching vocation. The under-graduates and postgraduates on this project have really been able to enhance the philosophical enquiry that the children and teachers have engaged with because their roles and methods have been very clearly defined.

This training has a number of components. The first is the use of modelling whereby the students observe the course leader and classroom teachers leading sessions throughout the school. Mindful of the fact that often good practice can be invisible to the uninitiated, these model sessions are followed up with lengthy guided analysis, which draws attention to key moments in an enquiry, both deliberate and serendipitous.

This practical experience is accompanied by theoretical readings that address emergent issues of philosophical significance, among them questions such as: Can children do philosophy, and should they? What is a community of enquiry? What is the role of the facilitator? And what – if anything – is philosophical about P4C? The last of these questions reveals the way in which the course provides students with a forum within which to discuss matters of fundamental importance to their core study, something recognised by former student Sophie Collins: 'During the programme, serious academic thought is put into question such as "What is philosophy?", something which stretches the students understanding of their own subject.'

This is not a coincidence; in fact, any discussion of philosophy with children proceeds from an understanding of what philosophy is, and this understanding is open to dispute. Students on the course ask, some for the first time, 'What is philosophy, what are its aims, and what is its value?' Courses for philosophers on philosophy with children create an opportunity to discussions of this nature – discussions that are often missing in the undergraduate study of philosophy.

> Surely it must be by a rather special, ruthless, act of will that this question is held to one side, or ignored in favour of other questions. For it remains a striking fact that there should be a discipline the nature of which is a problem internal to itself. It is almost a defining trait of philosophy that its own existence is a problem internal to itself.
>
> *(Danto, 1968, p. 16)*

Another key element of the project is the use of mentoring to support the planning and review process. Students are assigned a mentor with both an academic and a practical background who supervises all their sessions, while teachers receive mentoring on several occasions throughout the year. The introduction of mentors is a response to the observation that students and staff tend to reflect quite superficially on their early practice – or are polarised in their conclusions regarding sessions as unmitigated disasters or successes. Mentors provide a second set of eyes on the session, and through strategic questioning afterwards help practitioners identify specific learning and respond to it in future sessions.

The nature of the planning and review cycle itself contributes to the success of the programme because of its detailed nature but also because it draws attention to the specific dynamics of a session and the reasons that motivate, or justify, particular decisions. Students are expected to make session plans that include a rationale for and evaluation of all their own planned interventions. They are also encouraged to identify key spontaneous elements of the session and to recognise the integral role they play in giving the sessions their dynamism and energy.

Clearly, the teachers on the course cannot devote this level of attention to P4C; however, the students' efforts have an impact on their practice by illustrating the quality of reflection possible and distilling some of that analysis in weekly digests, which they share by email. The purpose of all this reflection is to help students and teachers become more perceptive and to raise the quality of philosophical enquiry as a result.

Finally, students are by assessed by means of a reflective journal containing annotated session plans, by a presentation on a theoretical issue drawing on the literature, and by a teaching observation. These modes of assessment are carefully designed to capture essential areas of competence in P4C: perceptive planning and evaluation, theoretical understanding and interest, and effective classroom practice. Students and teachers have made significant gains in all three areas.

Since Leeds Philosophy Exchange was first established, in collaboration with SAPERE, a sister project was established at the University of Bristol under the leadership of Thinking Space practitioner Ellie Hart. This growth has made experimentation possible and Bristol Philosophy Exchange has since adopted a model of mixed undergraduate and postgraduate volunteers working across multiple primary schools. At the University of Oxford, a pilot project with philosophy students and teachers from a local primary school has been completed and there are ambitions to support similar projects at other institutions. In all these projects, children from diverse social and cultural backgrounds encounter not only philosophical enquiry but also the possibilities of a university education and an introduction to philosophy as an academic subject as well as a versatile methodology. Students are asked to examine philosophy's aims, methods and value as well as the role it might play in their own future, which for many of our students has meant teaching. Finally, teachers involved in the programme embark on a long-term programme of professional development, which supports sustainable whole school practice.

Symposia, conferences and publications

The contribution philosophical enquiry can make within higher education was explored in a collaborative one-day symposium in December 2013 involving Heythrop College (University of London), SAPERE and Thinking Space, sponsored by the Higher Education Academy. This introduced aspects of P4C practice to university lecturers and explored where such practice might find a use within HE teaching. Two additional events at Heythrop College in 2013 and 2014 brought together school teachers and university students from around the country for similar discussions.

The conversations continued in July 2015, when the University of Leeds hosted 'Philosophy in Schools with Students', a one-day conference in collaboration with Thinking Space. The conference highlighted practical and philosophical issues arising from the work of various organisations and institutions attempting to form stronger links between schools and universities, among them SAPERE, Thinking Space, the Philosophy Foundation, Philosophy in the City at the University of Sheffield and Blooming Minds at the University of Greenwich. As the community of people involved in P4C swells to include (or more accurately to include once again) those in higher education, so do the opportunities to engage practically and theoretically with the many questions this exciting work raises. There are plans for more symposia, conferences and publications in the future.

Conclusion

We have briefly reviewed a number of projects in the UK that bring together academics, university students and school teachers in collaborative work on philosophical enquiry in schools. Such work is still in its infancy, but these pioneering projects are quickly demonstrating their potential for transforming the place of philosophy in primary and secondary education, as well as their relevance to university teaching. From our experience we believe that forming relationships between academics and teachers is central to maximising these benefits.

References

Daniel, M. (1999) P4C in pre-service teacher education: Difficulties and successes encountered in two research projects. *Analytic Teaching*, 19(1), 15–28.

Danto, A. (1968) *What Philosophy is: A guide to the elements*. London: Pelican.

Dewey, J. (1965) *The Relation of Theory to Practice in Education*. In M. L. Borrowman (ed.) *Teacher Education in America: A documentary history* (pp. 140–71). New York: Teachers College Press. Originally published 1904.

Floden, R. E. and Buchmann, M. (1989) *Philosophical Inquiry in Teacher Education*. Michigan: National Center for Research on Teacher Education.

Friquegnon, M. L. (1997) What is a child? *Thinking*, 13(1), 12–16.

Kennedy, N. and Kennedy, D. (2011) Community of philosophical inquiry as a discursive structure, and its role in school curriculum design. *Journal of the Philosophy of Education*, 45(2), 265–84.

Lipman, M. (1991) *Thinking in Education*, 2nd edn. New York: Cambridge University Press.

Matthews, G. (1994) *The Philosophy of Childhood*. Cambridge, MA: Harvard University Press.

Naji, S. (2013) Recent interviews with philosophy for children scholars and practitioners. *Childhood and Philosophy*, 9, 153–70.

12

THE PRAXIS OF P4C IN TEACHER EDUCATION

Fufy Demissie

Introduction

Teacher quality is one of the most important factors in raising the level of pupil outcomes. According to recent published studies, effective teachers have good curriculum and pedagogic knowledge, use carefully chosen questions to engage and challenge learners, and use reflection to make good judgements about their practice. However, although much has been written about teacher knowledge and teaching approaches, the issues around student teachers' reflection are not as fully explored. This chapter focuses on whether philosophical enquiry can be a tool for supporting student teachers' dispositions for reflection. In particular, I refer to their willingness to consider alternative perspectives about pedagogy and practice. In this chapter, I outline the role and problematic aspects of reflection in initial teacher education (ITE), and what role if any philosophical enquiry can play; present the research and theoretical evidence base for using philosophical enquiry in teacher education; and propose a strategy for integrating philosophical enquiry into ITE programmes.

Reflection and the ITE context

The benefits of systematic reflection by teachers for professional growth and development originates from John Dewey's ideas. He argued that compared to 'impulsive and routine activity', action that is informed by reflective behaviour is likely to lead to 'intelligent action' (1933). By reflective behaviour Dewey was referring to an individual's dispositions for reflections (such as open-mindedness) as well as their ability and willingness to recognise a problem, ask questions, explore different strategies and use the evidence to identify the best course of action. Dewey's ideas have been highly influential on the approaches used to promote teachers' professional learning, such as through action research and teacher education curricula. For example, in the English teaching standards, reflection is regarded as 'critical to improving teachers' practice at all career stages', and their ability to 'think systematically about their practice and learn from experience' is a core principle in the US teacher standards.

Reflection – the challenges for student teachers

For many student teachers, however, reflection is a challenging concept. Reflective behaviour requires skills, knowledge and attributes that they have yet to fully develop. For example, to systematically analyse their teaching they need to draw upon their knowledge of the curriculum, pedagogy, pupils' expected levels of learning, and their common misconceptions. This is important for reflection because it gives teachers benchmarks and criteria for comparing, evaluating and analysing their practice on which to base their judgements. For example, sound knowledge of children's social and emotional development is likely to enhance teachers' reflections on the effectiveness of different behaviour management strategies. Similarly, good knowledge of the curriculum and pupils' common misconceptions is likely to enrich judgements about lesson quality. The problem is compounded when student teachers (as in the case of British primary schools) have to teach a wide range of curriculum subjects.

One way to strengthen student teachers' practice knowledge is to spend more time in school during the training period. This can certainly provide much-needed practice knowledge that can support their reflections on practice. However, many educationalists have also argued that simply increasing the time spent in school is not sufficient on its own for in-depth reflection. Student teachers also need to relate their practice experiences to relevant theory and research evidence to help them analyse and evaluate their own and others' classroom practices.

The process of reflection also presents additional difficulties. In addition to curriculum and pedagogical knowledge, student teachers also need to develop certain personal and professional attributes and dispositions. Reflection, among other things, requires open-mindedness, readiness to look at alternative perspectives, curiosity and a self-critical attitude. For example, curiosity about classroom incidents and events is likely to lead to questions such as such as, 'I wonder what would happen if …?' 'How do I know that?' Such questions are likely to lead to reflection and evaluation on practice. But for many student teachers, and others on non-teaching degrees, the 'natural' tendency is to search for certainty and fool-proof teaching ideas rather than doubt and uncertainty. Jenny Moon's (2008) work on university student teachers' capacities for critical reflection suggests that the tendency to see knowledge as certain and unquestionable is one reason why many student teachers find reflection difficult. That is, if knowledge is seen as a given, it is unlikely to lead to inquisitiveness and curiosity about why things are as they are or how they might be.

The ability to analyse and evaluate evidence and to recognise assumptions and inconsistencies and to ask questions is also important for reflection. However, these are skills that students often seem to lack when starting university, and even when they have been taught how to use them, many find it difficult to put them into practice. Studies cite several reasons for this. Calderhead (1989), for example, argued that long-ingrained beliefs about 'right' teaching and learning (that often stem from their own schooling experience) limit their ability to analyse their own teaching critically. Many also find it difficult to assert their personal views about classroom practice and/or challenging their own and others' practice; this is something inexperienced student teachers' are often reluctant to do, as 'being critical' can be viewed in a negative light. This reluctance to ask questions, for example, can be exacerbated by the prevailing accountability culture, where to lessen the likelihood of 'failure' they seek seemingly fool-proof approaches and lesson plans. Such a culture is likely to discourage them from using the critical reflective skills that can support the systematic analysis of their and others' practice.

Approaches to teaching reflection

Teacher educators have used a range of strategies to nurture and develop their student teachers' reflections. Seminar discussions, reflective logs and journals in assignments, tutorials and structured rubrics for reflection are common in many teacher education programmes. However, while these approaches are often found to be useful, few of them put a sufficient focus on developing students' dispositions for reflection. Instead, most of these approaches seem to assume that student teachers already have or can easily learn the skills or dispositions for reflection. For example, Tripp's (1993) widely used reflection rubric (a series of questions such as, 'What happened? What do you think about it? Why?'), operates within the assumption that student teachers already have the necessary and skills, attitudes and dispositions (such as open-mindedness and evaluation skills) for reflection.

Neglecting to nurture and develop the dispositions and skills for reflection is likely to impact on the quality of reflection. In a recent classroom observation, a student taught a science lesson that was carefully planned, appropriately resourced and effectively executed. However, although familiar with the concept of reflection, she found it difficult to consider how the lesson could be improved (e.g. through effective questioning). The quality of reflection was limited because the student did not have, or was unable to draw on, her curriculum and pedagogic knowledge.

It is perhaps unsurprising that student teachers may find reflection difficult. As discussed earlier, having the necessary knowledge and the confidence to ask questions, being open-minded and able to critically engage with their practice are not easy things to do. Student teachers have a bigger and a more immediate problem to deal with, in the form of the basics of teaching and classroom management (the aspects on which they are judged). For teacher educators, it raises interesting questions about how existing approaches to teaching reflection in ITE could be enhanced in ways that take into account what student teachers find challenging about reflection.

Philosophical inquiry and the pedagogy of reflection

Matthew Lipman designed his Philosophy for Children (P4C) programme to improve children's thinking so they might grow up to be more reasonable adults. In other words, he wanted children to learn how to recognise assumptions, unsupported statements and good evidence, as well as to justify their views with good reasons, and be willing to reconsider and change their views. But such an outcome depended on a particular environment where ambiguity and uncertainty are welcomed and teachers are seen as fallible rather than the font of all knowledge. For this purpose, he offered the philosophical community of enquiry, which is based on dialogue, promotes reasonableness and encourages pupils to listen to each other and build on each other's ideas using critical, creative and caring thinking.

The process and outcomes of philosophical enquiry parallel the reflective dimension of teacher education. In terms of process, Philosophy for Children (P4C) is underpinned by the four Cs – the critical, caring, collaborative and creative dimensions of thinking that facilitate reflective thinking. Through the facilitator's guidance, participants are encouraged to draw on the four Cs to address the community's question and to make reasonable judgements. Thus, through statements and questions such as, 'How do we know that?' (critical), 'I have a different idea' (creative), 'My ideas connect to X's idea' (collaborative) or 'X's points have clarified my ideas for me' (caring), the facilitator helps participants to notice when they are being inconsistent or making assumptions. Student teachers can also make use of these language models when evaluating what they read and what they experience in the classroom. For example, to justify that their teaching has been effective, they need to ask, 'How do I know that?', so they will be able to give persuasive evidence to support their conclusions.

With regard to the outcomes of reflective thinking, Lipman is clear that it is reflective thinking that facilitates judgement. But he also saw the significance of judgement for the education of the professions. Judgement informs teachers' future actions, but can also challenge their existing views and perspectives about approaches to teaching. However, there are better and worse judgements. Good judgements are informed by thinking that is supported by 'good' reasons, and is aware of its assumptions. Thus, when good teachers make decisions, they seek the relevant facts and evidence, are aware of their own values and assumptions, and are ready to change their minds if presented with evidence that challenges their own views. Thus, judgement is vital to the development of the professions and the reason why its cultivation should be key to professional learning.

P4C and reflection

As outlined above, there are parallels between the skills, attributes and knowledge that student teachers need to become more reflective and the ones that a community of enquiry attempts to promote. To systematically reflect on their practice, student teachers need to question their judgements, such as how to organise the classroom and what to seek as evidence that supports a particular course of action, to consider alternative approaches to teaching, as well as questioning their assumptions, such as children's abilities in relation to setting. They need to be able to ask why they do what they do and explore the implications of their judgments.

There are several reasons why providing student teachers with similar experiences could support the development of their own reflective thinking. For many student teachers, anxieties about questioning their own and others' views or dealing with uncertainties are often barriers to reflection. In contrast, when taking part in philosophical enquiries, they report more confidence in expressing their views and questioning others' perspectives. Several aspects of P4C can help to remove some of these barriers. In P4C, the 'rules of the game' are explicit and understood by everyone. For instance, the ground rules before the start of any enquiry provide a supportive environment, where fears and concerns have been aired and the community has agreed on how to deal with it. Thus rules such as respecting others' views, active listening and being aware of confidentiality help to create a safe environment for reflection. Moreover, participants expect ideas to be challenged and justified, and assumptions to be questioned, because a skilful facilitator will ensure that the principles of philosophical enquiry are carefully explained before and throughout the inquiry.

Doing philosophical enquiry also provides a unique opportunity to experience reflection in a community of peers rather than as an individualised experience. As the facilitator models the language of reflection, such as, 'Why do you think that?', 'I agree/disagree,' they experience first-hand the language of reflection. Finally, by providing philosophy as the context for reflection, philosophical enquiry also limits the problems that arise with student teachers' insufficient curriculum and pedagogical knowledge. Philosophical concepts such as 'beauty', justice' and 'revenge' enable them to draw on their own experiences of these concepts.

Some aspects of the above are illustrated by the following example from a group of second-year student teachers undertaking module on Philosophy for Children. They were presented with photographs of classrooms from around the world. The question they voted to discuss was, 'Are children in developing countries learning in classes of 50 lucky or unlucky?' The group participated in a rich discussion that also explored the concept of 'luck' through questions such as, 'Is there a difference between luck and fate?' and 'What would it be like if everyone got lucky?' The discussion was deep and thoughtful, showing elements of critical thinking, enquiry and open-mindedness that they rarely showed in other seminars. This suggested that focusing a discussion on something that the participants cared about in a supportive context, such as P4C, can be a powerful vehicle for introducing the craft of reflection and the associated reflective behaviours.

Theoretical and research evidence

The principles of philosophical enquiry are underpinned with influential learning theories. For example, in Piaget's theory (Piaget and Inhelder, 1966), young children's approach to learning – for example, inquiry, investigation, testing and forming conclusions – is not too dissimilar to the process of engaging in inquiry and dialogue. Engaging in philosophical enquiry requires participants to be open-minded, questioning, willing to test out the validity of ideas and make judgements. Similarly, the community of enquiry mirrors Vygotsky's (1978) highly influential learning theory. Learning happens first in the inter-personal level (with collaboration and through social interaction) before it becomes internalised by individuals. Lipman argued that in a similar way the community of enquiry is the social context where individuals learn to become critical, caring, collaborative and creative thinkers before they internalise the skills for themselves.

There is emerging evidence to suggest that using a philosophical community of enquiry can benefit teacher learning. In Scholl's (2011) study, P4C was found to be a catalyst for in-depth reflection because of the way it challenged and extended teachers' pedagogical orientations towards learner-centred and enquiry-based approaches. Brownlee et al.'s (2014) findings with student teachers also found that P4C provoked in-depth reflections about student teachers' assumptions about children's capacity for learning through enquiry. The recent Education Endowment Foundation study in England (Gorard et al., 2015) reported on P4C's impact on learning gains made by 10 year olds. Teachers in the study also reported unexpected effects on their pedagogic approaches outside the P4C structure. Facilitating philosophical enquiries changed their practice in relation to their approaches to collaboration in the classroom, their questioning approaches and the way they listened to children's responses.

Qualitative data from a group of second-year student teachers (Demissie, 2015) further illustrates P4C's potential for promoting student teachers' dispositions for reflection. As a result of taking part in a P4C module, the students claimed that they had reconsidered their perspectives of knowledge and the role of the tutor. For example, early in the module some had represented their idea of learning as defining knowledge, for example mathematical notation such as 2 + 2 = 4, or rows of tables and chairs with a teacher at the front, to illustrate their notion of the transmission of knowledge. But by the end of the module, most had reconsidered their views and had produced new drawings to show pupils' sitting in a circle and speech bubbles to illustrate dialogue as a tool for learning and constructing knowledge. A comment by one of the students further illustrates the extent to which her experiences on the module led to reflections about important pedagogical concepts such as ownership, the learning environment, the importance of dialogue and the importance of critical thinking.

> The importance of ownership for them and how I want all of the learning to come from them and to be led by them … how I want them to be critical and all of these skills … It definitely changed how I want to teach … all the time, not just in a P4C session … how much everything needs to be about talk, and discussion, and I want them to be cohesive, I will always want my class to be communicating well … I think that is important to have when you grow up and how that is neglected …

How P4C can be incorporated in ITE

There is growing interest in including P4C in ITE programmes, fuelled by student teachers' enthusiasm and interest in the methodology and the emerging evidence on pupil outcomes. Several teacher education departments are currently trialling the most effective way of incorporating P4C into tightly packed programmes. The consensus seems to be that student teachers benefit from encountering the methodology in the early stages of their training. For BA student teachers, this could be introduced in an introductory lecture and a taster small group enquiry within a professional studies module, for example, on reflective approaches to thinking and writing. By the second year, a more formalised introduction could be introduced where they are provided with a SAPERE accredited four-hour introductory course, during which they are introduced to the principles and aims of P4C and take part in two philosophical enquiries. However, this could be further embedded through other modules where the aims and principles of P4C resonate, such as Inclusion modules, religious education, mathematics and literacy. In the final year, if they haven't started already, student teachers should revisit the approach, and begin to develop a more informed understanding by taking a critical perspective on the aims, purposes and practice as well as the possible limitations of the pedagogy. They could by this stage start to enact the insights they gained from doing and reflecting on P4C into day-to-day teaching so that they begin consolidate their conceptual understanding of curriculum content knowledge, and use this understanding to plan and teach highly effective lessons.

Conclusion

Making judgements about teaching strategies, assessments and meeting children's needs is a key part of teachers' professional role. At the same time, we also know that good judgements arise out of reflective thinking – that is, thinking that is 'aware of its own assumptions' as well as 'being conscious of the reasons and evidence that support this or that conclusion'. But for many, reflective thinking is problematic as they have yet to develop the necessary curriculum and pedagogical knowledge that can support their reflections. At the same time, they also often lack the skills (such as critical thinking) and dispositions (curiosity, open-mindedness) that facilitate reflective thinking. However, while teacher education programmes are well equipped to develop student teachers' curriculum and pedagogical knowledge, there is less emphasis on the development of reflective behaviours. In this chapter, I have proposed that participation in a sustained programme of philosophical inquiry can provide an important space for student teachers to learn the craft of reflection and the necessary reflective behaviours within a supportive community of peers.

References

Brownlee J., Curtis, E., Chesters, S., Cobb-Moore, C., Spooner-Lane, R., Whiteford, C. and Tait, G. (2014) Pre-service teachers' epistemic perspectives about philosophy in the classroom: It is *not* a bunch of 'hippie stuff'. *Teachers and Teaching*, 20(2), 170–88.

Calderhead, J. (1989) Reflective teaching and teacher education. *Teaching and Teacher Education*, 5(1), 43–51.

Demissie, F. (2015) Promoting student teachers' reflective thinking through a philosophical community of enquiry approach. *Australian Journal of Teacher Education,* 40(12), 1–13.

Dewey, J. (1933) *How We Think: A restatement of the relation of reflective thinking to the educative process.* Chicago: Henry Regnery.

Gorard, S., Siddiqui, N. and See, B. H. (2015) *Philosophy for Children – Evaluation report and executive summary*. London: Education Endowment Foundation.

Lipman, M. (2003) *Thinking in Education*, 2nd edn. Cambridge: Cambridge University Press.

Moon, J. (2008) *Critical Thinking: An exploration of theory and practice*. London: Routledge.

Piaget, J. and Inhelder, B. (1966) *The Psychology of the Child*. London: Routledge and Kegan Paul.

Sahlberg P., Broadfoot P., Coolahan J., Furlong J. and Kirk G. (2014) *Aspiring to Excellence: Final report of the international review panel on the structure of initial teacher education in Northern Ireland.*

Scholl, R. (2014) Inside-out pedagogy: Theorising pedagogical transformation through teaching philosophy. *Australian Journal of Teacher Education*, 39(6), 89–106.

Tripp, D. (1993) *Critical Incidents in Teaching*. Abingdon: Routledge.

Vygotsky, L. (1978) *Mind in Society*. Cambridge, MA: Harvard University Press.

13

CHALLENGING ASSUMPTIONS AND MAKING PROGRESS

Georgia Prescott

Introduction

Our role as teacher educators in higher education (HE) is two-fold. First, we need to educate trainee teachers at their level, and second, we need to educate them about different pedagogies to use in their own classrooms with children. Using the community of enquiry or Philosophy for Children (P4C) approach with students can enable us to do both; the student is engaging at their level, while experiencing how the process works as a participant, before going on to consider how to apply this in their classrooms. This approach to teacher education in ITT follows one that was also advocated some years ago by Matthew Lipman (1988, p. 27):

> By and large, teachers should be taught by the very same procedures as those that they are expected to employ in the classroom ... If the teachers of children are to encourage thinking for oneself, then professors of education must encourage thinking for oneself among teachers in training.

Within the field of primary religious education (RE), using a community of enquiry approach is invaluable both in helping trainee teachers to understand how P4C works, and its impact, and in helping to challenge (often negative) assumptions, misconceptions and stereotypes about religions, religious people and religious concepts. Using engaging activities, students can be helped to understand the value of using this approach as teachers themselves. P4C is also powerful in helping to challenge the facilitator's assumptions about the children/students that they teach. It can reveal a lot about our students or pupils that may not emerge when using other teaching approaches. Through case study and examples, this chapter explores the power of P4C in helping to challenge assumptions, and the obstacles this can present.

In school, pupils make real progress when P4C is used as a regular approach to learning. They can develop the skills (Cam, 2006) to ensure that they are making progress on different levels. With students in HE, this is more challenging for a number of reasons. This chapter explores ways of making progress in P4C and the real challenges for HE in making this happen.

Challenging assumptions in P4C

The role of P4C in challenging a learner's assumptions at any level is essential. Lipman (1988, 1991, 1993), in advocating that children participate in philosophical enquiry from primary (elementary) level, is steadfast in his beliefs about the benefits it can bring, if done in the right way, to encourage and develop enquiry and thinking as a community. His vision of education, influenced by, among others, Dewey (1933), puts enquiry at the heart of learning in order to develop skills such as thinking, articulation and reasoning. He defines enquiry as 'the self-corrective exploration of issues that are felt to be both important and problematic' (Lipman, 1988, p. 20). It is this notion of 'self-corrective exploration' that can involve the learner in challenging the assumptions of others (Lipman, 1991; Sharp, 1993) in having their own assumptions challenged, and reframing their ideas as a result. Lipman (1988, p. 26) felt that children need to be made aware of their own 'mental acts', among which he names 'assuming' as one. If they become aware of these acts, they are better equipped to become self-monitoring thinkers. Sharp (1993) lists 'discovering assumptions' among the cognitive behaviours that are present, or to be encouraged, in a community of enquiry. This implies that before children can challenge assumptions, they need first to become aware of or recognise them (Cam, 1995). There is a sense that assumptions would be challenged directly in the process of the community of enquiry by children and their peers, and where appropriate by the facilitator, and ultimately again by oneself, if the process is truly encouraging a self-corrective approach. Children are invited to explore ideas as a community and to begin to reframe or restructure their original thinking as a result of that process. Haynes (2002) asserts that in P4C, 'everyday-ness is examined'; the community begins to explore the fundamental assumptions, which we may not even recognise unless challenged to do so.

Lindop was critical of thinking skills programmes that were failing to 'overcome student incoherence in the formulation of explanations and arguments, in the ferreting out of underlying assumptions and implications, or in the unification of meanings. All of which one would expect of anyone we would describe as a good thinker or reasoned' (1993, p. 676). Lindop was writing with particular reference to Lipman's P4C programmes, which he supported. However, his notion of good thinking involving the 'ferreting out assumptions' is one that is of real relevance here. Fisher (2009, p. 84) discusses the importance of children being 'taught to look out for assumptions being made and then to challenge them' as part of a process of developing effective verbal reasoning skills. Fisher also distinguishes between uncritical thinking, which involves 'basing argument on unstated assumptions', and critical thinking, which is 'being open to self-criticism and self-correction' (2013, p. 40).

Cam (2006, p. 105) discusses the notion of 'uncovering' assumptions. Furthermore, he explores using assumptions as tools 'for the purposes of testing out an idea. It is equivalent to suggesting a hypothesis.' This would involve the community in 'hypothetical reasoning', enquiring into whether if X was true, what the consequences would be (p. 107). This adds another layer to the notion of challenging assumptions in P4C.

Challenging assumptions about each other

Much of the literature explored above discusses the vital role P4C plays in challenging the learner's assumptions, largely in relation to knowledge or concepts. There is another element to this, which is where P4C can play a part in challenging the assumptions that all the members of the community of enquiry can make about one another on a more personal level.

Box 13.1: Challenging assumptions about self and others

A Year 5/6 class who were very experienced in P4C and who participated in weekly sessions included a few children who had pronounced specific learning difficulties, including one Year 5 girl. One week, out of genuine interest in it, the class chose her question as the one they most wanted to discuss. Their assumptions of her as someone who was unable to ask such questions were significantly challenged, and they displayed real caring thinking by acknowledging this, without directly expressing it. The teacher was also really surprised at the level of question asked. Most importantly, though, the real pride and pleasure of the girl whose question was chosen was almost tangible, and was pivotal in helping to develop her self-esteem. This was a girl who had trouble accessing most of the rest of the curriculum with her peers. From this point on, she felt a real member of their community of enquiry and a full participant in the process.

In many ways this links to the notion of 'caring thinking' (Fisher, 2013, p. 42; Hymer and Sutcliffe, 2012, pp. 100–1), in that part of an effective community of enquiry involves being aware of and respectful of all members of the community and listening to others' ideas in order to examine your own.

First, P4C can profoundly challenge the assumptions that a facilitator makes about participants, particularly if the facilitator is a teacher who works regularly or exclusively with that class. It is not always easy to predict which children will shine or excel in P4C. This is one of its most powerful features. Children classed as 'high ability' because they are skilled at English or maths are not always able to cope with the uncertain nature of P4C and the need for 'self-corrective' thinking. On the other hand, children who find some academic elements of school difficult can really excel in P4C, because they enjoy the way it can value, affirm and challenge their thinking, and the voice that it gives them within the group. This can surprise the teacher, in terms of challenging the ways in which they categorise or label their children (Dweck, 2000; Nottingham, 2013); and it can surprise the children themselves because they begin to see their peers, and sometimes even themselves, in a different light. Box 13.1 shows a simple example to illustrate this point.

Finally, particularly in relation to student teachers and beginning teachers, P4C often challenges their assumptions about the levels of thinking children are able to engage with. When students and experienced practising teachers hear an audio recording of a discussion a Year 5/6 class had about their understanding of 'What is heaven?' (for a transcript excerpt see Prescott, 2015, p. 44) they are astonished at the depth of discussion children are capable of. This illustrates the levels of thinking children can reach when they become well practised at it. Box 13.2 further illustrates this point.

Challenging assumptions about concepts in RE

In my field of RE, P4C can be used to help children unpack concepts (Cam, 1995). They can really engage with both religious concepts and universal concepts that are familiar to many religions (Erriker *et al.*, 2011). Activities that involve concepts such as 'charity' or

---

Box 13.2: Challenging teachers' assumptions about children's thinking capacity

At an RE conference held by Cumbria Standing Advisory Committee for Religious Education (SACRE) in Penrith, Cumbria in June 2015, Jane Yates and her Year 5/6 pupils from Armathwaite CE school in Cumbria held an enquiry in front of an audience of 60 teachers to demonstrate their P4C skills in the context of RE. They discussed a question already chosen beforehand: 'Do you choose religion or does religion choose you?' The level of their thinking, articulation and reasoning skills astonished and impressed many people there. This enquiry was a convincing argument in favour of regular sessions, as it showed the potential and huge progress that children can make in P4C if it is embedded as a regular feature in their curriculum.

'worship' – for example, sorting statements into 'charity' or 'not charity', or 'valuable' or 'not valuable' (Prescott, 2015, p. 42; Cam, 2006, p. 79) – can be adapted for either child or adult learners and help to develop the skills such as reasoning that are at the heart of P4C. In teacher training, this approach can also help trainee teachers begin to unpack their own assumptions and develop thinking about concepts at their level. I often say that I hope they will leave my sessions a lot more confused than when they came in! Nottingham (2013, pp. 74–5) refers to this as 'cognitive conflict' and suggests that 'confusion leads to wisdom'. This confusion can be created by including an activity offering a collection of statements to sort that are deliberately ambiguous and problematic. This leads to real questioning about the concept and the assumptions that we can tend to make about it. In RE, it is useful to explore a concept like 'charity' before going on to explore specific religious concepts such as Sewa in Sikhism or Zakat in Islam.

Another approach to this is to use logo-visual thinking (LVT) (see www.logovisual.com/) to explore preliminary ideas about a concept, and to begin to think about it in more depth. I use this approach to explore generic religious concepts such as 'worship'. This catalyst for thinking can be used as a stimulus to generate questions for a P4C enquiry.

Students really enjoy these sessions and the opportunity to be involved in thinking activities at their level. They can see first-hand the benefits this type of approach could bring to the classroom. Box 13.3 shows some examples of their module evaluation comments about this.

Box 13.3: Examples of student evaluation comments

- Continue modelling interesting and engaging teaching and learning activities.
- The quality of teaching and learning has been engaging with lots of chances for questioning.
- I learned more than I thought and I feel much more confident.
- I enjoyed the discussion and the free questioning.

Box 13.4: When cognitive challenge goes too far

A class of Year 3/4 children at Goodly Dale Community Primary School in Cumbria were sorting a set of statements into 'stealing' or 'not stealing'; they were exploring the concept of stealing by being encouraged to recognise that moral dilemmas or judgements are not always straightforward. At the beginning of the session, the class were largely convinced that stealing was 'wrong'. In sorting the statements they began to recognise that this might be case-dependent. Statements such as, 'You find a £5 note on the road and keep it', and 'You eat a piece of your sister's Easter egg without asking', created lively debate. After sorting the statements, the children were invited to move any statements they disagreed with if they could provide a good reason for doing so. The end result was that virtually all the statements ended up being classified as 'not stealing'. The teacher became worried by the subsequent discussion; in attempting to help the children recognise the ambiguity of moral issues, some of them had taken this to mean that stealing was acceptable if there was a good reason for doing it. She later unpacked this further with them to help redress the balance.

This approach works to help learners to explore moral dilemmas as well. Cam (2006) uses an example about stealing which I have used in the classroom both in school and in university. Again, in RE, these dilemmas can be explored as an introduction to studying the moral teachings of a religion, or a religious story with a moral message. This helps children become more involved in what they are learning about. However, there can sometimes be an issue with this type of thinking activity, which needs unpacking or following up. In our desire to create cognitive challenge, we may unwittingly give over subliminal messages that could be counter-productive. Box 13.4 shows an example of this happening.

Challenging assumptions about religion

In my work in primary RE with mainly undergraduate QTS students, I use P4C approaches and strategies to help highlight to students some of the assumptions that they make about religions and religious people. There is often a confusion, which may be widespread in the community in general, between what is religious and what is influenced by culture. Of course these are intertwined and inextricably linked in many cases, as religion is based within and influenced by a predominant culture. There is also evidence of some bias and prejudice. These ideas may be formed as a result of images and language used and perpetuated by the media. They may be shaped by family and people's experiences of religious people in their own neighbourhoods; their attitudes can sometimes reflect tensions within their own communities, at both local and national/global level. They are often reflective of a lack of knowledge generally, founded on headlines and face-value interpretations, or a lack of awareness of what surrounds them. I consider it a duty to work to challenge the kinds of assumptions I hear expressed in RE both overtly and covertly, particularly as these HE students are preparing to become people of influence in young people's lives as primary teachers.

Box 13.5: Images of Jesus

Trainees look at a set of images of Jesus represented by artists from different cultural backgrounds (for examples of images see Blaylock (2004) or www.rejesus.co.uk/site/module/faces_of_jesus/). As an introductory activity I ask them to choose one they are most drawn to and share that with the group, saying why. They then use this and the images to create questions for a P4C enquiry. The images should be challenging in some way, either because they portray Jesus in an unfamiliar way (e.g. as a Chinese person, or a black African), or even shocking because they show an aspect of Jesus people can be uncomfortable with. (A picture of 'The Tortured Christ' sculpture by Guido de Rocha is one I use with adults.) This activity begins to highlight a common assumption that Christianity is solely a British religion and show that the figure of Jesus was at times controversial. What is interesting about it is that students often choose an image they are drawn to as one that has challenged them in some way. However, others choose the image that upholds their stereotype, perhaps a very white Sunday-school style one as a portrayal of Jesus that they are familiar with and feel at home with.

One of the things I try to do is to help students recognise their assumptions, and begin to challenge their stereotypes through a community of enquiry. Lipman discusses the important role of the community of enquiry as 'a highly promising process by means of which stereotypical thinking can be replaced by thinking that is more fair towards others and more accepting of others without destroying the positive self-images of the participants' (1991, p. 255). Boxes 13.5 to 13.7 give examples of the types of activity that can be adapted for use in school and university that can help to raise awareness of stereotyping and begin to challenge this.

Although many of these examples relate to Christianity, I point out to students that it is equally important to depict all religions as diverse and different, and to challenge stereotypes across all religions in RE (Fisher, 2013). It is not possible in a short module on RE to begin to explore all assumptions that students make; however, some of their assumptions can be highlighted through these kinds of activities, helping them to reflect on how their teaching

---

Box 13.6: Photographs of Christianity

I have a set of images of Christianity gathered mainly from the internet, but also from my travels. These are laminated as a set. In a logo-visual thinking activity, school pupils or students are asked to group the images in any way they choose. They then give each group a heading or title. Next they have to select a group of eight to ten images that 'show a well-rounded view of Christianity as a global religion'. This can be used as a starting point for a P4C enquiry. Again, as in 13.5, many students still choose as part of their set images of a Christianity they are familiar with (i.e. white, middle-class, Protestant), even though the images show Christianity in many forms, denominations, cultures and countries.

Box 13.7: Visits to places of worship

As part of a core RE module I take students on visits to places of worship in the local area. I try to show the variety of religion at a local level, so that each group will visit churches from different denominations of Christianity, such as the Baptist, Methodist, Salvation Army, free churches or the Society of Friends. I also use contrasting churches within the Church of England, which would be classed as 'high' or 'low' churches. These visits really help to develop the students' knowledge and awareness of Christianity as a diverse religion.

---

might challenge or support the kinds of assumptions the children they will be working with might hold.

Making progress

In my experience in primary schools, there is no doubt that real progress, both directly in P4C itself and indirectly in its impact on attainment in other areas (Fisher, 2013), occurs when P4C is used regularly and throughout the school, starting in the Early Years. Box 13.2 refers to a class of Year 5/6 children who had been doing P4C regularly throughout their primary school years, and this was reflected in the sophistication of their enquiry. Lipman (1988, 1991) specifically developed his programme of P4C to build in progress at different levels of primary and secondary education. Some of the ways in which children can make progress are as follows.

Development of community

As children become regularly exposed to working in a community of enquiry, they make progress in coming together and working as a community. We do this through community builder activities, and through skilled facilitation, building up the elements of working as a community such as listening to one another, responding to or building on what someone else has said, and learning to disagree respectfully. These form part of what is known in P4C as the four Cs: caring, collaborative, creative and critical thinking (Buckley, 2011, 2012; Fisher, 2009, 2013; Hymer and Sutcliffe, 2012). In the beginning, the teacher has to work hard as a facilitator to help the children develop these skills. Some sessions with very young children will be planned specifically to develop skills such as taking turns, or learning to listen. With practice and experience, the teacher can begin to take a back seat, and allow the children to run an enquiry themselves, only stepping in where necessary.

With adult learners in HE, this aspect of community is usually in place and needs only minimal interjection from a facilitator. What is interesting, though, is that working in this way can help the student community to come together as a group, or to begin to see one another in a different light. It is also the case that in a student group, just as in a primary classroom, there can be members who are dominant in an enquiry and those who do not contribute so much, and the facilitator will need to work to try to encourage the community to give everyone who wants it a voice.

Development of skills

Regular use of P4C in the classroom can help children to make progress in existing and working as a community. Alongside this, however, we need to help children develop key philosophical skills appropriate to their age and experience. These skills include elements such as questioning, reasoning, making distinctions and connections, giving counter-examples, recognising and challenging assumptions (Cam, 2006; Fisher, 2009, 2013). As well as running regular enquiry sessions using the P4C format, it is important that we sometimes build in sessions with exercises designed to develop some of these specific skills. This is more difficult to do in an HE setting with trainee teachers, because we are not able to have regular P4C sessions with any one group, mainly because there are competing demands on their timetabled sessions.

Development of thought

Regular use of P4C in school can also help children to develop their levels of thinking in terms of the kinds of concepts and ideas they can engage with. The important thing is that younger children need to explore concepts that are concrete and based within their experiences of the world. Later, into Key Stage 2, and Key Stages 3 and 4, children can engage in enquiries that are about more abstract and complex concepts. Again, in an HE context, progress is more difficult to achieve in this area as we are unable to have regular sessions using P4C; it tends to be on an ad-hoc basis, wherever we can fit it in.

Supporting progress

There is no doubt that children can make progress in all the above areas if P4C is taken on board by a head teacher as a whole school priority and structured to ensure progression in all areas. This is much more difficult to achieve in a university setting with trainee teachers, because we cannot ensure regular exposure to P4C in their training programme to build up the progression. As with in schools, in order for this to happen there has to be real commitment at senior management level to allow P4C to be built into programmes, and for a significant number of staff to be trained up and be able to deliver it properly.

Conclusion

In this chapter we have explored the key role that P4C can play in helping to challenge assumptions about concepts, about members of the community, and specifically in the case of RE, about religions. This is an important aspect of becoming 'self-corrective' thinkers and can help in 'counteracting stereotypical thinking' (Lipman, 1988, 1991). Although the context here is RE, it could equally be applied to other areas where stereotypes prevail, such as geography. The examples in this chapter are ones that have been adapted for use both in primary classrooms and undergraduate teacher training situations.

The progress that can be made in either context is in relation to progress in the skills of operating as a community, such as the skills of thinking and reasoning and the level of concepts explored. This progress is dependent, however, on the commitment made at institutional level to ensuring regular access to P4C sessions. In reality this is much more difficult to achieve in

HE, but what we can do is seek to expose our trainees to P4C in order that they develop their own interest in it and seek to further develop their expertise when they become teachers themselves. In modelling P4C in our classrooms we can seek to light the fire of enthusiasm in the teachers of the future and hope that this is sustained as they take up roles in their own classrooms.

References

Blaylock, L. (2004) *Picturing Jesus: Worldwide contemporary artists.* Birmingham: RE Today.

Buckley, J. (2011) *Thinkers' Games: Making thinking physical.* Chelmsford: One Slice Books.

Buckley, J. (2012) *Pocket P4C: Getting started with philosophy for children.* Chelmsford: One Slice Books.

Cam, P. (1995) *Thinking Together: Philosophical inquiry for the classroom.* Sydney: Hale and Ironmonger.

Cam, P. (2006) *Twenty Thinking Tools.* Camberwell: ACER Press.

Dewey, J. (1933) *How We Think.* Boston, MA: D. C. Heath.

Dweck, C. S. (2000) *Self-Theories: Their role in motivation, personality and development.* Hove: Taylor & Francis.

Erriker, C., Lowndes, J. and Bellchambers, E. (2011) *Primary Religious Education – A New Approach: Conceptual enquiry in primary RE.* Abingdon: Routledge.

Fisher, R. (2009) *Creative Dialogue.* Abingdon: Routledge.

Fisher, R. (2013) *Teaching Thinking,* 4th edn. London: Bloomsbury.

Haynes, J. (2002) *Children as Philosophers: Learning through enquiry and dialogue in the primary classroom.* Abingdon: Routledge Falmer.

Hymer, B. and Sutcliffe, R. (2012) *P4C Pocketbook.* Alresford: Teachers' Pocketbooks.

Lindop, C. (1993) Critical thinking and philosophy for children: The educational value of philosophy. In M. Lipman (ed.) *Thinking Children and Education* (pp. 676–81). Iowa: Kendall/Hunt Publishing Company.

Lipman, M. (1988) *Philosophy Goes to School.* Philadelphia: Temple University Press.

Lipman, M. (1991) *Thinking in Education.* Cambridge: Cambridge University Press.

Lipman, M. (ed.) (1993) *Thinking Children and Education.* Iowa: Kendall/Hunt Publishing Company.

Nottingham, J. (2013) *Encouraging Learning: How you can help children learn.* Abingdon: Routledge.

Prescott, G. (2015) Creative thinking and dialogue: P4C and the community of enquiry. In S. Elton-Chalcraft (ed.) *Teaching Religious Education Creatively* (pp. 35–50). Abingdon: Routledge.

Sharp, A. M. (1993) The community of enquiry: Education for democracy. In M. Lipman (ed.) *Thinking Children and Education* (pp. 337–45). Iowa: Kendall/Hunt Publishing Company.

14

THE IMPACT OF P4C ON TEACHER EDUCATORS

Babs Anderson and Karen Rogan

This chapter examines the long-term impact that experience with P4C in the classroom with children and young people can have on the repertoire of learning strategies used by teacher educators within a higher education (HE) institution in the UK. It takes the form of a dialogue between the two authors, who are HE lecturers/tutors, one with an early childhood background, the other with secondary English as a subject specialism. Through this dialogue, the formative experiences of the lecturers are foregrounded in order to illuminate professional learning gains possible for practitioners across all the phases of education, statutory and voluntary.

For both lecturers within the HE context, the democratic nature of the P4C process is used to extend and deepen the students' engagement with their learning at undergraduate degree level, giving ownership to the participants in an enquiry. This appears to match stated intentions of the purpose of a university degree in the UK as fostering the development of autonomous learners. Characteristics of such may be the capability to evaluate sources of knowledge in a robust manner and the ability to construct for themselves a corpus of knowledge, understanding and skills, which embody democratic, inclusive principles. These principles have a wider reach than the classroom or campus environment, illuminating the wider community and society.

The framework for Higher Education Qualifications (FHEQ) indicate that by level 6 of this framework (Bachelor's degree with honours in England and Wales), students must be able to:

- apply the methods and techniques that they have learned to review, consolidate, extend and apply their knowledge and understanding, and to initiate and carry out projects
- critically evaluate arguments, assumptions, abstract concepts and data (that may be incomplete), to make judgements, and to frame appropriate questions to achieve a solution – or identify a range of solutions – to a problem
- communicate information, ideas, problems and solutions to both specialist and non-specialist audiences. (QAA, 2014, p. 26)

These recurring themes of evaluation, the exercise of significant judgement and accountability for choices are not disembodied tasks, set outside the learning environment within the HE classroom. On the contrary, the need for an active embodiment of critical thinking skills is set precisely within these learning spaces. This is too important to leave to chance.

Critical thinking, according to Beyer (1990), includes the ability to assess the authenticity, validity or worth of knowledge and arguments. One application of this in practice may be the student body being able to comprehend a diverse range of interpretations of data sources, to evaluate the evidence base and to synthesise an argument taking into account these interpretations holistically. This is more likely to be achieved through seminar and group tutorial formats of learning and teaching sessions as vehicles for social construction. During these sessions, students are encouraged to engage with ideas and concepts together with others, so that they may come to their own understanding. The traditional lecture format with intentions of knowledge transmission provides less of an opportunity for students to evaluate and problem solve.

The former links to the notion of student autonomy as learners, giving students practice at evaluating sources of knowledge and evidence bases, using the skills of analytic philosophy, such as the systematic application of logical principles in determining coherence, relevance, probability or consistency of argument.

It is useful to deliberately contest the view of factual knowledge as being a finished product, set in stone that is incapable of change. Dewey (1933) suggests that it is necessary for education to reveal the processes that have illustrated our knowledge and commonly agreed version of the textbook 'facts' of subjects, including all the revisions and reconstructions leading to their current forms. We can do this overtly when we model a process of scribing P4C enquiries, checking with the participants as to whether this fully represents their sense of the discussion. Having a visual record enables this revision and reconstruction to be made explicit. It also allows the facilitator to add to the record, as a form of extending the dialogue.

The conversation

Babs Anderson: Given that our own teaching expertise comes from very different groups of children and young people, nevertheless do you think there are common threads to the way this approach works for us now with students in higher education?

Karen Rogan: Yes. It's based on the expectations of the participants whether they are children, young people or students, both from the tutor and their peers. The expectations are set that the learning will take place in a collaborative, rather than an individual, research project.

BA: Yes, but this requires a relationship of trust, so that the HE tutor must trust that learning will take place, without the intended learning outcomes promoted through constructive alignment, such as Biggs and Tang (2011) might suggest are required for effective curriculum planning and assessments.

How have you found that using a community of enquiry approach has impacted on your philosophy of teaching as a lecturer in higher education?

KR: For me, it's the reciprocal nature of the P4C experience as the foundation of dialogic teaching. This means that participants socially construct their knowledge and understanding by engaging in speaking and listening to themselves and others.

BA: So we might question the nature of knowledge and how this is constructed by using the P4C approach. For me it works as a process of participation and engagement in making sense of the physical and social world through active enquiry within a collective.

KR: I'm interested in the question of how do we learn?

BA: For me, at undergraduate level it's being able to articulate one's own ideas, beliefs and values in a way that others can comprehend. It's also about tuning into the ideas, beliefs and values of the people within the dialogue, comparing and contrasting them with our own positionality. So it's about listening to others' ideas and thinking about them. It's sorting those ideas that can be assimilated into our own theoretical constructs or schema and those that cannot, which then give rise to cognitive dissonance. The ideas that we cannot fit into our current way of thinking create a sense of disequilibrium or cognitive discomfort and with it the potential for accommodation as a shift of understanding to a more comprehensive or specific construct. This gives an opportunity to explore the liminality of threshold concepts, that space of cognitive challenge and learning potential (Land *et al.*, 2010).

So, how does this impact on our work as lecturers? The theoretical framework underpinning many teaching sessions in a higher education context is that of social constructivist theory, where knowledge and understanding is constructed within a group. This is far more complex than a simple sharing of prior knowledge. It requires a process, which sets the conditions for collaboration, including the socio-emotional micro-climate of the classroom. It also has to take into account the wider student experience of being a student at a particular university, within a particular set of norms and expected behaviours.

KR: As tutors, we also need to activate prior knowledge, so that connections can be made between the subject at hand and a diverse knowledge base that has arisen from previous learning experiences of the participants within the group.

BA: Yes, and we need the ability to facilitate the discourse so that all can contribute and this knowledge be made manifest for all. We need to act on the recognition that encouragement to contribute for one individual may appear intrusive to one person, yet enabling for another. We need to find a nurturing way of encouraging participants to be involved. We need to remind ourselves that it's not about learning, but about the level of thinking which facilitates learning.

Certainly for me, one of the issues inherent in this is that the sharing of knowledge moves to a collective rather than individualistic standpoint, but the majority of assessed assignments at university are individual. When recognising the importance of visual mapping and the graphical representation of the shared knowledge through the facilitators' scribing of the enquiry, we have to question, who has ownership of this shared knowledge?

KR: The physical environment of a circle may influence the process; understanding the impact of the environment as a deliberate use of space can lend itself to different power structures, including a movement in the direction of equality of status away from static power relations of tutor and student.

BA: That's why circle time in primary schools is overly formalised for my thinking, so that the child, who has an idea, must wait until they have the speaking object, which gives them their turn to contribute. As the object moves around the circle, each child has to engage with all the separate strands of thinking from all the other circle members. For some children, particularly the younger ones, having to cognitively process all the information is too challenging. P4C, on the other hand, allows for a chain of thinking to develop, a connectivity of responses that build on the previous ones so that a communal argument is created.

KR: Individuals will show an interest in their own opinions, and conversely be interested in the opinions of others, especially where they agree or disagree with their own. P4C allows the opportunity of higher order thinking, for example synthesising your own ideas with another person, as a collaborative endeavour.

BA: It's about inculcating a position for learning and engagement with value laid on the diversity of opinion through the culture and ethos of the classroom.

KR: Working with a lack of absolutes. Tuning into the group as a community requires a sensitive and proactive understanding of the diversity of the individuals comprising the group. It also means not being fearful of silence as this may mean that thinking is actually taking place. It's about engaging with deep-level thinking rather than surface-level quick thinking. If someone poses a challenging question, we can model giving ourselves the space to think about it rather than respond with a quick and ready answer.

BA: Loosening the strings of control can be challenging.

KR: Yes, P4C has made me analyse my own practice as a teacher and how I share the learning environment. It's about the democratisation of the learning community.

BA: I'm also questioning the ubiquity of stated learning outcomes by considering the use of objectives for teaching sessions rather than learning outcomes. In this way, the topic to be explored is shared, but the learning trajectory is not predetermined as this results from the composition of the group, their knowledge and interests. Each enquiry will be different because it is a different group of participants.

KR: Using the P4C approach has made me re-examine other pedagogical oracies. It can be used as a very effective strategy within a wide repertoire so that it is not the only approach.

BA: Yes, oracy is flexible and fluid, whereas text can come across as static, although still open to range of interpretations.

KR: In schools and universities, it's not about setting up a separate room to do P4C, a singular dedicated space for this type of activity.

BA: No, it's a philosophy, a pedagogical approach, not an isolated subject. The approach works through the discipline context, so that in HE contexts, the subject of the enquiries relates to those threshold concepts belonging to the subject.

KR: It's about raising the quality of the questions that show a cognitive search for validity and meaning.

BA: Unfortunately, some young children learn early that their questions are not valued and the consequence of this is that they stop asking questions. Often in traditional classrooms, questions are used as behaviour management tools rather than open-ended searches for knowledge and understanding. This reduces the teacher's ability to model open-ended questions, as the children associate questions posed by adults as ones to which the adult already knows the correct answer.

KR: So we know that P4C can enhance children's questioning, that their questions can be supported to develop a more open-ended quality, which supports this search for meaning.

BA: That's what it amounts to in the end, no matter what the age of the participant in an enquiry. It's the critical evaluation of the expressed ideas through reasoning that gives opportunities for enhanced thinking. And this links back to our starting point of the capabilities of an undergraduate student, the characteristics of being an educated individual.

References

Beyer, B. (1990) What philosophy offers to the teaching of thinking. *Educational Leadership*, 47(5), 55–60.

Biggs, J. and Tang, C. (2011) *Teaching for Quality Learning at University*, 4th edn. Maidenhead: OUP/ SRHE.

Dewey, J. (1933) *How We Think*. Boston, MA: D. C. Heath.

Land, R., Meyer, J. H. F. and Baillie, C. (2010) *Threshold Concepts and Transformational Learning*. Rotterdam: Sense.

QAA (2014) *UK Quality Code for Higher Education, Part A: Setting and Maintaining Academic Standards, The Frameworks for Higher Education Qualifications of UK Degree-Awarding Bodies*. Gloucester: Quality Assurance Agency.

15

BEING AND BECOMING A PHILOSOPHICAL TEACHER

Joanna Haynes

Introduction

The Philosophy for Children programme, outlined by Lipman *et al.* (1980), has spawned a host of related ideas and practices since it first emerged in the USA in 1969. While Philosophy for Children *is* for children, and proposes a curriculum for schools, it is *not only* for children, and it does much more than provide questioning activities and guidelines for teaching thinking – it is a radical proposal for education as a whole (Lipman, 1993). It is a philosophical and educational project that raises questions about the nature of philosophy, both as a subject and as a practice. It proposes that all schooling should nurture the capacity to philosophise and that both curriculum and individual subjects[1] are enriched when their methods are made explicit and their central concepts are problematised and explored (Lipman, 1991). The proposal is underpinned by a reflective model of educational practice.

Ways of working associated with communities of philosophical enquiry have been taken up by formal and informal educators in diverse contexts, giving rise to significant research and scholarship around the world.[2] So why do these ideas have such an enduring appeal for a growing number of educators and what relevance might they have for student teachers and teacher educators today? In what ways might Philosophy for Children offer a philosophical framework for teachers and teaching? This chapter has the modest intention of elaborating on those questions and offering a brief account of some of my own critical engagement with its philosophy of teaching, highlighting things that have been important to my development as an educator, in the hope of provoking readers' curiosity and desire to find out more.

The BBC television documentary *Socrates for Six Year Olds* (SAPERE, 1990) helped to generate UK teachers' awareness of the Philosophy for Children programme. The title is rather misleading as the programme shows not only six year olds but also high school students engaged in philosophical enquiry, led by graduate students of philosophy, who in turn discuss classroom events with experienced teachers and their academic tutors: a kind of intergenerational reflective circle. In this documentary Matthew Lipman asks what the world would be like if education were based on thinking. It's an apparently simple and wonderfully provocative question.

Philosophy for Children proposes education based on critical and relational enquiry and dialogue, rather than transmission and delivery. It is critical because its proper practice entails deep thinking: putting ideas *and* its own methods into question; it is relational because it involves dialogues with others along with ongoing negotiation of the terms of intellectual, emotional and social engagement, in shared spaces of living and learning. This ethical, epistemological and pedagogical framework is as relevant to teacher education and professional development as it is to classrooms in schools or any learning context. Knowledge, understanding and action emerge through lived experience and relations and take shape through our dialogues with one another. These ideas and interactions have real purchase and agency in education and everyday life. Learning to teach, an always unfinished, troublesome (impossible?) and rather elusive project, is very well served by this practical philosophy and reflexive paradigm.

Drawing on experiences of working with children, students, student teachers and teachers in primary and secondary schools, in writing this chapter I have reflected on ways in which this imaginative, critical and practical philosophy of education has informed my thinking and teaching over the last 20 or so years. I discuss elements of my approach to 'being and always becoming' a philosophical teacher: the mode of philosophising – child as philosopher and philosopher as child; the significance and role of narrative in enquiry-based teaching; the reflexive paradigm and practical philosophy of teacher development. I argue that it is important to think deeply about our reasons for engaging in Philosophy for Children, to keep hold of a vision of education, and to put things in place to remain imaginative, critical and attentive. I conclude with my position of 'critical advocacy' in relation to P4C.

The P and the C in Philosophy for Children

I begin my discussion with a playful picturebook analogy for Philosophy for Children, as a way into exploring the philosophy of education that underpins its practice. If you have already experienced Philosophy for Children, you may have worked with picturebooks as a starting point for enquiry, whatever the age group you teach.[3] In *Picturebooks, Pedagogy and Philosophy* (Haynes and Murris, 2012) we discuss the reasons why many contemporary picturebooks and graphic novels are so thought-provoking. We mark them as philosophical texts, outlining the characteristics that draw readers into enquiry (pp. 119–21). In our work with teachers and students of all ages, we have found that picturebooks are truly ageless and boundary-breaking texts. They seem to speak to adults and children alike, providing a very direct and creative way into deliberation of philosophical and educational questions.

In recent presentations and writing I have drawn on the well-known story of *The Princess and the Pea* to illustrate ideas about the kind of philosophy and child implied in Philosophy for Children (P4C) and to reflect on the implications for teachers who want to philosophise. Children's author Lauren Child has written a witty, ironic version of this tale to delight older children and adults, which includes images of wonderfully detailed miniature 3D sets, photographed by Polly Borland (2006). It's a classic fairy tale in which the prince is looking for a 'real princess' to marry. His mother the queen naturally wants to be sure that her son's bride is the real thing and sets up a special royalty test. One stormy night a princess arrives at the door in search of shelter. The queen offers her a bed made up of a pile of mattresses and beneath the very bottom layer is a small green pea. The princess passes a completely sleepless night, because of her sensitivity to the pea. This sensitivity shows, of course, that she is a true princess and therefore suitable to marry the prince.

How might we use this analogy to unpack ideas that underpin Philosophy for Children? In the paragraphs below I offer interpretations of the P and the C in P4C and argue that 'wakefulness' might be a useful quality for a philosophical teacher to cultivate.

The P in P4C

For me the pea symbolises the impulse to philosophise that keeps the philosopher-princess awake and thinking. The provocation is so strong that the pea can be felt in spite of all the padding and her need and desire to sleep. We are often drawn into philosophical thinking by the questions and problems that emerge in our lives with others and in our effort to make sense and meaning out of being in the world. Sometimes these are 'big' and urgent questions of the kind that have been the subject of philosophy for centuries. Sometimes they are small questions that are significant in particular situations and for which we struggle to find an answer. Sometimes other people bring these questions to our attention when we least want to examine them. They are the questions that perplex us and that sometimes matter a great deal. They have agency – they attract us towards them, and our ways of bringing them into question and thinking them through makes a real difference.

Typically (although not slavishly) P4C practice involves those who take part in generating and selecting the philosophical questions that they find truly thought-provoking. These questions sometimes arise from resources introduced by the teacher and sometimes, particularly when philosophising becomes a 'habit', out of their own thinking and experience. The creation, presentation and negotiation of questions all take time and are an important part of philosophical practice in their own right. These aspects of participation and articulation seem to be significant in terms of people's motivation and affective engagement with the matters in hand. In classrooms, this participatory and democratic approach to making and enacting the philosophical enquiry stands in contrast with a pattern of pre-set curricula or lesson plans. Enquiries tend to be prepared for rather than tightly planned; possible lines of thinking are anticipated, but not scripted. These ways of understanding the 'agency' of the questions, the shared responsibility for pursuing them and the living impact of these processes are distinctive features of philosophy in P4C. The power of this dynamic and unpredictable philosophising is often very striking, to newcomers and experienced practitioners alike. The comparative freedom of philosophical enquiry seems to generate renewed energy for thinking, learning and action (Haynes, 2007a).

The C in P4C

The test to see whether she is a 'proper' princess (philosopher) in the story of *The Princess and the Pea* alludes to debates about whether non-professional philosophers – young people, and particularly little children – can philosophise. Some have challenged the integrity of P4C and the philosophy that children do in classrooms and asked whether children are really capable of philosophical reasoning and whether young ones should spend time philosophising when they are inclined to play (Fox, 2001). P4C values playfulness, the disposition to wonder and question, and argues that these seem to come easily to young children, by virtue of their newness in and openness to the world (Haynes, 2014; Lipman, 1993; Matthews, 1980). Whereas most often it is children's lack of experience that tends to be highlighted in education, we might argue that there is a certain epistemic privilege that accompanies coming to the world with fresh eyes. In educational terms it is something to be cultivated and nurtured, a virtuous orientation that might lead to better understanding and wiser judgment.

Scholarship in P4C has brought new thinking to childhood and youth studies, interrogating essentialist ideas that seek to define childhood or adolescence in some universal way, challenging assumptions about what children are capable of, and raising questions about inter-generational relations.[4] More than 30 years ago, philosopher of childhood Gareth Matthews drew attention to the tendency in child development studies to neglect children's philosophical capabilities, and argued for 'the need to rethink the child, not as an ignorant being, but as a rational agent who already has the capacity to reason philosophically' (Matthews, 1980, p. 172). In some quarters progress has been made in challenging such deficit models of childhood, but prejudice and narrow age=ability thinking remains powerful.

We can also consider childhood as not only referring to a period of time in early life, but as shaping aspects of being that, throughout our lives, remind us strongly of childhood and strike us with the same intensity. Like Lipman and Matthews, teachers of P4C today are often surprised by qualities of openness and immediacy that children and 'amateur' philosophers bring to enquiry. This is not to dismiss the value of knowledge, experience, insight and training offered by 'educated' or 'academic' philosophers. Rather, it is to argue that philosophy is, and should be, open to everyone. It is to claim that qualities often associated with childhood, such as playfulness, rule-breaking and experimentation, help keep philosophy refreshed and alive. John Dewey, a philosopher of education whose thinking is an important influence on P4C, wrote that 'with respect to sympathetic curiosity, unbiased responsiveness, and openness of mind, we may say that the adult should be growing in childlikeness' (Dewey, 1916, p. 50). This meeting between philosophy and childhood engenders 'children as philosophers' but also 'philosophers as children' (Gregory and Granger, 2012).

Being sleep deprived or choosing to stay up all night

Being wakeful and playful philosophical teachers might engender a desirable state of eagerness and attentiveness in the classroom. But there is another side to insomnia. The padding of the mattresses on which the princess lies restlessly is a reminder of the piles of policies, curriculum and assessment documents that often seem to overcrowd the minds of teachers and make it difficult to think clearly or creatively. This is the more anxious dimension of sleep deprivation, the overthinking and horribly unsettled mind. We know that neither overload nor anxiety helps students and teachers to flourish.

However, philosopher Maxine Greene's (2000) interpretation of 'being wide awake' is given as the opposite to indifference. She explains it as a kind of alertness to and curiosity about the mystification of our being in the world. Being awake represents a break with the mundane and taken for granted, what she calls the cotton wool. Greene proposes that imagination is central to the ethical exercise of choice and freedom, and that more than any other capacity it is the release of imagination that dispels our 'inertia of habit' to give us courage and enable us to generate alternatives. In the version of the princess and the pea story I have mentioned, the (informally dressed) princess wanders the forest freely at night alone. The tale has the usual conclusion, but the irony of the text and humour of the images communicate the sense that this could be a thoughtful and egalitarian kind of love and partnership. I want to suggest that it is in these kinds of ways that teachers could stay wide awake.

Narrative understanding in Philosophy for Children

It is not only to make some of these points about the nature of philosophy and child in P4C that I have introduced a narrative. The use of narratives to provoke philosophical questions and communicate philosophical ideas is a highly distinctive feature of P4C. In the 1970s Lipman and his colleagues at the Institute for Advancement of Philosophy for Children (IAPC) devised a curriculum and teaching activities to engage children with the ideas and themes in a series of philosophical novels. Their narrative form was deliberately designed to enable shared reading and imaginative engagement with the lives of the characters in the novels, their inner dialogues and interactions with others. I'm convinced that it is the use of narratives, in many forms (either the novels of this programme, or the picturebooks, fairy tales, news stories, poems, thought experiments and dramatic scenarios, narrative still and moving images), that has persuaded many teachers that Philosophy for Children is possible. They provide a particular kind of entry point into philosophical thinking.

Lipman (1991) makes a series of ethical and epistemological arguments for the adoption of narrative texts for teaching in terms of first and third person voice, based on a critique of traditional educational and philosophical methods. He argues that the third person voice[5] 'is the voice of the all-seeing, all-knowing, totally rational Other. It is the objective, authoritative, legitimate voice' and the voice of the social establishment (Lipman, 1991, p. 214). He posits the first person voice as the voice of dissent from within. This analysis of the character of first and third person voice reveal the extent of Lipman's insights into the power of text forms used in education settings, learning processes and learners. Students at all levels of learning can recognise these aspects of reading and struggle with texts, and that struggle can be productive or off-putting. It can be empowering to think about our varying relationship with texts and how we stand as readers. In his discussion of stories, Lipman questions the claims made for the superiority of expository text over story-based text and their association with factual knowledge and rationality over mere fancy and emotion. It is not that he suggests only using stories for teaching. Instead he suggests 'monologue and dialogue, rationality and creativity are simply warp and woof of the texture of thinking', an inter-relationship that is necessary for higher order thinking (Lipman, 1991, p. 216). Lipman and his colleagues also proposed that story texts and the dialogues between the characters could teach readers to think philosophically and develop more fruitful enquiry. The narrative form of the novel was attractive because it allowed for the fictional 'modelling' of a community of inquiry.

The narrative form of philosophical texts adopted for P4C expresses its strongly relational, participatory and situated pedagogy. The sharing of stories and anecdotes, and the collaborative conversations and reflections they engender, are critical dimensions of its democratic power and of its claims to be socially and intellectually transformative. Choosing texts is one of the most important and powerful things that teachers do and this issue provides a rich seam for educational thinking. Strong interest in narrative understanding, and its place in philosophical enquiry, continues to flourish among P4C scholars and practitioners. This is not necessarily in terms of the kind of modelling of philosophising that Lipman had in mind, but in terms of opening up the curriculum and pedagogy as a whole.

Advocates of picturebooks for P4C (for example Murris, 1992; Haynes and Murris, 2012) offer various reasons for this choice of philosophical text for enquiry. Narrative frameworks work with the capacity for metaphorical and imaginative thinking that generate alternative scenarios and lateral solutions to philosophical questions and problems. The modes that are possible in a narrative context (dramatic, artistic, aesthetic, bodily, creative, poetic) make the thinking and communication of ideas more experimental, multifaceted and explicitly inclusive of the intra-actions of bodies, affects, space and objects, rather than striving for abstraction and representation through language alone. They give us a sense of the dynamic play of material, ideas and beings. Murris offers both theory and an array of examples of these methods in her new book *The Posthuman Child: Educational transformation through philosophy with picturebooks* (2016), drawing on her work with student teachers.

In terms of developing creative and inclusive practices through narrative approaches there is a great deal for philosophically inclined teachers to learn from early years' practitioners in P4C. Sara Stanley (2012) uses dolls, figures and puppets to develop enquiry within the story worlds she co-creates with children. She works with the magical and other worldly elements they contain, perhaps a key, a magic lamp or some gold coins and the fantasy characters that people the tales, such as giants and witches. She draws parents into these conversations through journals, photographs and invitations to talk at home with children about questions that have emerged in class. As well as drawing from fairy tales, like many early years practitioners in P4C, Stanley also works with contemporary picturebooks, creating philosophical enquiries inside the texts and between the text and children's talk. Stanley uses her close listening and tuning in to children's engagement with everyday concepts such as fairness or friendship to open up enquiries connected to children's lived experiences, in highly integrated and imaginative ways.

In introducing Philosophy for Children to student teachers I have found picturebooks to be an immensely powerful medium. Secondary school teachers are often surprised to discover artist-authors of 'crossover' visual texts, such as Shaun Tan, Gary Crew, David Wiesner or Neil Gaiman. Growing up with exposure to digital media, secondary school students are often adept at the sophisticated reading of images that such complex and rich works demand.

Having described some of the characteristics of philosophical teaching in the manner of P4C I want to discuss some of the reasons why teachers are often drawn towards this mode of reflexive educational practice. Alongside this I want to consider some of the arguments put forward for including philosophical enquiry in the curriculum, and to ask how much weight these arguments should be given.

Why Philosophy for Children?

Many of the education students I work with in university settings have strong ambitions to be teachers and to make a difference in the world, but they are very concerned about the climate of measurement, competition and performativity in schools. They are often drawn towards 'alternative' education ideas and practices, as I have also been throughout my career. Equally many teachers I meet tell me that philosophising with children in their classes brings them closer to the kind of teaching and relationships to which they aspire, creating opportunities to become deeply absorbed in thinking and to listen as if they do not already know the answers and engage in open-ended dialogue with their students.

It is not unusual to express this ambivalent attitude to compulsory and formal schooling, particularly when it is fuelled by a concern that the schooling system is part of the problem of continuing inequality. Working as a school and community teacher in the UK cities of Glasgow and then Bristol in the 1980s and 1990s I was first drawn to Philosophy for Children because of its emancipatory flavour. Just as primary school student Jason reported to an audience of educators at a London conference a few years ago – that philosophy made it possible for him to go to school (Haynes, 2007b) – Philosophy for Children somehow enabled me to continue to work in mainstream schooling and teacher education systems. What was attractive for me was its playful approach to philosophy; the freedom to be inquisitive, childlike and amateurish (Haynes, 2016; Murris, 1992). During a period of seemingly unstoppable innovation and policy intervention in schools I would argue that P4C has created an exceptional space for listening to children and being moved by the dialogue. It is a time out in which to forget about rank and measurement. It provides a means to mediate some of the negative effects of curricular and pedagogic reforms, characterised by the metaphor of 'delivery'.

One of the things that drew me towards Philosophy for Children was my experience of the 'training' offered to teachers and the ways in which it practised the community of enquiry approach that it proposed should be adopted in school classrooms. In other words, the model of teacher education directly mirrored what was being advocated. I remember being profoundly struck by the kind of thinking and conversation that became possible. The slow and deliberative space for thinking and reflection that is opened up through this approach is one of the characteristics of the practice most often commented upon. Again a rather simple yet radical idea: pause a moment; make time and space for thinking in classrooms. The philosophical thinking and conversation is an end in itself, and the effects are palpable (Haynes, 2008).

Advocates of Philosophy for Children give many different reasons for taking it up and in presenting it to others. A factor impacting on the introduction of P4C in schools has been the difficulty of providing funded and/or accredited professional development courses without linking this to central policy agendas and school development plans. Thus P4C has often been bought and sold on the back of 'raising achievement' or 'improving self-esteem'. P4C has also been 'piggy-backing' on other educational policy agendas, such as citizenship, sustainability, and literacy enhancement. These areas of education are politicised and controversial and have provoked considerable debate among practitioners.[6]

Thinking about why we might adopt different educational approaches requires careful consideration. Let's have a brief look at some of the major reasons that are given for including P4C in the school curriculum:

- It has a persuasive theoretical, pedagogical and philosophical underpinning, drawing on a strong body of work by educationalists, social psychologists and philosophers of education and childhood. It has 'roots' and something of a track record.
- There is a large body of research evidence to indicate that, when practised in a coherent and sustained way, it has many positive and lasting impacts on learning (particularly higher order thinking); well-being; and relationships in education settings (see IAPC website for further details of research studies and meta-reviews).
- Particular reasons given by teachers include the 'growth' of intelligence, the boosting of self-esteem, the impact on academic achievement and the improvement to behaviour in school.
- Other reasons given by teachers and children include the sense of space, freedom and calm it creates, the satisfaction of having one's thinking taken seriously, the confidence it generates, the enjoyment it provides.

Arguments based on 'evidence' are often needed to make the case for educational changes. Philosophy makes a great deal of use of the 'what if' question. What if we did not have this evidence – what if the evidence showed no significant impact on achievement? How would we respond to the policy-makers – how could we justify its inclusion in this age of measurement? Critics have challenged the instrumental use of P4C to achieve particular educational ends such as improving test scores. This is not because they think that such improvement is necessarily a bad end, but because the focus on attainment might limit or undermine the value inherent in the activity of philosophising. Concern has also been expressed about the marriage of P4C with policy agendas focused on the formation of certain kinds of subjects or citizens and the production of certain kinds of rational thinker. What is clear to me is that both the ends we have in mind, and the reasons we adopt particular 'teaching strategies', have a profound effect. Avoiding narrow instrumentalism, listening to the dialogue and responding to the threads of enquiry as they emerge, are part and parcel of a focus on philosophy as an experience of thinking. Gregory and Granger (2012, p. 12) put it like this:

> The primary value of philosophy, for children as for adults, is not that it makes us smarter or more successful. Rather, it offers us a method of inquiry and a history of ideas that can help us in our struggle to make sense of academic knowledge, of the world of our immediate and our mediated experience, and of our place in it.

What kind of teacher to be and become?

Philosophy for Children is a methodology I have both consciously and intuitively internalised and made my own through engagement with its theory and practice and through participation in networks of practitioners with similar concerns, a practical everyday philosophy. I put the reflexive and practical methodology to work. It informs my approach to teaching and to continuing to develop and grow as a teacher, in response to my experiences of teaching. I take an enquiring stance towards my practice.

For Lipman, reflection includes 'any methodical activity' (1991, p. 11) and the reflective paradigm of critical practice implies a restructuring of the entire educational process, so both teaching and research take the form of enquiry, directly informing one another. Some assumptions within Lipman's (1991, p. 14) perspective include the views that:

- knowledge and understanding emerge from participation within enquiry where the goal is good judgement;
- enquiries are prompted by a perception of the world as mysterious and ambiguous, of knowledge as provisional; by the understanding that the relationship between the disciplines of knowledge to their subject matter is problematic;
- the teacher/researcher adopts a fallibilistic rather than an authoritative stance, 'ready to concede error';
- the focus of education is on understanding relationships between subject matters under investigation, rather than on the acquisition of information.

Dewey's ideas have exerted a strong influence on the methodology of Philosophy for Children, in respect of such ideas about learning as inquiry and the school/education setting as a form of community life. Dewey criticised the 'spectator theory' of knowledge, whereby knowledge is understood as a kind of detached seeing. He valued experience and regarded learning as inquiry, via progressive problem-solving, the means by which the growth of the mind and the self is sustained. He proposed that the educational process should draw upon, and enlarge, the experiences of learners, using, testing and developing knowledge in the process of tackling real problems. He regarded this process of inquiry as inherently social. His theory of knowledge was a theory of active inquiry, deeply connected to real things and their uses, and extended to life in the wider community. This theory is related to his social and political philosophy, the role of education in the sustenance of a deliberative democracy and his view of democratic life as a mode of associated living.

Morwenna Griffiths (2003, p. 21) argues that a practical philosophy aims to engage with the conditions of all people and 'is interested in the empirical world as a way of grounding its conclusions in interaction between thinking and acting'. She suggests that practical philosophy is 'with and for' rather than 'about or applied to' people and contexts. The little words matter. Practical philosophy acknowledges its origins in the communities in from which it springs.

I studied philosophy as an undergraduate but it was my encounter with the ideas and practices of Philosophy for Children some years after qualifying as a teacher that set me on a particular pathway of being and becoming a philosophical teacher. This was to entail study and research, changes to my classroom practice and work with fellow teachers and student teachers. Most importantly, it led to my doctoral study, which involved working in one particular school over a five-year period, experimenting with Philosophy for Children and developing a practitioner research enquiry focused on what it meant to listen to children and young people in a philosophical way (Haynes, 2007b). While engaged with this study I wrote and published my book based on my practical philosophical enquiry, *Children as Philosophers* (2002). I felt that there was a need to communicate to teachers the ways in which P4C might be adopted in an English school, how it might map onto the curriculum and ways of working, how it might 'fit in'. I used case studies and examples from my experiences of working philosophically with children in one school to show the many different ways in which they were working philosophically, what I learned about myself as a teacher and the challenges that this presented me. It involved the willingness to take risks and make mistakes; to listen to the children's suggestions; to carefully document the work, and use this to inform thinking and future practice.

The methodology I adopted in my doctoral work (Haynes, 2007b, pp. 32–69) emerged directly from my understanding of the views of Lipman *et al.* (1980, pp. 207–15) regarding teacher education and professional development in situ. These proposals mirror the P4C programme through the emphasis on participation in collaborative enquiry and poly-vocal dialogue. They aim to produce teachers who have 'a strong empathy with children's needs and interests' and 'a love of ideas for their own sake' (1980, p. 210). I took the principles of philosophical enquiry and applied them to events that were happening in my classroom, cultivating my awareness to significant moments in my practice, the memorable episodes that provoked questions about what it might mean to listen in a philosophical way, with that kind of empathy and love of ideas.

Critical advocacy and wriggle room

As I have shown in this chapter, Philosophy for Children has provided a kind of home or family for my educational thinking over the last 25 years. This is not nostalgia or sentimentality, but alludes to that sense of long-term connection with a group of people, practical involvement, shared values and commitment. I am a 'critical advocate' of Philosophy for Children. I am an advocate because it is a deep approach to pedagogy, founded on critically constructive educational aims and understanding of good conditions for learning to take place. I have directly experienced the satisfaction, pleasure, struggle and new thinking and sense of freedom of taking part, felt by others as well as myself; I have reviewed the various sources of evidence that there are other educational and social benefits for school children. It all adds up. Philosophy for Children can be embraced as a critical pedagogy.

I remain cautious and critical because I believe that my enthusiasm *must* be tempered by the knowledge that it is all too easy to gloss over the deep inequalities in the school system, to forget one's position of privilege, partial perspective and authority. This is critical because of the positive changes it can make when open-ended philosophising and community building are taken seriously. There are important choices to be made. Of course there are limitations on structural changes individual teachers can make – but you only have to visit different schools and colleges to know that there are enormous differences between those that are genuinely seeking to be egalitarian and inclusive, to challenge injustice, and those that prefer the status quo. Teachers do have important wriggle room to make significant differences to the learning and classroom experience of their students and to create conditions for listening to their students, through which they come to have a much better sense of their students' perspectives. In the wriggle room we have as teachers there are many opportunities to work with colleagues, parents and the school community to pursue the topics, questions and problems that are generated from within – sometimes immediate and sometimes far-fetched – responding to the draw of the yet-to-be-thought.

Notes

1 For discussion of how enquiry approaches can be applied in different subjects in the secondary curriculum see, for example, Lewis and Chandley (2012). Chapter 12 of *Children as Philosophers* (Haynes, 2008) discusses thinking across the primary curriculum.
2 Professor Maughn Gregory has compiled an extensive P4C bibliography, and among and with others created a thematic record of published research on Philosophy for Children, which can be found on the IAPC website: www.montclair.edu/cehs/academics/centers-and-institutes/iapc/research/.
3 If not, you might want to start by looking at *Storywise* by Murris and Haynes (2010) or consult the Philosophy Cooperative at: www.P4C.com.
4 In addition to sources cited in the text, readers interested in following up ideas in philosophy of childhood might start with work by Karin Murris (2016), David Kennedy (2006) and Walter Kohan (2015), as well as the online journal *Childhood and Philosophy*. Those interested in older children and adolescence could consult Hannam and Echeverria (2009).
5 I think this is the voice that students assume is required for all assignments. 'Am I allowed to use the first person I in my essay?' is the question I have been asked most often in my university teaching. It is a small but revealing question.
6 More recently this has generated debate about whether, for example, the community of enquiry offers a way for schools to explore 'fundamental British values' or to address the duties outlined in the government's Prevent duty guidance for Scotland and England and Wales (www.gov.uk).

References

Childhood and Philosophy (ICPIC journal). Online at: www.periodicos.proped.pro.br/index.php/childhood.
Child, L. and Borland, P. (2006) *The Princess and the Pea*. London: Puffin.
Dewey, J. (1916) *Democracy and Education*. New York: Macmillan.
Fox, R. (2001) Can children be philosophical? *Teaching Thinking*, 4, 46–9.

Gov.UK (2015) *Prevent Duty Guidance for England, Scotland and Wales*. Online at: www.gov.uk/ government/publications/prevent-duty-guidance.

Greene, M. (2000) *Releasing the Imagination: Essays on education, the arts and social change*. San Francisco, CA: Jossey-Bass Education.

Gregory, M. and Granger, D. (2012). Introduction: John Dewey on philosophy and childhood. *Education and Culture*, 28(2), 1–25.

Griffiths, M. (ed.) (2003) *Action for Social Justice in Education: Fairly different*. Maidenhead and Philadelphia: Open University Press.

Hannam, P. and Echeverria, E. (2009) *Philosophy with Teenagers: Nurturing a moral imagination for the 21st century*. London: Continuum.

Haynes, J. (2002, 2008) *Children as Philosophers: Learning through enquiry and dialogue in the primary school*. London: Routledge.

Haynes, J. (2007a) Freedom and the urge to think. *Gifted Education International*, special issue on Philosophy for Children, ed. B. Wallace, guest ed. B. Hymer, 22(2/3), 229–37.

Haynes, J. (2007b) *Listening as a Critical Practice: Learning through philosophy with children* (doctoral dissertation). University of Exeter.

Haynes, J. (2014) Already equal and able to speak: Practising philosophical enquiry with young children. In S. Robson and S. F. Quinn (eds) *The Routledge International Handbook of Young Children's Thinking and Understanding*. London: Routledge.

Haynes, J. (2016) Philosophy with Children: An imaginative democratic practice. In H. E. Lees and N. Noddings (eds) *The Palgrave International Handbook of Alternative Education*. London: Palgrave Macmillan, in press.

Haynes, J. and Murris, K. (2012) *Picturebooks, Pedagogy and Philosophy*. New York and London: Routledge.

International Institute for the Advancement of Philosophy for Children. Online at: www.montclair. edu/cehs/academics/centers-and-institutes/iapc/.

Kennedy, D. (2006) *The Well of Being: Childhood, subjectivity and education*. New York: SUNY Press.

Kohan, W. (2015) *Childhood, Education and Philosophy: New ideas for an old relationship*. London: Routledge.

Lewis, L. and Chandley, N. (2012) *Philosophy for Children through the Secondary Curriculum*. London: Continuum.

Lipman, M. (1991) *Thinking in Education*. Cambridge, MA: Cambridge University Press.

Lipman, M. (ed.) (1993) *Thinking, Children and Education*. Duboque, IA: Kendall/Hunt.

Lipman, M., Sharp, A. M. and Oscanyan, F. S. (1980) *Philosophy in the Classroom*, 2nd edn. Philadelphia: Temple University Press.

Matthews, G. (1980) *Philosophy and the Young Child*. Cambridge, MA: Harvard University Press.

Murris, K. (1992) *Philosophy with Picture Books*. London: Infonet.

Murris, K. (2016) *The Posthuman Child: Educational transformation through philosophy with picturebooks*. London: Routledge.

Murris, K. and Haynes, J. (2010) *Storywise: Thinking through stories*, international e-book version. Johannesburg: Infonet. Online at: www.mindboggles.org.za/index.php/publications/books/storywise.

P4C Cooperative, online at: http://p4c.com/.

Prevent Duty Guidance for England, Scotland and Wales (2015), online at: www.gov.uk/government/ publications/prevent-duty-guidance

SAPERE (1990) *The Transformers: Socrates for Six Year Olds*, television series episode. In Communities of Enquiry. London: BBC TV. Online at: www.youtube.com/watch?v=fp5lB3YVnlE.

Stanley, S. (2012) *Why Think? Philosophical play from 3–11*. London: Continuum.

INDEX